The New Student Left

The New Student Left

AN ANTHOLOGY

EDITED BY MITCHELL COHEN

AND DENNIS HALE

WITH A FOREWORD BY CAREY MCWILLIAMS

REVISED AND ENLARGED EDITION

BEACON PRESS BOSTON

The editors wish to thank the authors of essays in this volume for permission to reprint, and the following publishers:

motive magazine for the essay by Philip Altbach, reprinted from *motive*, November 1962. Copyright © 1962 by the Division of Higher Education of The Methodist Church, P. O. Box 871, Nashville, Tennessee.

Venture magazine, a former publication of Students for a Democratic Society, for the essay by Robert A. Haber.

Humanity, Berkeley, California, for the essay by Mario Savio.

"God in the Colleges: The Dehumanization of the University," by Michael Novak, by permission of the author, copyright © 1961 by Harper and Row, Publishers, Inc.

The New York Review of Books for the essay by Stokely Carmichael, reprinted from *The New York Review of Books*, September 26, 1966. Copyright © 1966 by The New York Review.

Revised and enlarged paperback edition first published in 1967

Published simultaneously in Canada by Saunders of Toronto, Ltd.

Beacon Press books are published under the auspices
of the Unitarian Universalist Association

Printed in the United States of America

TO MARCHAMONT NEDHAM (1620–1678)

who recognized the value of dissent in a world whose dogmas always fall short of the truth

CONTENTS

FOREWORD

by Carey McWilliams

It is ironic that at a time when the possibility of actually creating a utopia, any kind of utopia, did not exist—for lack of know-how and wherewithal—the projection of utopias was a favorite pastime of historians, scientists, philosophers, and statesmen. Meagerness of resources did not dim but seemed rather to stimulate the utopian imagination. Today we have, as never before, the resources, the wealth, the science, the technology, the organizational skills which could be used to fashion utopias without end. In one year Gross National Product shot up by something like $44 billion—more than the total GNP of Canada in the same year. And only recently Vice-President Humphrey spoke of a trillion-dollar GNP as being "in the offing." Yet despite the prodigious resources now available, utopias have gone out of fashion; indeed anti-utopias are "in," and utopias are "out."

In part the eclipse of the utopian element in politics reflects the contemporary tendency to denigrate politics. Practical politicians, "real pros" as they like to think of themselves, are constantly reminding us that politics is the art of the possible and that progress is made through consensus. Obsessed with power, adept in the carrot-and-stick technique, these operational schemers would accept, if they were familiar with it, Harold Lasswell's conception of politics as the science of who gets what, when, and why. But politics involves more than wheeling and dealing, more than patronage and appropriations, more than image-making and news management. Politics, Louis Brandeis once said, is the art of making possible that which seems impossible; it is concerned with the highest goals that action can achieve. Subtract the utopian element and politics becomes tedious and trivial, tawdry and tiresome. Complaints on this score have been multiplying of recent years. "What can be detected," *The Wall Street Journal* observed some time back (November 2, 1962), "is a certain sense of disenchantment with politics and politicians. . . . National politics today is pretty much a vacuum or at least a desert. It is arid of ideas. . . . The nation isn't getting debate but political shadow-boxing, a careful dancing around the real issues." Other and more sweeping denunciations of contemporary politics are not hard to find. "The truth is," writes Allan Temko, "that we have no politics . . . if politics is to be understood as it has been by civilized men since Aristotle as rational control of human affairs. Instead of politics, the twentieth century has power, and power, as Henry Adams wryly observed half a century ago, is poison."

In part, too, the current low estate of politics is due to the strange way in which the future has dissolved into the present; the pace of change has been so swift that we seem to have lost the sense of the future in our wonderment with the present. Our phenomenal success in creating an enormous wealth-producing apparatus has blinded us to the implications; we do not know what should come next because we scarcely know what it is that we have achieved. In the process, means have come to be confused with ends; the technique of getting things done crowds out any sense of the worth or value of what it is that we are supposed to be doing. At times we act as though production were an end in itself, as though there were no higher goal or larger purpose. The failure to keep goals and purposes in mind, the eclipse of any utopian vision, has made our politics seem petty and meaningless.

In describing what has happened to the most durable and pervasive of our utopian visions—the American Dream—Dr. Grayson Kirk in a commencement address at Columbia in the spring of 1965 suggested how and why it is that the future has dissolved into the present:

> Our country has rounded a corner in its history, and the road which led to that corner no longer beckons us on ahead with the same legible signposts that guided our fathers. In one sense the American Dream is over. Many of the beliefs of our national youth

no longer seem to fit the conditions of life in our time. In consequence, it is fair to say that our people appear to be in a greater state of national confusion than at any time in their peacetime history. The future once seemed to be so sure, so certain and so alluring. Now we appear to be unsure of ourselves, of our course, and of our prospects.

Once we were busy with the physical building of our country. A vast and virgin land had to be peopled, tamed and developed. Because we were safe from the threat of external menace, and because were were proud of the speed with which we had subdued the forces of nature about us, we could be free to indulge ourselves in romantic dreams of our future. Our political system, obviously the best that man had yet devised, was destined to spread throughout the world, to topple monarchs from their thrones and tyrants from their seats of arbitrary power. Our free economic system would bring us affluence, and affluence would bring us happiness and the leisure that would enable us to cultivate the gentler arts of civilized society. It was to be our destiny, through precept and example, to lead the world into a new and golden age. And if precept and example did not suffice, there were among us those who were prepared on occasion to contemplate even the use of force to help pull the world after us into utopia.

But now the glow of this youthful enthusiasm has faded. We have discovered that our form of government is not in every respect ideally suited even to our present-day needs, and that it is not generally regarded as a panacea for other countries in various stages of national political and economic development. We have discovered that the non-western world is not filled with simple heathen people awaiting the Midas touch of our grace, but that, on the contrary, it is a complex of ancient and sophisticated civilizations whose leaders judge us freely, unsparingly and unsentimentally. Further, we have come to realize that our physical power, though the greatest ever possessed by any state in history, cannot in our time assure either our safety at home or the automatic implementation of our national will abroad. And, finally, we have become uncomfortably conscious of the fact that, though our history is, on balance, a success story without parallel, we continue to have a multitude of ugly and difficult domestic problems that cause much of the world to look upon us with a judgment that is far from that which we would wish them to have.

* * *

To date our politics has not even begun to assimilate this rather matter-of-fact statement of where we are and of what has happened to us. In consequence, the new generation—always the first to sense a crisis in the prevailing value system—has broken violently with the norms of "consensus politics," of politics as usual, and has taken to the streets with marches, protests, demonstrations, all-night vigils, teach-ins, picket lines, and assorted forms of unconventional action. From these activities the substance of a new politics will emerge; in fact it is emerging, as the contributions in this volume, by a representative group of activists, clearly attest. What our politics has lacked is precisely what these contributions provide—a new infusion of utopian idealism. "The student revolt," of which we have heard so much but about which we know so little, is the most impressive political development of the postwar period. In this movement, new insights are being accumulated and new values are being forged from which, in time, the new vision will emerge. Always quick to pick up any new development that holds even a hint of threat to Establishment values, the mass media have pounced on "the student unrest" and have tried not so much to explain it as to smother it in a froth of words. Flattering as this attention may be, it is not intended to be helpful and in fact it isn't. All the more reason, then, for a reliable guide to this many-sided and rapidly changing movement.

The papers that have been gathered in this volume represent an initial attempt by students themselves—by the activists of the new left—to give direct voice to their discontents and their anticipations, to say what they think the new left is all about, and to trace the genesis of the movement. There is, of course, never any substitute for the real thing. In these pages one can see the new left as the new left sees itself, not as someone else imagines it to be. In retrospect the collection is certain to rank high, I should think, as a significant political testament. Here, then, is a volume which examines and rejects values no longer relevant or acceptable, which gives direct voice to the new generation's dissatisfactions and discontents, and which recaptures for all of us a sense of the future. We must be grateful to the authors and editors, to the staff of *The Activist*, and to their faculty advisers for giving us this volume—

a welcome omen that politics is being restored to its old estate. In recapturing the sense of the future which we lost in the swift onset of "affluence" and the fever we mistook for prosperity, the activists have bridged the gap between the generations and pointed the way to tomorrow.

New York
November 18, 1965

PREFACE TO THE PAPERBACK EDITION

Of all books, an anthology should entertain the fewest pretensions. This anthology concerns the "new left," a political movement which is at once fluid and anarchic: Consequently, our book can make few claims at 100 per cent inclusiveness or accuracy. Rather than attempt a detailed portrait of the entire movement, we have decided to concentrate on a much more important and (at least) interesting question: "What are these kids really talking about?"

Some of these essays were written for public consumption; most were not. Some pieces are propaganda; others are critical of the movement itself. Some pieces try to explain the movement to the outside; some try to find *within* the student community some consensus on goals and tactics. Some articles try to serve all these functions at once.

But out of this welter of material, there will emerge a mosaic which may help the initiate to understand the eclectic, radical spirit that is common to us all. Pundits aside, the "new left" *does* have an "ideology." It should not go unnoticed simply because it is unexpected.

Our position as editors should be made clear. We are both publishers of a student political journal, *The Activist*, which has been printing student writing for the past six years. Therefore we have been able to watch the student movement from the vantage point of a sympathetic but critical review. The journalist is always in an odd position regarding political struggles: part advocate and part critic, he must also be a translator. Our view of the "new left" grew up under just these circumstances, and was shaped by them.

What we said in the Preface to the first edition still holds:

... We felt the time had come for students to attempt a systematic analysis of their own movement, in the words of its own partisans. Others have tried, using the values and experiences of another generation. Comparisons have been made to the thirties which tend to obscure the radically different nature of the sixties. ...

"Men when they age," Machiavelli reminds us, "lose their strength and energy, whilst their prudence and judgment improve; so the same things that in youth appeared to them supportable and good, will of necessity, when they have grown old, seem to them insupportable and evil; and when they should blame their own judgment, they find fault with the times."

A few content changes must be explained. We have removed a few essays which are no longer of much relevance, and have added some that are. We have also appended a small section on the "antiwar" movements and the war in Vietnam. This should not be mistaken for the entire peace movement, but it will give the reader a good sample of the students' thinking on war, international politics, and American foreign policy. Otherwise, the arrangement of the book is unchanged. The first part deals with the role of the student in society, the second with the civil rights and antipoverty movements, and the third with university reform.

We want to reacknowledge our debts to Wilson Carey McWilliams for his work on behalf of *The Activist* and this book. He is still a fine teacher and an even better friend.

New York City
August 1966

M. C. and D. H.

INTRODUCTION

I

We are people of this generation, bred in at least modest comfort, housed in universities, looking uncomfortably to the world we inherit. . . .

The Port Huron Statement
SDS, 1960

The increase in student political activity during the past five years has called forth no end of praise and denunciation from the liberal and respectable among the public, most of it addressing itself to the paradox implied by the statement above. This is, indeed, an age of "modest comfort," but it has nevertheless generated among its younger generation a sizable minority who are not impressed. What is to explain this disaffection of the young? Some point to the fact of youth itself, and declare that youth always rebels, and that age always misunderstands the rebellion. Some point to more sinister forces: communism, atheism, the breakdown of traditional morality. Others (mainly, unfortunately, among the liberal press) declare that the student, faced with the most incredibly complex industrial society any generation has had to face, is lost in a welter of conflicting signals, where the old values have lost their meaning and where none have appeared to take their place. In other words, the students are confused, and not a little bored with the world they are supposed to "inherit." Nathan Glazer explained the student revolt at Berkeley as a case of student *malaise* that had little if anything to do with free speech: "only homosexuality or perversion, it seemed, could make an issue at Berkeley."[1]

[1] Nathan Glazer, "What Happened at Berkeley," in *The Berkeley Student Revolt*, Seymour Martin Lipset and Sheldon S. Wolin, ed. (Garden City, Anchor, 1965), p. 287.

If this seems an odd explanation, it is nevertheless typical: the peculiar biases of the liberal tradition in America find little room for legitimate radical political movements. Those that do appear must be explained away as aberrations: as the result of alien political forces or unhealthy psychological ones. But there is a kernel of truth in the psychological explanation: if the student of the "new left" is angry, he is also (as he would be the first to tell you) confused. But he would then point to the twenty-five million Americans who voted for Barry Goldwater and tell you that students are not the only ones who neither like nor understand the age in which they live; or, as Kenneth Keniston argues, that the alienation of the young is merely a particular symptom of the general alienation of American society.[2]

If the student is part of a larger cultural environment, he is also part of a special one as well, the world of the university, which has a style and a set of problems all its own. It is to this world that we must look for an understanding of the *specific* reasons and nature of the student revolt. Much of the student's behavior can be explained by his existence in these two worlds simultaneously: the student community—"the perfect model of the society of the alienated and uprooted"—is a transient one, in passage from the world of the child to the world of the adult. It is from this "non-community" that the student views, with some apprehension, the world he has been prepared to take over. That that world should frighten and sicken him is perhaps understandable: after all, many others in America react the same way. That he should react in the *particular* way he has requires some further explanation.

First of all, there is a certain inevitability in the contempt with which the new left views the American educational establishment. Educational authority is the first authority the student confronts outside the home; those in revolt, remembering a long train of past conflicts, are likely to view the administration of a university as Reaction incarnate. But although the rebel looks upon the educational hierarchy with disfavor he is not, of course, entirely inde-

[2] Kenneth Keniston, "Alienation and the Decline of Utopia," *The American Scholar* (vol. 29, 1961).

pendent of it. The mental pattern cultivated in high school and college is likely to be pervasive, if not permanent in many of its more important features. There are many facets to this dependence: what interests us here, however, is what the educational system teaches and implies about the political world.

The first thing the student is likely to discover is that he is an apprentice, that his education consists of "education for life," or for citizenship, or some other idea. The outside world may still seem strange, and hostile, to him, but there is little doubt in his mind that becoming a *functioning part* of it is the main object of his education. He soon discovers, moreover, that "becoming a functioning part" does not include becoming a *critical* part. "Now," goes the high-school principal's introductory speech, "you will be treated as adults, and you will be expected to behave as such. Observe and learn." That is a falsehood, of course. The student is not treated—nor is he expected to behave—as an adult; but the point is made. Throughout the next eight years, the behavior of his adult guardians is offered as an example of how he—whether he likes it or not—will behave at the appointed hour.

Nowhere is that behavior more consistent or more effective than in its portrayal of politics and political behavior. If a person is to appreciate the importance of political issues, he must see them as relevant—whether positively or negatively—to his personal fortunes. The paternalism of the American secondary school and college, as Thomas Hayden argues, achieves precisely the opposite: the fatalistic view, popular among many students—and many nonstudents—that "politics doesn't matter," that it is "unreal," "dirty," or "futile."[3] This appraisal is quite accurate as far as university politics are concerned: student councils usually *are* irrelevant and "unreal;" educational authority usually *is* distant and unresponsive. But the attitude can be fatal when applied consistently to the outside world, where the public order is decidedly *not* irrelevant. *In loco parentis,* however, occupies so much of the intellectual ground

[3] Thomas Hayden, "Student Social Action."Hayden notes the reaction of one group of students to a poll on the "great issues of our time." The students acknowledged the possibility—even the likelihood—of nuclear war, but did not consider it to be one of the "great and important issues."

of the American school that the student will usually enter the world of professions or graduate study quite convinced that authority is right in at least one thing: that the important thing in life is to look out for Number One and eschew any involvement with the collective problems—or actions—of men.

Kenneth Keniston has discussed another important aspect of the student's political education: the destruction of "positive myths" and the hostility toward utopian thinking. Alienation may be defined, Keniston argues, as a deliberate and frustrated withdrawal from the world of the "public," and the inability to formulate any mythical alternatives to that public which might be translated into reality. The myths of this age are myths of estrangement and isolation, not of hope: "Horatio Alger is replaced by Timon, Napoleon by Ishmael, and even Lincoln now seems pallid before the defiant images of 'hoods' or 'beats.' "[4] Utopian systems, in which men have traditionally placed their most hopeful visions for the future, come to us today in the form of negations: *Nineteen Eighty-four*, *Brave New World*, and *The Stranger*. Those who might be imbued with hope—the intellectuals—are instead wrapped in despair: "So here we stand," writes one student, "limp, questioning, even scared. . . . To the question, 'What can we do?' one finds the . . . huge, bold answer, 'Get ready to die.' "[5]

The student's predicament is in part a manifestation of a larger problem, that of society as a whole. ". . . More and more men and women are fundamentally alienated from what their culture offers them," which they see as nothing more than a world of useless work, boredom, routinization, and conformity. Consequently, "hopeful visions of the future, idealisms, and utopias become increasingly rare and difficult."[6] The frustration and alienation are in turn heightened by a process which Keniston argues is becoming synonymous with the transition from childhood to adulthood: the destruction of imagination. Imagination is essential to the formation of ideology, and ideology to the construction of alternatives to the present. But American society, with its increased special-

[4] Keniston, *op. cit.*, p. 161.

[5] Thomas Hayden, "A Letter to the New (Young) Left."

[6] Keniston, *op. cit.*, p 162.

ization and abstraction of occupations (life on the assembly line or at the computor), encourages a "dissociation of fantasy" and imagination from everyday life:

. . . Our shared fantasies are almost entirely contrasts to daily life: they contrast with the *lack of violence or intense passion in the average man's life, and with the specialization and abstraction of his work*. Thus, they seldom serve to enrich life, but rather to vitiate its imaginative vitalities. [emphasis added][7]

If adults are becoming increasingly disenchanted with their lives, the adolescent increasingly sees adult life as a dull and unexciting business:

The [child] abandons a world of directness, immediacy, diversity, wholeness, integral fantasy, and spontaneity. He gains abstraction, distance, specialization, monotony, dissociated fantasy and conformity. Faced with [this] . . . transition . . . the youth can only hesitate on its threshold. . . . The humanization of childhood has been accompanied by a dehumanization of adulthood. . . .[8]

Thus, the student is torn between two alternatives: to enter the world of the adult on *its own terms*, or to remain a part of the student world until he can enter the adult on *his terms*. Yet it is difficult to enter on any terms *but* the given, precisely because it is hard to formulate any *other* terms, any alternatives to the present, any "positive myths" about the future and how it should be faced. If the student recoils immediately from this predicament, and proceeds no further in his analysis, he becomes "knowing," "cynical," determined to "get his" while he still possesses a modicum of freedom. Another, more difficult alternative is rebellion: but even here the student remains caught in the predicament. In order to be successful in his revolt, he must steer clear of the adult community: consequently, rebellion often leads to the construction of a very personal, private, and highly individualistic world of vehement nonconformity and gratification—*Playboy Magazine* affluence for the conventional; drugs and existentialism for the bohemian.

[7] Keniston, *ibid.*, p. 168.
[8] Keniston, *ibid.*, p. 172.

As an example of this tendency, Irving Howe points to the emphasis on "personal style" among many of the new left partisans, and suggests that *style* has in many cases taken precedence over the *content* of revolt, i.e., that the existential act of rebellion, whatever its forms, has come to be enough.[9] It is plausible, perhaps, that one reason for emphasis on style over content is that many students have become convinced that content *does not matter any more*; the public world is doomed, and the best one can do is dissociate oneself from it as quickly as possible.

Traditional political thought has always held that the most effective response to frustration among large numbers of people is collective action toward changing the institutional structure of society. Few on the left would dispute that, in theory. But collective action implies alliances, whereas the student who sees rebellion as a private act usually decorates his world view with extremely militant and exclusive moral imperatives. Morality and politics seem to be incompatible. Translated into tactics, this attitude often takes on the appearance of hostility toward the adult world, and has led many observers to interpret the student movement as one more manifestation of the conflict between the generations. But it is something more than hostility toward adults *qua* adults. The fear of distasteful alliances—of "selling out"—is partly a fear that, in spite of everything, the student will eventually be co-opted by Suburbia. And for much of the new left, that means the end of a decent human existence. Here, for instance, is Mario Savio during the sit-in at Sproul Hall:

American society is a bleak scene, but it is all a lot of us have to look forward to. Society provides no challenge. American society in the standard conception it has of itself is simply no longer exciting. The most exciting things going on in America today are movements to change America. . . . The "futures" and "careers" for which American students now prepare are for the most part

[9] Irving Howe, "New Styles in Leftism," *Dissent* (Summer 1965). See also W. C. McWilliams, "Students and Politics: The Would-Be New Rulers Against the Old," *motive* (vol. 25, 1964). Examples of this type of rebellion are legion: here we will mention only the recent draft-card burnings and self-immolations in the Vietnam demonstrations.

intellectual and moral wastelands. This chrome-plated consumers paradise would have us grow up to be well-behaved children.[10]

So it appears that Suburbia, as well as the proverbial Bomb, is one motivation for the present rebellion. It is at this point, when the rebel confronts the world he has been trained to "take over," that the handicaps of his origins become most apparent and most troublesome. Trained to think of the Public Order as irrelevant, he nevertheless fears it and is made uncomfortable by it. Unequipped to deal with it, he can only shrink in fear from the prospect of becoming one of its parts. Above all else, the rebel fears that he will become, inevitably, a part of that world, the adult world which beckons benevolently, and which holds out numerous material rewards in exchange for his soul. So the movement turns back, into itself, in a frenzied attempt to save its own before it is too late. It is possible that the new left does more good for its own members than for anyone else. But even that is a significant accomplishment. the present generation may one day have to live with Big Brother; they will never learn to love Him.

II

So we would participate. If this fever is contagious, we are harboring a revolution: the Western world has for two thousand years seldom known such a thing. Its resistance might be weak. But it takes a mighty swarm of mosquitoes to poison a Leviathan. And would not such a swarm be a Leviathan itself?

—Christopher Reiner

For many students the civil-rights movement was a direct challenge to the official version of American life, and at the same time a possible way out of the dilemma sketched above. Here, finally, was a cause worthy of the name. Here was an idea that could be carried into the adult world as a shield with which one might ward off the sterility of a normal American life. The intellectual and the student, says Paul Potter of SDS, have found a new home, outside of the university, in "agitation and movements for social change," a home that is more hospitable than the old one. If the

[10] Mario Savio, "An End to History."

fifties proclaimed the "end of ideology," the sixties would proclaim the "mystique of participation."

The story of the civil-rights movement has been told and retold a thousand times: for our purposes here we are mainly interested in it as a starting point from where the new left has moved in a number of directions, often farther than the civil-rights movement itself. In many ways, the history of the new left is one of the application, with varying degrees of success, of the lessons learned in the civil-rights movement to a number of different problems.

The trend within the student civil-rights organizations has been away from emphasis upon purely racial goals to an awareness of the relation of class *and* racial oppression.[11] A corollary of that trend has been an increased understanding of the common plight of both the Negro and white poor, especially in the North. Implicit in much of the analysis of SDS is a kind of populist excitement with the idea of a political coalition that would form along class, rather than racial or ethnic, lines.

Also implicit in SDS's analysis (and SNCC's as well) is another important assumption about the political characteristics of the poor, white and black: that the poor, by having "less stake" in the system, are therefore potentially more radical than anyone else. ". . . People strongly affected by the rottenness of our society," writes Todd Gitlin of SDS, "are best capable of exorcising that rot."[12] This is an assumption shared historically by many radical movements, but it has not gone unchallenged. Kimberly Moody, also of SDS, has argued that the poor cannot be thought of as a homogeneous class whose interests are at all times identical, and that the fact of poverty is not enough to produce a rebellion:

From an historical point of view, I believe it is fairly clear that it has *never* been the poorest sector of society that has rebelled. Rather, it has been that sector or those sectors that have been most

[11] See, for example, the difference in emphasis in the following pieces in this volume: "Spiritual and Moral Aspects of the Student Struggle in the South," by Charles McDew (1961); "Only Connect: Reflections on the Revolution," by Jonathan Eisen (1964); and "An Interracial Movement of the Poor?" by Thomas Hayden and Carl Wittman (1965).

[12] Todd Gitlin, "The Battlefields and the War."

pressed by the prevailing structural contradictions of the society at that time.[13]

According to this criticism, we might expect middle-class Negroes to be more ready for organization in civil-rights groups than their counterparts in the ghetto. To a large degree this has been true: no civil-rights group to this day has been able to gain a loyal following in the urban ghettoes.

SDS and SNCC suffer from a complication faced by most radical groups that see themselves as "unions": should they "represent" their constituents in the struggle for material and political goods, or should their main emphasis be upon "bringing down the system" regardless of the wishes of those the society has oppressed? The labor movement has opted for the first role, and SDS and SNCC seem to be doing the same. In spite of the concern for "working outside the system," projects like the Congressional challenge and the rent strike are clearly system-oriented. What could be less radical than demanding representation in Congress?

Beyond the debate over working within or without the system, SDS and SNCC face a second tension common to radical movements: the problem of leadership and democratic control, of "indigenism" versus "elitism." Indigenism refers to the theory that the exploited know best how to solve their problems, but are lacking organizational and administrative skills which it is the role of the student organizer to provide. This is a commonly accepted theory within SDS, and the debate is usually couched in terms of helping the poor to discover their "real" needs. The instincts of the "underclass" are basically accurate; it remains, however, to banish those misconceptions the poor have inherited from middle-class culture:

The problem is that needs immediately felt are not the only needs people have. . . . One of the diabolical successes of this organized society is that it perverts people's notions about themselves into fantasies that perpetuate an unjust system. . . . If you can get to the suburbs you'll be green, safe, and happy. . . . What you really need is Dial Soap and tail-fins. . . . Cultural and commercial pres-

[13] Kimberly Moody, "Can the Poor Be Organized?"

sures generate artificial "needs" that, in the minds of the victims, displace more genuine human needs.[14]

Unlike radical movements of previous generations, there are few in the present movement who are open advocates of elitism. Elitism occurs as an issue only in a negative way, as something to be studiously avoided. "We have been taking the greatest pains," writes Carl Wittman of an SDS project in Chester, Pennsylvania, "to develop grass roots leadership in the neighborhood organizations. Democracy does not come easily to people who have never worked with it and who do not believe in it; and when they accept it, they accept it in form only, and not in content. But slowly, people in the neighborhood . . . are rising, and displaying their potential."[15]

But the discussion of indigenism is as much one of goals as of means, for the two are clearly inseparable. An uncomfortable question lies in the back of the student's mind: is it not possible that we are leading the poor in the *wrong* direction? Is it not possible that we are leading them back into the middle class? This is a natural question for someone as anti-bourgeois as the student radical. But the answer is unavoidable: providing the underclass with the material and political power of the middle class (good housing, education, steady jobs, and so on) will *quite possibly* make them think and act like the rest of the middle class. But for the student—who has in many cases translated his hatred for middle-class culture into the belief that the culture of the poor is better—this is an unthinkable prospect. He immediately accuses himself of being an elitist, guilty of leading his people into a false Promised Land. In all this, of course, there is a valid point: what, beyond economic, political, and racial inequality, is wrong with this country? The new left's answer is that there is plenty more wrong, that the standard American way of life is incompatible with a decent human existence. The fear of creating a "new middle

[14] Todd Gitlin, "The Battlefields and the War." See also the discussions of leadership of the war on poverty in "The War on Poverty: Notes on Insurgent Response," by Rennie Davis.

[15] Carl Wittman, "Students and Economic Action," an SDS working paper which can be found in the original edition of *The New Student Left*, pp. 170–180.

class" rests, ultimately, upon an accurate perception of the inadequacy of middle-class culture.

But there is another dimension to this fear. Let us return for a moment to the radical as student. He is first of all a product of something: of that university toward which he has such ambivalent feelings and which he has not yet fully escaped. In the university he encounters a decision-making structure which purports to be democratic, but which is in fact paternalistic, and a political ideology which deprecates politics. As he begins the process of defection from the university system, he comes to the conclusion that the university—and, by extension, the society—is governed by irresponsible elites. Hierarchy and authoritarianism become synonymous.[16] The hostility toward "elitism" stems from the fear that the organizer will create, and become part of, a new hierarchy, one that will eventually be as unresponsive to the needs of the poor as the Welfare Department. Participatory democracy, then, is a way to purge American politics of hierarchy and elites, and to prevent their substitution by new ones.[17]

This hostility toward hierarchy and the plea for participatory democracy are never really reconciled with another important element in the new left's ideology: the belief, implicit in most of its writings, that industrialism is a fact of life, and probably a good thing. These are not Populists, and they do not advocate agrarian virtues. Unlike most American radical movements, the environment of the student revolt is purely urban; even its music comes from the cities. Only in an industrial society, moreover, can poverty be eliminated, cities rebuilt, or a number of other projects accomplished which the new left has advocated. The conflict may be posed in the following question: are the ideas of participatory democracy and community organization compatible with the growth of industrialization and urbanization?[18] There occurs

[16] David Esmond, "Community and its Nemeses: The New Left and International Politics," *The Activist*, November 1965.

[17] As of this writing, SDS is discussing the abolition of the offices of president and vice-president of the organization, on the grounds that they are incompatible with the theory of "consensus politics."

[18] Bruce Payne, "SNCC: An Overview Two Years Later."

among the students little if any overt criticism of the idea of participatory democracy, but there are indications that they have not answered the question to their own satisfaction. Beneath the surface can be detected a suspicion that the problems of an industrial society are not amenable to purely local—or even democratic—solutions:

. . . A major problem faces us in Chester [Pennsylvania], and will face all areas which begin similar [community] movements in the North: if one puts all one's hopes in a national solution and therefore a national movement, how will Chester hook up with this national movement, and what form will such a movement take? . . . Chester will soon reach the end of the number of projects which can achieve some success on the local level, and if leadership is good enough, Chester will soon face squarely the fact that national unemployment is the key issue, that working on other issues is dilatory. When Chester comes to that point, must it stagnate, die, or wait for the rest of the North to catch up . . . ?[19]

That, in fine, is the problem. If national solutions are, in fact, necessary—and it is difficult to imagine a non-national solution to unemployment—then are not the possibilities for local leadership severely circumscribed?

This does not mean, however, that local leadership is useless. In the most unreconstructed parts of the South, and in the cities, what the students have created so far resembles in many important respects a revamped "city machine," as yet powerless, but nevertheless responsive to the needs of the people it serves. The typical ERAP project operates with the intent of giving its people some feeling that, in the language of the old machine, "somebody cares."[20] Beyond that the hope is that by assisting the poor in their confrontations with the outside world, the student can give them some feeling of power, some notion that the outside world is accessible. And just as the old machine instructed the immigrant in the ways of the city and country he had adopted, the community project and the Freedom School instruct the indigent in the ways

[19] Carl Wittman, "Students and Economic Action."

[20] Cf., Rennie Davis, "The War on Poverty: Notes on Insurgent Response."

of the bureaucratized technology that confronts him. How does one go about moving a recalcitrant welfare office? How does one get a job when jobs are scarce? How can the police department be made receptive to the needs of the poor? In each instance the goal is more than immediate: the long-range goal is *control*, and the perception that certain means lead to certain ends, and that there are alternatives to the present. This is the prime function of any political leadership, and in spite of the "anti-leader" style of the new left, this is what it has been most successful at.

III

Last summer I went to Mississippi to join the struggle there for civil rights. This fall I am engaged in another phase of the same struggle, this time in Berkeley. . . . The same rights are at stake in both places—the right to participate as citizens in democratic society.

–Mario Savio

Rebellion, Albert Camus tells us, implies an affirmation as well as a negation. The student, in his university environment, searches for something to affirm. War is bad, he is told, but one is not to agitate for peace. Discrimination is bad, but one ought not to break Jim Crow laws. Poverty is inexcusable, but one is not to affirm the rights of the poor too stridently. The student senses, but does not really know, what is wrong. "Something" is wrong; "they" are messing things up terribly. The times seem to call for more, not less, passion; but the student is told to separate his values from his daily existence, to be "objective." The times seem to call for more, not less, inquiry, but he is told that the really important questions have all been asked and answered satisfactorily: "ideology" has come to an end because it is merely a way of asking questions, not of verifying answers. Long before the rebel confronts the power structure of the South, he has come into conflict—often serious—with the establishment of the university. It was inevitable that the movement should eventually turn, as at Berkeley, upon its most dangerous and most efficient enemy, the Multiversity.

In many important ways the structure of the university reflects, on a smaller scale, much of the social and political conflict of the outside world. Here, too, the student encounters an "unresponsive hierarchy," conservative and bureaucratic in its style and thought. Here, too, he encounters specialization, isolation, "bigness," and abstraction. The university appears to him as one more corporation, indistinguishable in its style from General Motors.

Faced with this impersonal structure, the first critical question the student is likely to ask is "What is it all for?" He may receive many answers to that question, but the most frightening is some form of the answer provided by Clark Kerr in *Industrialism and Industrial Man*. Kerr predicts that industrialism will move American society inevitably down a path toward a new class structure: the managers and the managed. The new structure implies a new purpose for the university: the production of managers for an ever-increasing industrial sector.[21] Students, while they are in the university, are part of the "managed" class. The function of the student once he has left the university is clear: he is to take his place at the machine. Kerr's thesis is both descriptive and normative: this is how the university is tending and the tendency should be encouraged. As Bruce Payne and his colleagues suggest, to the extent that Kerr's theory is descriptive, the new structure of the multiversity is enormously significant: in the budding class structure of Kerr's vision can be seen the source of the alienation of the American student.[22] The student response to this vision of the university was predictable—when the university treats its students as something less than human, as something resembling a cog in a machine, it can expect in return to be treated as something less than a university. Mario Savio stood atop a police car at the University of California and exhorted students to throw their bodies "upon the gears and upon the levers of the machine, and to indicate to the people that run it, that if you are not allowed to be free, the machine will be prevented from running at all."

But this structure has its advantages as well as disadvantages. In a smaller environment things can be seen in their essential rela-

[21] For a discussion of Kerr's philosophy and its effects upon the Berkeley campus, see Bruce Payne, David Walls, and Jerry Berman, "Theodicy of 1984: The Philosophy of Clark Kerr."

[22] Bruce Payne, *et al.*, "Theodicy of 1984: The Philosophy of Clark Kerr."

tionships, stripped of ambiguity. The vague distrust of the middle-class adult world can be translated into a specific disgust with Clark Kerr's vision of the multiversity. Power, to paraphrase Norman Mailer, has a face, and can be attacked. Public decisions can be seen as relevant to the personal problems of undergraduate life: the administrative mentality of *in loco parentis* can be identified, as Thomas Hayden argues, as the source of the frustration and boredom that stifles rebellion and creativity.[23] The great problem of the American student—his failure to perceive the political world as relevant to his personal fortunes—is made explicit and is largely resolved by the university's willingness to constrict his behavior and thought. One observer of the Berkeley revolt has this to say of the effect of the revolt on the political awareness of the student body:

> There were others in the outer ring of students [around the police car] who sympathized with the demand for free speech. Normally, they feared to act because of anxiety regarding clearances for jobs, or were unable to act for lack of a vehicle of expression. Some who felt politics to be "unreal" still felt it unjust to whisk a student off in a police car for so trivial an offense; *indeed, it was unjust because politics was unreal.*
>
> For all these reasons, the students of a large, anonymous university lost, for a moment, their feeling of being strangers to one another. Different in their motives, they lost their fear of difference in a common feeling of rebellion, and in a sense of equality in banding together.[24]

In addition to the process of the revolt at Berkeley, its goals represent a significant departure from orthodox student thought on the university. Students—even the conventional ones—have usually looked upon the university as being a temporary phase and as such not very important. Paul Potter, for instance, argues that the university, in spite of its conservatism, can be "used" by the movement for purposes of research, public relations, and financial aid, in the form of grants and fellowships. Rather than a "commu-

[23] Thomas Hayden, "Student Social Action."

[24] Joseph Paff, *et al.*, "The Student Riots at Berkeley: Dissent in the Multiversity."

nity of scholars," the university can be thought of as a "recruiting center" and way station, where the radical takes time off from his battles to renew contacts and do research.[25] But the Free Speech Movement realized that neither the student nor American society can remain independent of one of our most influential social institutions. The university will be, in DuBois' terms, a "center of polite society," or it will be "the organ of that fine adjustment between real life and the growing knowledge of life . . . which forms the secret of civilization." Or, as Michael Novak argues, the dehumanization of American culture will not be arrested if its roots run deep in the educational process itself.[26] The university is critical, and until it is reformed, the student movement and the American Left—to say nothing of American society—will go their way permanently scarred by their sojourn in 1984.

The vision of the political art is necessarily a public vision, one that demands a careful conceptualization of what the future ought to be. But the "utopias" of the past have been replaced by an apprehension, shared by rebels as well as conformists, a fear that the years to come hold only misery. The liberal creed once held that history moves endlessly upward. History is now seen as simply endless, with a slight suspicion that it is probably moving downward as well. History still progresses, but we have ceased believing in the particular brand of progress our culture has invented. We are living, as Michael Harrington tells us, in an "accidental century," and our public vision has been replaced by a private vision of hell.

We have been in this predicament before. The present generation is often compared with that of the thirties, but a better comparison might be with the generation of the twenties, who also sensed that their times were out of joint and that progress had become a dizzy spiral downward. They, too, because they no longer trusted history, no longer believed in any public vision that might redirect it. History became a monolithic "They." The reaction of the present generation is similar. The fear of the middle

[25] Paul Potter, "The Intellectual and Social Change."
[26] Cf., Michael Novak, "God in the Colleges."

class is really a fear that time will make even the rebel into a suburbanite. The point is not that the rebel should accept the public order of things: on the contrary, his analysis of history's downward trend may be accurate. The point is, rather, that the public order cannot be escaped: not by drugs, not by escape into the world of corporations, not by escape into the world of the poor. It must be dealt with. The revolt at Berkeley, insofar as it dealt with the university in a constructive and ruthless way, recognized that the public order might be forced to play an active role in the reconstruction of human existence. In so doing, it laid the foundation for a new ideology, a new utopia that reaffirmed the right of the underclass to be a *part* of society, and not just a rebellious or acquiescent outcast.

1. Agenda for a Generation

College administrators must face up to their public function. Gone are the good old days when school spirit meant hazing the freshmen, eating goldfish, and raiding the sororities. May I propose that all college administrators help tell our people what college study really means—what we must demand of our students—if we hope to make them active Americans. Make our people safe for students with ideas, and you will be performing a real service for America. You will be halting the epidemic of social hysteria that is spreading across our nation under the libelous labels of secret societies.

Far from discouraging your students' social and public interests, I propose that you positively exploit them. Here is an honorable source of college spirit; here is a worthy unifying and organizing principle for your whole campus life. I say: Thank God for the spectacle of students picketing—even when they are picketing me at Sacramento and I think they are wrong, for students protesting and Freedom Riding, for students listening to society's dissidents, for students going out into the fields with our migratory workers, and marching off to jail with our segregated Negroes. At last we're getting somewhere. The colleges have become bootcamps for citizenship—and citizen-leaders are marching out of them.

For a while, it will be hard on us as administrators. Some students are going to be wrong, and some people will want to deny them the right to make mistakes. Administrators will have to wade through the angry letters, and colleges will lose some donations. We Governors will have to face indignant caravans and elected officials bent on dictating to state colleges and faculties. But let us stand up for our students and be proud of them. If America is still on the way up, it will welcome this new, impatient, critical crop of young gadflies. It will be fearful only of the complacent and passive.

GOVERNOR EDMUND G. ("PAT") BROWN
from a Commencement Address
University of Santa Clara, 3 June 1961

A LETTER TO THE NEW (YOUNG) LEFT

by Thomas Hayden

In a publication such as *The Activist*, written and read by a community sharing some degree of consensus regarding political values, it should not be necessary to labor in detail over the several challenges confronting the peoples of the world, and especially confronting those who claim to be of the Left. However, in part:

Internationally, the growing power and even higher expectations of the "underdeveloped" nations; the numerous issues directly relating to man's nuclear arsenal; the population problem; the influence of the Cold War conflict on seemingly every private and public facet of the common life; the polarizing effects of the Cold War; the disintegration of easily-grasped categories like "democratic," "undemocratic," "neutral"; the evolution from Stalinism to ? in Russia; the hazy and threatening future of China; the movement of power away from the West in the United Nations; the development of outer space; the coming of new communications systems. . . .

Domestically, the failures of the welfare state to deal with the hard facts of poverty in America; the drift of decision-making power away from directly representative, legislative or executive institutions into corporate and military hands neither checked by nor responsible to the courted "public"; the persistence of a racism that mocks our principles and corrupts everyday life; the encroachment upon our civil liberties seen in the intellectually-masked "balancing" theory of the five Supreme Court judges as well as in the naked paranoia of our most rabid Communist-phobes; the resurgence of a leaderless McCarthyism raising the flag and fist in every city across the land; the near-total absence of left position in an incredibly conservative Congress; the growing dominance of the military over formerly civilian decisions; the decline of already-meager social welfare legislation in the face of larger defense appropriations; the squandering and continuous—though somewhat checked—exploiting of our natural resources; the ugliness and ill-planned nature of our cities; the development of a technology great in its potential. . . .

Educationally, the endless repressions of free speech and thought, the stifling paternalism that infects the student's whole perception of what is real and possible and enforces a parent-child relationship until the youth is suddenly transplanted into "the world;" the sterility of the student government and the general student community; curriculums conspicuously anachronistic in the fields of Africa, Asia and Latin America; whole new areas of study in astronomy and nuclear physics. . . .

The problems are immense. We of the Left, however, find no rest in theory, and little hope in leadership. Liberal philosophy has dealt inadequately with the twentieth century. Marx, especially Marx the humanist, has much to tell us but his conceptual tools are outmoded and his final vision implausible. The revolutionary leaders of the rising nations have been mostly non-ideological, either forced to be so or preferring (as is the case of Guevara) to forge their political views in the heat and exigencies of revolution and the present. The American intellectuals? C. Wright Mills is appealing and dynamic in his expression of theory in the grand manner, but his pessimism yields us no formulas, no path out of the dark, and his polemicism sometimes offends the critical sense. The others? There is, I find, an inhibiting, dangerous conservative temperament behind the facade of liberal realism which is so current: Niebuhr in theology; Kornhauser, Lipset, and Bell in political science and sociology; the neo-Freudians in psychology; Hofstadter in history; Schlesinger and others of the ADA mind in the Democratic Party. Their themes purport to be different but always the same impressions emerge: Man is inherently incapable of building a good society; man's passionate causes are nothing more than dangerous psychic sprees (the issues of this period too complex and sensitive to be colored by emotionalism or moral conviction); ideals have little place in politics—we should instead design effective, responsible programs which will produce the most that is realistically possible. . . . Here and there, from the pages of *Dissent* or from isolated radicals and scholars, including Mills himself, come cries: No! You false liberals are suffering from the failure of your youthful dreams; you are eviscerating the great optimistic tradition of liberalism from the Enlightenment to the twentieth century; you are justifying disinterest in morality; you are eliminating emotion, dissent, outrage and, yes, the wellsprings of life itself.

So here we stand, limp, questioning, even scared. Our jokes run something like the cover of a recent *Liberation:* scrawled in the manner one finds covering rest room walls is the question "What can we do now?" and the huge, bold answer, "Get ready to die." It is not as though we can dismiss the world; some of us know people who already have contracted radiation disease. It is not as though we can change things; Mills was pretty accurate with his description of the monolithic power elite. It is not as though we even know what to do: We have no real visionaries for our leaders, we are not much more than literate ourselves. And it is not as though, I also fear, we even know who we are. What has made me so strangely sensitive when my brothers seem so acquiescent, what has made me call insane what the experts call the "hard facts of power politics," what has made me feel we are on the threshold of death when others excitedly say we are on the New Frontier, and why have I turned with trembling and disgust from the Americans who do recognize peril and recoil into shelters full of the comforting gadgets the culture has produced? A more blinding situation is difficult to imagine. War, ironically, would be cathartic—though the release would be grimly brief.

In the unpredictable meantime, there are classes to attend; there are drinking bouts ahead, new friendships to be formed, loves to be experienced, parents to relate to—in short, lives to be led, no matter what the tension.

But there are more than normal lives for us to lead. The felt truths of this age call us to incorporate new dimensions into our existence. Those dimensions will constitute our response to the challenges of modernity I have briefly mentioned. Here a fundamental point should be made: "Challenge" implies not only threat but opportunity. We have access to more knowledge, more potential and actual and varied power than ever before, and in the endlessness of change lies always the possibility of making new and revolutionary departures.

How, then, shall we respond? I should like here to separate style of response from program of response and claim that both our style and our program can tend toward either a defeating dogmatism or a hopeful radicalism.

By dogmatism of style is meant the style which employs stereotypes, untested concepts, easy answers, ritualistic language. Red-baiting, especially the loose use of "stalinoid" and "stalinist" is usually either paranoiac or begs the central question: It attacks motivation or psychology without substantively addressing whatever issue is really at hand, e.g. whether or not democratic social control is evolving in the Soviet Union, whether or not the Hungarian revolution was a fascist-inspired uprising. Red-baiting is no more or less dogmatic, I should add, than its current opposite, "anti-anti-communism," or "issues orientation," which tends to seal off critical, freewheeling discussion in the worthless name of "group unity." The "issues orientation" tendency says essentially: Let us join together in action wherever we agree upon the specific, isolated issue, regardless of our differences over any other issues; let us find an ideology "inductively," through group action, rather than starting with an ideology and running off into sectarian corners to spar. The danger in this course of action has not been, as fearful persons would allege, "fellow travelling" and "fronting," but, more concretely, the subversion of the possibility of lending a persuasive, insightful intellectual content to protest. "Ban the bomb" is a sentiment we all share intestinally, but it makes a movement appear mindless to the decision-makers. Furthermore, it communicates no challenge to the Rand or Nato intellects, and most important, it has no permanent educational effect upon participant, audience, and society.

The radical style, on the other hand, takes as its presupposition Dewey's claim that we are free to the extent that we know what we are about. Radicalism as a style involves penetration of a social problem to its roots, to its real causes. Radicalism presumes a willingness to continually press forward the query: Why? Radicalism finds no rest in conclusions; answers are seen as provisional, to be discarded in the face of new evidence or changed conditions. This is, in one sense, a difficult mental task and, in a more profound moral sense, it represents a serious personal decision to be introspective, to be exposed always to the stinging glare of change, to be willing always to reconstruct our social views. Who likes to understand himself, or be without his personal Bible, be it that of Marx, Freud, Darwin, or Christ? Radicalism of style asks us to go beyond the State Department lies about the U-2, or the simplistic view that Khrushchev dropped the fifty-megaton bomb for purposes of pure terror, or that democratic socialism solves all the problems of individual development. In its harshest condensation, radicalism of style demands that we oppose delusions and be free. It demands that we change our life.

All this circumlocution is not intended to suggest that simple moral statements or concerns are meaningless. On the contrary, I think most persons who lean to the left politically are moved by quite important feelings of solidarity for the impoverished, the oppressed, the debased, and all of suffering mankind; by a commitment to the general ideals of Western humanism, particularly, the freedoms of speech, thought, and association; by a distrust of selfish, competitive individualism operating in the economic sphere (or any other); by a belief in cooperation and collective planning balanced against the necessity for individual consent; and so on. These, however enthralling, are not worthy of our allegience as abstraction. It is their infusion into practical life which gives them true content and determines the extent to which we shall value them. The things we are for or against are quite simple at the level of abstraction; it is in the test of their practical meaning that we must make our judgment—not between good and evil, but the more difficult distinction between better or best, or the hardest choice of all, that of the necessary evil. Radicalism, it seems to me, does not exclude morality; it invites and is given spirit by the quality of *reflective commitment*, the combining of our passion and our critical talents into a provisional position. To remove an idea from the plane of abstraction, it should be added, means to inject its meaning into our total life—to send telegrams of support to Southern students means to *live one's solidarity with them*, not to belie glorious phrases by private selfishness or tolerance of local discrimination.

Radical program is simply the radical style as it attempts to change the practical life. As with style, a radical program is not one that rests before it has plumbed to the basis of the problem it confronts. We should not be satisfied with going by "back door" methods (however "realistic") to persuade President Kennedy to wire a telegram of encouragement to a jailed Martin Luther King. That is problem-mitigating, not problem-solving. That is useful, preventive, and even opinion-changing, but not radical for it in no sense identifies and deals with the underlying political-economic-historic-psychological bases of the problem.

All this is not to say we should diminish our urgency or reduce our passions—we should not. This is not to say we should go off in corners to study "both sides of the issue"—we should, but not exclusively. This is simply to say that the student movement which has rejected so many institutions and instruments of social change—the Southern courtrooms, by and large the Democratic Party, the military, often the Congress—has invented no substitute save a noble morality and in some cases a commitment to non-violence that will dissipate soon if not secured in new social structures. An essential phase of radicalism is the decision to disengage oneself entirely from the system being confronted (segregation for example) so that the structure sustained by our former attitudes can no longer endure. Another essential, however, is that we visualize and then build structures to counter those which we oppose. This extends from the concrete formation of a national student organization to the conceptual—for the time being—formation of a different society.

Instead of this we find ourselves making the understandably frequent mistake, for example, of confusing target with goal. This is true of the campaign to abolish the House Committee on Un-American Activities. HUAC is surely no more than a target, but our passions have made its abolition, in fact, a goal. The danger here is that in our failure to formulate a comprehensive personal vision of a social goal beyond the abolition of HUAC, abolition itself may not carry with it a scourging effect on the society. The deeply rooted strands of nationalism, fascism, and racism will be newly woven in new HUAC's by our fearful public. Similarly, the lunch counter sit-in movement has been forced to develop a broader, more complex vision of the future—inter-relating targets with goals—to remain successful.

Thus far we have been quick to know what we oppose: racism, militarism, nationalism, oppression of mind and spirit, unrestrained capitalism, provincialism of various kinds, and the bombs. It has been an almost instinctive opposition. We have been hurt by what exists, and we have responded in outrage and compassion. However, the times are too threatening for us to respond simply as comforters of the oppressed. Keeping sentiments as our base, we must move ahead concertedly with our goal—the changing of society, not the assuaging of its continuous ills. That means politics as well as sentimentality. That means writers and theoreticians as well as organizers and picketers. That means drawing on what remains of the adult labor, academic and political communities, not just revolting in despair against them and the world they have designed for us. Contrary to what our passions demand, our struggle will not be brief and cataclysmic–unless terminated in the roaring climax of nuclear war. Our gains will be modest, not sensational. It will be slow and exhaustingly complex, lasting at the very least for our lifetimes. For many of us it will not and cannot be a college fling, a costless, painless tugging at our liberal sentimentality. It will be longer, and the cost great.

What is desperately needed, I think, is the person of vision and clarity, who sees both the model society and the pitfalls that precede its attainment, and who will not destroy his vision for short-run gains but, instead, hold it out for all to see as the furthest dream and perimeter of human possibility. I am beset by doubt at this point; so, perhaps, are we all. We doubt our ability to effect change, we doubt our ability to understand enough, we doubt the validity of time-honored liberal notions, we doubt the right and wrong of it. I do not recommend that we banish doubt and rush forth under the banal slogan "where there is a will there is a way," but I would suggest that it is possible and necessary to begin to think and act—provisionally yet strongly—in the midst of our doubts. We must begin to see doubt, not as a reason for inaction—that way leads to intellectual sterility. We must see it as a reminder that infallibility is not the property of any single man and, moreover, that compassion for enemies is not simply a heroic show, but a manifestation of our deepest moral anxiety.

Thomas Hayden is a past president of Students for a Democratic Society and a staff member of the Newark Community Union Project (ERAP) in Newark, N. J. "Letter to the New (Young) Left" originally appeared in The Activist, *Winter 1961.*

FROM THE *PORT HURON STATEMENT*

We are people of this generation, bred in at least modest comfort, housed in universities, looking uncomfortably to the world we inherit.

. . .

Our work is guided by the sense that we may be the last generation in the experiment with living. But we are a minority—the vast majority of our people regard the temporary equilibriums of our society and the world as eternally-functional parts. In this is perhaps the outstanding paradox: We ourselves are imbued with urgency, yet the message of our society is that there is no viable alternative to the present. Beneath the reassuring tones of the politicians, beneath the common opinion that America will "muddle through," beneath the stagnation of those who have closed their minds to the future, is the pervading feeling that there simply are no alternatives, that our times have witnessed the exhaustion not only of Utopias, but of any new departures as well. Feeling the press of complexity upon the emptiness of life, people are fearful of the thought that at any moment things might thrust out of control. They fear change itself, since change might smash whatever invisible framework seems to hold back chaos for them now. For most Americans, all crusades are suspect, threatening. The fact that each individual sees apathy in his fellows perpetuates the common reluctance to organize for changes. The dominant institutions are complex enough to blunt the minds of their potential critics, and entrenched enough to swiftly dissipate or entirely repel the energies of protest and reform, thus limiting human expectancies. Then, too, we are a materially improved society, and by our own improvements we seem to have weakened the case for change.

Some would have us believe that Americans feel contentment amidst prosperity—but might it not better be called a glaze above deeply-felt anxieties about their role in the new world? And if these anxieties produce a developed indifference to human affairs, do they not as well produce a yearning to believe there *is* an alternative to the present, that something *can* be done to change circumstances in the school, the workplaces, the bureaucracies, the government? It is to this latter yearning, at once the spark and engine of change, that we direct our present appeal. The search for truly democratic alternatives to the present, and a commitment to social experimentation with them, is a worthy and fulfilling human enterprise, one which moves us and, we hope, others today. . . .

Values

Making values explicit—an initial task in establishing alternatives—is an activity that has been devalued and corrupted. The conventional moral terms of the age, the politician moralities ("free world," "peoples democracies") reflect realities poorly, if at all, and seem to function more as ruling myths than as descriptive principles. But neither has our experience in the universities brought us moral enlightenment. Our professors and administrators sacrifice controversy to public relations; their curriculums change more slowly than the living events of the world; their skills and silence are purchased by investors in the arms race; passion is called unscholastic. The questions we might want raised—what is really important? can we live in a different and better way? if we wanted to change society, how would we do it?—are not thought to be questions of a "fruitful, empirical nature," and thus are brushed aside.

Unlike youth in other countries we are used to moral leadership being exercised and moral dimensions being clarified by our elders. But today, for us, not even the liberal and socialist preachments of the past seem adequate to the forms of the present. Consider the old slogans: Capitalism Cannot Reform Itself, United Front Against Fascism, General Strike, All Out on May Day. Or, more recently, No Cooperation with Commies and Fellow Travelers, Ideologies Are Exhausted, Bipartisanship, No Utopias. These are incomplete, and there are few new prophets. It has been said that our liberal and socialist predecessors were plagued by vision without program, while our own generation is plagued by program without vision. All around us there is astute grasp of method, technique—the committee, the *ad hoc* group, the lobbyist, the hard and soft sell, the make, the projected image—but, if pressed critically, such expertise is incompetent to explain its implicit ideals. It is highly fashionable to identify oneself by old categories, or by naming a respected political figure, or by explaining "how we would vote" on various issues.

Theoretic chaos has replaced the idealistic thinking of old—and, unable to reconstitute theoretic order, men have condemned idealism itself. Doubt has replaced hopefulness, and men act out a defeatism that is labelled realistic. The decline of utopia and hope is in fact one of the defining features of social life today. The reasons are various: The dreams of the older left were perverted by Stalinism and never recreated; the congressional stalemate makes men narrow their view of the possible; the specialization of human activity leaves little room for sweeping thought; the horrors of the twentieth century, symbolized in the gas ovens and concentration camps and atom bombs, have blasted hopefulness. To be idealistic is to be considered apocalyptic, deluded. To have no serious aspirations, on the contrary, is to be "tough-minded."

In suggesting social goals and values, therefore, we are aware of entering a sphere of some disrepute. Perhaps matured by the past, we have no sure formulas, no closed theories—but that does not mean values are beyond discussion and tentative determination. A first task of any social movement is to convince people that the search for orienting theories and the creation of human values is complex but worthwhile. We are aware that to avoid platitudes we must analyze the concrete conditions of social order. But to direct such an analysis we must use the guideposts of basic principles. Our own social values involve conceptions of human beings, human relationships, and social systems.

We regard *men* as infinitely precious and possessed of unfulfilled capacities for reason, freedom, and love. In affirming these principles we are aware of countering perhaps the dominant conceptions of man in the twentieth century: that he is a thing to be manipulated, and that he is inherently incapable of directing his own affairs. We oppose the depersonalization that reduces human beings to the status of things. If anything, the brutalities of the twentieth century teach that means and ends are intimately related, that vague appeals to "posterity" cannot justify the mutilations of the present. We oppose, too, the doctrine of human incompetence because it rests essentially on the modern fact that men have been "competently" manipulated into incompetence. We see little reason why men cannot meet with increasing skill the complexities and responsibilities of their situation, if society is organized not for minority participation but for majority participation in decision-making.

Men have unrealized potential for self-cultivation, self-direction, self-understanding, and creativity. It is this potential that we regard as crucial and to which we appeal—not to the human potentiality for violence, unreason, and submission to authority. The goal of man and society should be human independence: a concern not with image or popularity but with finding a meaning in life that is personally authentic; a quality of mind not compulsively driven by a sense of powerlessness, nor one which unthinkingly adopts status values, nor one which represses all threats to its habits, but one which has full, spontaneous access to present and past experiences, one which easily unites the fragmented parts of personal history, one which openly faces problems which are troubling and unresolved—one with an intuitive awareness of possibilities, an active sense of curiosity, an ability and willingness to learn.

This kind of independence does not mean egoistic individualism; the object is not to have one's way so much as it is to have a way that is one's own. Nor do we deify man—we merely have faith in his potential.

Human relationships should involve fraternity and honesty. Human interdependence is contemporary fact; human brotherhood must be willed, however, as a condition of future survival and as the most appropriate form of social relations. Personal links between man and man are needed, especially to go beyond the partial and fragmentary bonds of function that bind men only as worker to worker, employer to employee, teacher to student, American to Russian.

Loneliness, estrangement, isolation describe the vast distance between man and man today. These dominant tendencies cannot be overcome by better personnel management, nor by improved gadgets, but only when a love of man overcomes the idolatrous worship of things by man.

As the individualism we affirm is not egoism, the selflessness we affirm is not self-elimination. On the contrary, we believe in generosity of a kind that imprints one's unique individual qualities in the relation to other men, and to all human activity. Further, to dislike isolation is not to favor the abolition of privacy; the latter differs from isolation in that it occurs or is abolished according to individual will.

. . .

In the last few years, thousands of American students demonstrated that they at least felt the urgency of the times. They moved actively and directly against racial injustices, the threat of war, violations of individual rights of conscience and, less frequently, against economic manipulation. They succeeded in restoring a small measure of controversy to the campuses after the stillness of the McCarthy period. They succeeded, too, in gaining some concessions from the people and institutions they opposed, especially in the fight against racial bigotry.

The significance of these scattered movements lies not in their success or failure in gaining objectives—at least not yet. Nor does the significance lie in the intellectual "competence" or "maturity" of the students involved—as some pedantic elders allege. The significance is in the fact that the students are breaking the crust of apathy and overcoming the inner alienation—facts that remain the defining characteristics of American college life.

If student movements for change are rarities still on the campus scene, what is commonplace there? The real campus, the familiar campus, is a place of private people, engaged in their notorious "inner emigration." It is a place of commitment to business-as-usual, getting ahead, playing it cool. It is a place of mass affirmation of the Twist, but mass reluctance toward the controversial public stance. Rules are accepted as "inevitable," bureaucracy as "just circumstances," irrelevance as "scholarship," selflessness as "martyrdom," politics as "just another way to make people, and an unprofitable one, too."

Almost no students value activity as a citizen. Passive in public, they are hardly more idealistic in arranging their private lives; Gallup concludes they will settle for "low success, and won't risk high failure." There is not much willingness to take risks (not even in business), no setting of dangerous goals, no real conception of personal identity except one manufactured in the image of others, no real urge for personal fulfillment except to be almost as successful as the very successful people. Attention is being paid to social status (the quality of shirt collars, meeting people, getting wives or husbands, making solid contacts for later on); much, too, is paid to academic status (grades, honors, the med school rat-race). But neglected generally is real intellectual status, the personal cultivation of the mind.

. . .

Look beyond the campus, to America itself. That student life is more intellectual, and perhaps more comfortable, does not obscure the fact that the fundamental qualities of life on the campus reflect the habits of society at large. The fraternity president is seen at the junior manager levels; the sorority queen has gone to Grosse Pointe; the serious poet burns for a place, any place, to work; the once-serious and never-serious poets work at the advertising agencies. The desperation of people threatened by forces about which they know little and of which they can say less, the cheerful emptiness of people giving up all hope of changing things, the faceless ones polled by Gallup who listed "international affairs" fourteenth on their list of problems but who also expected thermonuclear war in the next few years—in these and other forms, Americans are in withdrawal from public life, from any collective effort at directing their own affairs.

Some regard these national doldrums as a sign of healthy approval of the established order, but is it approval by consent or by manipulated acquiescence? Others declare that the people are withdrawn because compelling issues are fast disappearing; perhaps there are fewer breadlines in America, but is Jim Crow gone, is there enough work and is work more fulfilling, is world war a diminishing threat, and what of the revolutionary new peoples? Still others think the national quietude is a necessary consequence of the need for elites to resolve complex and specialized problems of modern industrial society. But, then, why should business elites help decide foreign policy, and who controls the elites anyway, and are they solving mankind's problems? Others finally shrug knowingly and announce that full democracy never worked anywhere in the past—but why lump qualitatively different civilizations together, and how can a social order work well if its best thinkers are skeptics, and is man really doomed forever to the domination of today?

There are no convincing apologies for the contemporary malaise. . . . The apathy is, first, subjective—the felt powerlessness of ordinary people, the resignation before the enormity of events. But subjective apathy is encouraged by the objective American situation—the actual separation of people from power, from relevant knowledge, from pinnacles of decision-making. Just as the university influences the student way of life, so do major social institutions create the circumstances in which the isolated citizen will try hopelessly to understand his world and himself.

The very isolation of the individual—from power and community and ability to aspire—means the rise of a democracy without publics. With the great mass of people structurally remote and psychologically hesitant with respect to democratic institutions, those institutions themselves attenuate and become, in a fashion of the vicious circle, progressively less accessible to those few who aspire to serious participation in social affairs. The vital democratic connection between community and leadership, between the mass and the several elites, has been so wrenched and perverted that disastrous policies go unchallenged time and again. . . .

The first effort, then, should be to state a vision: What is the perimeter of human possibility in this epoch? . . . The second effort, if we are to be politically responsible, is to evaluate the prospects for obtaining at least a substantial part of that vision in our epoch: What are the social forces that exist, or that must exist, if we are to be successful? And what role have we ourselves to play as a social force?

The Port Huron Statement *was adopted by the Students for a Democratic Society at their convention in Port Huron, Michigan, in 1962. While not at present the official policy statement of SDS, it remains extremely influential, especially among those students just entering the movement.*

THE INTELLECTUAL AND SOCIAL CHANGE

by Paul Potter

All paths in the university seem to turn ultimately back upon the university and back upon the established order within it. The academic pecking order; the establishment of professional organizations and the criteria of excellence they set forth—all of these were turned back upon the bureaucratic organization of the university, upon the isolation of the intellectual, or upon his faithful service to the Establishment and to the status quo. This left those intellectuals who wished to play a dissenting role in a peculiarly exposed position. There was not a place for them to go. There was no home for them. The university, which was supposed to provide their home, was not willing to play that role. The agencies in which they might work, in which they were welcomed, were not agencies that wanted critical dissent; they were agencies that wanted expert advice in carrying out the already established programs. And this was a pattern, I think, which dominated the post-war era. There are exceptions to that. In some sense I make this position an archetype more than it may have been. But let me give a few specific examples of how the intellectuals were exposed.

I think the whole debate on civil liberties that raged in the post-war era and especially in the 1950's is a good example of this exposure. It was a debate that was divorced from any analysis of the problems of the society at large. It was a fraudulent debate. It was a debate which could only have been a significant debate in a society that was actually threatened by anarchy or by imminent revolution. It was not a real debate and yet the intellectuals participated in it with vigor because it seemed to be the only way of extricating themselves from the squeeze that they were in.

Another example would be the ADA and its development—the amalgamation presumably of labor and intellectuals into a vital political force, an amalgamation which in its very effectiveness led to the co-optation of more intellectuals into the power structure, rather than the freeing of the intellectuals from the burdens of an oppressive university system.

A final example, one which I'll return to later, of the impetus of the intellectual in the universities, was (and is) beautifully illustrated by faculty politics—the most petty, mundane, bureaucratically centered system of politics that I can imagine. It is not a set of political activities that has as its basis the idea of liberating the university from the society. It is a set of politics which is organized around personal advancement, prestige, centers of influence and power within the university—not within society.

But I think there has been a change, and the change is what I want to talk about most of all. For the first time, there are alternatives to the intellectual other than service to the Establishment or isolation from society, and those alternatives are being enunciated and proclaimed and implemented by social movements in the society. For the first time there is a base of power outside the university to which the intellectual can turn—which he can utilize in freeing himself from the strictures of the university system, in defending himself from the exposed position which he held in society until 1955 or later.

This, essentially, is another place to go. It is a home. It is not the home that any of us predicted. The home that we've been looking for is in the university, and the home the intellectual is finding is in social movements, political action, and agitation.

Out of this comes a new view, a new view that is expressed by an increasing number of intellectuals and students. . . . They no longer think of the university as a Gestalt—as a possibility of a new synthesis, of a deep and beautiful image shimmering in the far-distant future. They think of the university very concretely as a mechanism they can utilize, that they can manipulate to gain certain ends which they consider important.

. . .

Intellectuals want direct power. They no longer want to deal with power as an abstract symbol of the classroom and of lectures. They want to utilize power for social ends, and from this insurgency comes autonomy. . . . There is the paradox: Autonomy is not isolation. Autonomy is involvement, and this is the critical factor which I think we have submerged in our own particular ways of talking about university reform as the penultimate goal of our new society.

Let me skip back to the old order for a moment because I want to trace an important aspect of that order into the new. In the old order, with the pecking order, with the politics, with the service of the Establishment, with the isolation, there was a tremendous amount of cynicism. I think that if the universities were shot through with this cynicism (It has been called "goofing off"; Norman Mailer, I think, would call it a particular kind of academic hipsterism), then there was an understanding on the part of the intellectuals that the work they were doing was not important, that it was devoid of deep meaning for themselves. There was a peculiar kind of alienation for the intellectual which had expression in the rejection of Labor, in the rejection of the masses of the people, and a turning inward of the universities—looking at the navel and hoping to find a way out of the problems which had their roots in the social structure. This alienation had its expression in the students: A hundred thousand a year drop out because they can't take it any longer, because they find it detached and drifting away from the elements of life that are meaningful to them. The alienation is found in the introductory psychology lecture where the student is told as he walks in the door that nothing he learns is to be utilized in his life experience because it is esoteric. It is found in the elevation of all knowledge in sociology, in large numbers of fields, to the realm of esoteria and remoteness.

This cynicism remains, and if anything it has been strengthened. Yet in the past when intellectuals were cynical they dreamed of the day when the university might be reformed. Today, I think that is receding. And instead, intellectuals are thinking increasingly of how they can use the University to accomplish pragmatic ends. . . .

Why is it that the university tolerates being milked for money and being placed in a position where it is supporting movements which normally it would not desire to support? I want to bring out two points in answer to this. First of all, there's an inability of the Establishment today in American society to comprehend or to deal with the kinds of problems that are becoming increasingly apparent. And there's a need, an organic need, in the social system to loosen up and to allow people more freedom in exploring these problems. So there is a desire, increasingly on the part of informed Establishment members (and I include President Kennedy in that) to have new thought flowing up through the social structure, to allow some mobility, some freedom, and some leeway. That's one reason.

The other reason, and I think this is particularly significant, is the increasing inability of the social system to handle conflict. There is a minority of intellectuals, however, who are willing to talk publicly about the needs for change. The university system is buckling because it would rather pay off this group of intellectuals than continue to have the kind of adverse publicity which works to the detriment of the university system in the eyes of the State and the legislature and the other key institutions upon which the university depends for support.

How this change of which I've talked is coming about is an important new experience for intellectuals. There is an end, I think, of the old romance about power. Power was something that *Time Magazine* had, power was something that congressmen had, power was something that only the people at the pinnacles of bureaucratic structures could hold and the only way to obtain access to power was to serve those structures and exert minor influence on their peripheries. But there is a new understanding, gained through direct participation in social movements, that power is something that can be created, that it can be generated at the base of the social structure; and the intellectual can obtain power by involving himself in the emerging centers of power in society: the civil rights movement, the peace movement, the discussion of economic issues. So there is an end to the romantic vision of power as something that could not be touched, and there is a beginning of a self-conscious use of power for the accomplishment of certain goals.

. . .

So there aren't two communities; there is a series of communities and a kind of interchange of material and ideas and people that is going on within that series of communities. This interchange ranges from fairly esoteric research organizations on the economy or peace or conflict resolution, to the people who are in the field and on the line collecting signatures and picketing and going to jail. This kind of flow back and forth is the current dynamic which keeps the whole system operating. . . . We find a new sense of mobility, a self-conscious sense of the ability of the people to move in society, up and down in the social structure, in and out of roles, in and out of class conditions. Thus the university becomes a center for research, for training, for mobility . . . for inspiration, for new thinking—the list could go on.

. . .

What is happening is what in December I was wont to call "dropping out of the system." But what is critical about the new situation is that although people are dropping out, they are hanging on with one hand and are knocking the system for all it's worth. And they are getting away with it as well.

I think that now we must pause and think a bit about the attractiveness of the picture I've attempted to sketch, because if it is correct, it means that the romance is over. It means that in a sense the community of scholars is no longer something that is on the horizon. The community of scholars is drifting into the archives of the library and is being replaced by a much more explicit and comprehensive framework of social change. And I think that we have to understand this in all its implications; we especially have to understand that in giving up the conception of the community of scholars, we do not fail to replace it with another conception which is as coherent and humane and as beautiful as that conception was. We have to replace it, not with a revised conception of a community of scholars, but with a community of people—a community which includes not only scholars but workers and housewives and individuals from all walks of life who will, I hope, make up the kind of community in which the community of scholars would have existed, but in which there are much more attractive and meaningful alternatives to that once-heralded situation.

Paul Potter, a graduate of Oberlin College and a graduate student at the University of Michigan, is a past-president of the Students for a Democratic Society and is active in the Cleveland Economic Research and Action Project of SDS (ERAP). This article was originally published as an SDS working paper in 1964.

THE STUDENT AND RELIGIOUS COMMITMENT

by Philip Altbach

In this piece Mr. Altbach asks why the student "is alienated from one of the traditional sources of inspiration for social action, that of religious concern?" He comes to the conclusion that the movement of students out of our churches is one more symptom of the increasing secularizing of political ideology.

The recent rise of political and social action among students has caused some people to question the motives of this activity and to look for the basis of their discontent manifested in the student peace movement, in the civil rights and sit-in struggles, and in the fight for civil liberties. Religious leaders have noticed that students no longer seem to take religion as their basis for meeting social issues. They have bemoaned the fact that the students who are involving themselves in the fight for a better society are usually not those from the campus religious fellowships or the churches. They are, rather, secularly oriented and . . . uninterested in questions of theology and . . . often hostile to the religious establishment.

A number of observers have noted that the students who are doing the protesting and taking the moral stand these days also are not interested in . . . ideological considerations. . . . They are concerned with protesting a specific injustice or working for a concrete cause, be it the eradication of racial discrimination in the South (or the North), the halting of nuclear weapons testing, or the abolition of the House Committee on Un-American Activities. If anything, the present crop of concerned students is motivated by vague emotional feelings or "enlightened self-interest," rather than by a desire for service or responsibility to a higher force.

Why is it that the student is alienated from one of the traditional sources of inspiration for social action, that of religious concern? Religious leaders have questioned the motivation of the student movement. They have, however, been unable to make any real impact on the majority of the students involved in the movement in recent years. Much of the student activity of the thirties and before was based on a religious commitment. The YMCA was once one of the most important vehicles of social action among students. Thousands of students were involved in various social struggles from a specifically religious viewpoint. Their action in one or another organization was motivated by a commitment to a broader ideology, that of the church. Jewish students, also, participated in politics from a Jewish standpoint and committed themselves to act in keeping with the best traditions of the Prophets. Today, the "Y" movement is a shadow of its former self, and in very few instances is there any real grass-roots social action. Many Jewish students participate in the student movement and work actively for one cause or another, but very seldom as Jews, just as Christian students work actively, but seldom with any Christian identification. One of the serious consequences of this trend toward "noncommitment" among students in terms of social action is that a particular individual, having no real belief in any broader set of principles, will wander in and out of the student movement and be unwilling to make any extensive contribution. This is one of the reasons for the dismal failure of the civil rights movement in the North, where students supported the southern sit-ins for a time and then almost totally withdrew from the struggle. In addition, the collapse of the civil liberties movement among students, which so vigorously opposed the Un-American Activities Committee, . . . is another indication of the lack of broader basis and dedication in the student movement.

The challenge to the church is clear. If religion is to take an active part in the lives of concerned students, it must be made relevant to them. At the present time, the failure of religious institutions of the United States to present the students with a meaningful program is obvious. Despite the church's expenditure of large sums of money on staff and facilities, students are turning in ever increasing numbers to small organizations with much commitment but meager resources. The Protestant fellowships, the Hillel foundations, the Newman clubs apparently have not been inspiring commitment in the students. Even with professional staff, campus religious groups have not been meeting the needs of today's "concerned students."

. . .

An example of the importance of Christian motivation in one segment of the student movement will serve as a contrast with the mainstream. . . . The civil rights movement in the deep South found its stimulus in the Christian concern of students at a number of small and otherwise benighted denominational colleges. Although they are perhaps the last places that the trained social analyst would look for a grassroots movement for social change, these schools provided a basis for civil rights activity that was felt throughout the nation. Why did these students act? According to their leaders, one of the main reasons for their action was a realization that segregation and Christianity were incompatible. Many of the students who suffered beatings and jail sentences stated that their mainstay throughout these tribulations was their Christian witness coupled with a faith in nonviolence as taught by Jesus and Gandhi. Perhaps the reason that the Negro students in the South were motivated by religious principles to move toward justice is that only among the Negro minority is religion still an important factor in everyday life. The church is not only a means of social mobility and communication, but is also a mainstay of community life. This is not true of American society in general.

The nature of American religious life has played an important, if negative role in shaping the ideology of the college student. The move toward secularism among concerned students and the religious and social apathy of those students who nominally identify with the religious groups on campus are indicative of the present situation. Students who instinctively "want to do something" are often repelled by the hypocrisy of churches which engage in segregation while preaching equality. Stress on fund-raising and building programs rather than on feeding the poor and helping the needy is hardly in keeping with the teachings of Jesus or the tradition of the Old Testament prophets. The moral teachings which are inherent in both Christianity and Judaism no longer seem meaningful to those in charge of the nation's religious establishments, and organized religion seems to be concerned with the more mundane matters of social programs and seeing that seats are filled for services. The church has increasingly identified itself with the middle class to such a degree that it is difficult for sensitive young people to see that the values of the middle class cannot wholly fit into an ethical system consistent with the teachings of their religion.

The problem is clear. Ministers and others may bemoan the fact that fewer and fewer dedicated people are interested in religious activity, yet this trend will continue until some real changes are made in the religious institutions of this country. . . .

Why, one might ask, is the trend away from religious social action to be regretted? Can't such activity be carried on by nonreligious groups just as well? The present trend is alarming for two reasons. In the first place, it means that the churches are losing their vitality and appeal to concerned young people and that many of these young people are not being exposed to what used to be called the Social Gospel. Middle-class students often have never heard of some of the social problems facing the urban lower class and are not overly disturbed about the possibility of nuclear war or the situation in Asia and Africa. True, their attitude is generally that of their parents and teachers, yet it is unfortunate that the religious institutions have abdicated their role as a focus of concern and a "gadfly" to a materialistic and conformist world.

Secondly, . . . the present student movement lacks the perspective that the religious student community could bring to it. In order to be a participant in any social struggle, one must have some reason for action. One of the most compelling reasons for such participation is Christian concern. However, one of the hallmarks of the present student movement is the fact that students participating in it have no real ideological or moral reason for doing so, and often their action is of short duration and often not clearly thought through. The pacifist who is involved in the nonviolent struggle for peace or civil rights has the conviction to act consistently and effectively. The religiously motivated students who started the sit-ins in the South had the courage to face beatings and jail sentences. Many of the students who have participated in social action movements have not had this background of deep concern for human rights and dignity and, therefore, do not participate fully in the struggle. This has sapped the energy of the movement in some instances and has meant its collapse in others.

Because religion no longer offers a challenge to young people, they have had to seek challenge and vision elsewhere. Many have found it in the liberal student movement. Others have given up trying and have been "lost" (or beat) in terms of moral or religious responsibility. The restoration of religious concern to the movement and the revitalization of the churches themselves are difficult and far-reaching problems. Indeed, they seem overwhelming in the light of present trends in both religious and secular life.

. . .

What is the answer? It is clearly a revolutionary change in the religious institutions in this country. Ministers, rabbis, and educators must again preach and act, not soothe. They must be willing to risk as much as the sit-in students in the South risked in their actions. Only when students feel that the church is again the church will they be able to identify with it. Until that time, one of the most potent forces for justice and peace will remain without meaning for large numbers of concerned and active students.

Mr. Altbach teaches political sociology at Harvard University, and is a past president of the Student Peace Union (1959–64). He has written for the New Leader, The Activist, The Christian Century, *and* New Politics. *This article originally appeared in* motive, *November 1962.*

POLITICS AS ART: THE CIVIC VISION

by Christopher N. Reinier

"The constitution of man is the work of nature; that of the state the work of art." —ROUSSEAU

So we would participate; if this fever is contagious, we are harboring a revolution; the western world has for two thousand years seldom known such a thing; its resistance might be weak. But it takes a mighty swarm of mosquitoes to poison a Leviathan; and would not such a swarm be a Leviathan itself?

We admit that all life is action. But for the moment let us say that contemplation is non-action and that activity which brings us into contact with other things and other people is action.

And art is making or constructing. Good art is lasting, though further construction might be made upon it. Bad art carries in her bosom destruction.

Philosophers act in order to contemplate; political actors contemplate in order to act. Philosophers leave the cessation of their contemplation to death; men of action construct their own ending to contemplation. There lies the beginning of their art.

We want to be artists.

Hear Beethoven: "I will seize fate by the throat. It shall never wholly overcome me." Or da Vinci: "The painter contends with and rivals nature." Or Van Gogh: ". . .one must seize nature and that with a strong hand. And then after having struggled and wrestled with nature, sometimes she becomes docile and yielding." And Delacroix: ". . . in the work of a mediocre artist, one feels that he has not been the master of anything."

Artists need power.

The political artist's power is derived from other men; his object is other men. The means and the end of his art are identical. How he views the source of his power tends to affect the picture he strives to construct in his object. It matters, then, where the artist constructs the cessation of his contemplation. That work of art can be good or bad.

Two political "tactics"—Machiavellian and Liberal—have been suggested for discussion. Let us contemplate. . . .

Machiavelli was no Machiavellian! And, consequently, we have learned from him much about liberal tactics! In his more tempered *Discourses* he wrote: ". . . the world consists only of the vulgar, and the few who are not vulgar are isolated when the many have a rallying point in the prince." Yet, in his infamous work, he counseled: "I say that every prince must desire to be considered merciful and not cruel." The emphasis is, of course, on the word, "considered," but why?

Two possible answers. First, political men must appear good (though they are not) because men in general are so bad that they insist that others be good; they call it "projection." Or men are so good that they would not tolerate being led by an evil man; they call it "justice." Machiavelli was shrewd in seeing that in a liberal society there exists a system of values which is related to men only as a weapon to be used to punish other men. And such is the art of the liberal.

It is a very great problem, however, whether men were really so bad as all this before the liberal constructed a stopping-off place for contemplation which was so far from an accurate grasp of the nature of man that ultimately his art had to be destructive or bad.

Hear the first spokesman of the liberal state which Machiavelli foresaw, Thomas Hobbes: "And because the condition of man. . . is a condition of war of every one against every one. . .every man has a right to everything." Neither Aristotle nor Adam Smith first proclaimed the liberal conception of man as a natural material slave; it was Hobbes: "The value, or *worth* of a man, is as of all other things, his price. . . . And as in other things, so in men, not the seller, but the buyer determines the price."

But the liberal who put this conception of man in a way so inspiring that our Jefferson could not resist was John Locke. Locke's blissful state of nature, where men were really men, was peopled by "men being partial to themselves," and "passion and revenge is very apt to carry them too far and with too much heat in their own cases as well as negligence and unconcernedness to make them too remiss in other men's." Locke did not declare that men are morally bound to be good men.

He declared that men are morally bound to preserve their lives and their property; they are good men when they are selfish. Such is the meaning of the natural right to life, liberty, and property.

Now bad, free men need government to constrain the other bad, free men. And it was Madison's task to construct such a government. "So strong is this propensity of mankind to fall into mutual animosities," he wrote, "that where no substantial occasion presents itself, the most frivolous and fanciful distinctions have been sufficient to kindle their unfriendly passions and excite their most violent conflicts." Yet it would be "folly to abolish liberty" which allows this selfish conflict.

Madison's art was to establish a system of rules under which we evil men could struggle with each other over our respective rights, while none of us could gain ascendency. Hobbes, Locke, and Hamilton realized that such a system would require a very powerful government. History reveals that they were right.

Liberty has been an inglorious word in our tradition: It has been self-destructive. Throughout our history it has been the increasing of liberty, the defense of rights, which has been our essential political concern. Hear Hoover declare: "True liberal government is founded on the emancipation of men . . . .We propose to turn the whole direction of this country toward liberty, not away from it." Then compare his words with Roosevelt's: "Each group has sought protection from the government for its own special interests without realizing that the function of government must be to favor no small group at the expense of its duty to protect the rights of personal freedom and of private property of all its citizens."

When men claim rights or freedoms first, they leave the fulfillment of duty to the government, as Roosevelt observed. Our two major political parties are different, but only in the sense that one defends more different kinds of rights than the other does. They, because of us, have constructed a government which has burgeoned to the point that liberty is one of the larger jokes of our society.

But who can laugh? The energy which liberal political artists have expended on creating a system of rules, whereby evil men could not interfere with other evil men, is the *tragic* picture of artists defeating the possibility for good political art.

Socrates lamented that men who could not be bad could not be good.

One who knew Congress once told me: The purpose of our legislature is to prevent legislation.

Liberal politics is not the politics of construction. It is defensive; it is the politics of unmaking.

And when it comes to gaining the power to unmake, the art is so subtly bad art that only it apparently will destroy itself. But it might carry us unwittingly with it. So perhaps we had better not adopt a laissez-faire attitude.

Those rules with which the liberal artist is concerned have dealt essentially with the procedure of the political art. Since the liberal society assumes that man is evil, it must also be assumed that rules work only because we fear punishment for breaking them. Procedural rules about campaigning and electioneering, have simply not been frightening. There is nothing bad about that, except that since it is the duty of the government to enforce them, we can do anything we wish if the rules are not enforced. Rules are a blessed escape from responsibility.

A revolution would occur if one party determined to be responsible, however, and insisted that the other party be responsible as well. Rules are enforced by men. Campaign rules are not enforced because enough men from both parties have agreed not to enforce them.

Brother artists, we approach the beginning of the end of our contemplation.

Liberal contemplation overlooked Augustine's wise words: "For what are robberies themselves, but little kingdoms? The band itself. . .is knit together by the pact of the confederacy; the booty is divided by the law agreed on." Liberals could not hear Rousseau insist: "If the clashing of particular interests made the establishment of society necessary, the agreement of these very interests made it possible."

Many years ago, Aristotle declared that "a king is maintained by his friends; a tyrant has no friends." Stimpson Bullitt recently wrote about the liberal artist: "A politician has few friends, and he is sure of hardly any except those he knew when he was still unknown."

Is it possible that the end of the liberal political art has been the production of tyrants?

Yes, even the band of robbers is disintegrating.

Hobbes said that the price of a man is his power. In liberal politics, the value of a man is his price, his power, as seen by the buyer, the politician. For most of us, our value is only one vote; our value can be increased if we give time or money to the politician's efforts. Since few of us have money in an influential quantity and few of us will spend the time in an influential quantity, our value is our vote.

That vote in liberal politics is in the hands of a selfish man and it is to be secured by a selfish man.

Rarely among the fine artists does one hear a comment like Degas': "A picture is something which requires as much knavery, trickery, and deceit as the perpetration of a crime. Paint falsely, and then add the accent of nature." Does this sound like Machiavelli's description of the liberal political art? Does it sound like modern "image-making"?

Since the liberal artist can do anything to get that vote except what he is forced not to do, he can deceive as much as possible. He creates "images," "slogans," "flavors," which are supposed to attract us, and these attractions are presented, not directly, but through the mass media. His image may or may not be related to his self. In a world where friendship is not the foundation of power, I shall never really know the difference between, or the similarity of, the image and the self.

I consider myself free when I submit to the rule of another (if I have to submit to the rule of another) because I know rationally that the other is capable of ruling me in a way that allows and even helps me to be a good man.

When I cast my vote in our liberal drama, I shall not be free, for I shall not know whether our actors should lead me or not.

Now freedom is important to me because I want to be good; I am duty bound to my fellow citizens. Our art, however, has denied me a sense of goodness, for the possibility that I have made a good choice in casting my vote for an image depends on chance. When goodness or badness depends on chance, why bother?

I said Degas was a rarity. Most great artists struggle with nature in order to discover her essence that they might better follow her in ruling their stone or canvas.

Van Gogh: "I, for my part, know no other way than to wrestle so long with nature till she tells me her secret." And: "At bottom nature and the true artist agree." Delacroix: "Experience is indispensable for learning all that one can do with one's instruments, but above all to avoid that which should not be attempted .... It is only the fools and the impotent who torment themselves to reach the impossible." And Henry Moore: "But with more experience the completed work in stone can be kept within the limitations of its material, that is, not be weakened beyond its natural constructive build, and yet be turned from an inert mass into a composition which has a full form existence, with masses of varied sizes and sections, working together in spatial relationship." See Frank Lloyd Wright, Rodin, da Vinci, Reynolds, Goethe, Epstein, Mondriaan, *et al.*

We must not be too callous in our condemnation of our liberal tradition. When our liberal artists constructed the ending of their contemplation, they were looking at man as he already existed in the mammoth national state. Man had for centuries been denied the capacity to govern himself. Alexander and Caesar had constructed the Empire that precluded such self-government. What alternative was there to limiting one's concern for being a good man to the realm of one's private home or property? Since men in relating to the public realm could not govern themselves, how could they behave but with passionate defensiveness? Poor Rousseau had to retain the escape to primitivism as, at least, a better alternative to his small commonwealth than a life in the Empire would be. Life in the Empire would have to be viciously passionate. Life in the woods could at least be pleasantly passionate.

Our ancestors saw that vicious passion, and tried to erect a political art upon it. They could have had no success at all if they had been right. The state is not held together by antagonistic passion. Their art had to come to a bad end, for it tended to weaken society "beyond its natural constructive build."

"Idle tricks form a passing tie; only wisdom can make it lasting," lamented Rousseau.

I feel pity and terror.

Now one man's wisdom is another's tomfoolery. So be it. But perhaps there is even in the Empire an alternative to the liberal political art.

It is in the nature of man both to have to live with other men and to want to do so. It is in the nature of man to be both social and anti-social.

Man's natural place on this earth, however, seems to be that of living with other men, sharing with them the tasks of ruling nature for all of their benefit. It is natural for men to share life with each other, then, but it is not automatic. It seems most proper for men to be social and good, but they are not automatically so.

Whether men are good or bad is a work of human art. "At bottom, nature and the true artist agree." The political community must be one in which the art of goodness is not only possible, but encouraged.

Goodness is not a mystical thing. It is the simple but difficult day by day task of men, not saints, concerned with the welfare of their fellows. We know little of this today, but we know enough about it to understand its meaning. We do not mean charity; we mean friendship.

As political artists our power to act will always remain dependent upon other men. Our object is by definition other men. Our art is collective in its means and its end. In our empire, men will of necessity be partially enslaved. Such is the necessity for men in large spaces. But rather than exploit our limitations, we must make of our possibilities, and not as "fools" and "impotents."

If men assume political duty beyond that of the duty to secure rights, they, not the Leviathan, will gain greater self-government.

If we would create an "image," let us give men the opportunity to discover whether the image has any basis in nature. If we would buy a vote, let us make the purchase as directly face to face as possible. This art demands many participants. It is impossible with a small palette.

Liberal tactics have been successful in winning office, but they have been part of the destructive force tearing the common good, the social tie, to shreds. If winning office were our only concern, we too could be successful for a while—until the slaves of liberality revolt in outrageous, destructive passion.

We are citizens before we are partisans. If our immediate success is not built upon friendship, it is bad art. If our community is robustly concerned with its common good, even the immediate success of bad artists will be less likely. But if bad artists should reach high office, our art will have constructed a community which can endure beyond their caprice. Our first concern is with our community. We are needed. We need each other.

"To make us love our country, our country ought to be lovely." —Burke.

Christopher N. Reinier graduated from the University of California (Berkeley) and is now working as a legislative assistant to California Assemblyman Robert Crown. This article appeared originally under the title "Machiavellian versus Liberal Tactics" in the working papers of the National Conference on Campus Political Parties, Oberlin, 1962.

FROM PROTEST TO RADICALISM: AN APPRAISAL OF THE STUDENT MOVEMENT 1960

by Robert A. Haber

This year has been hailed as the coming of a new student radicalism. We have spoken at last, with vigor, idealism, and urgency, supporting our words with picket lines, demonstrations, money, and even our own bodies. We are talking about the specifics in terms of right and wrong. The decisiveness of our deeds leaves no room for vague notions of progress and the "principles" that rationalize injustice.

Curiously, however, our actions are magnified by both reactionaries and liberals—damned by one side, idolized by the other, and understood by neither. The sit-ins are seen as a prototype, and the other activities—the sympathy pickets, capital punishment, atomic testing—are given an equivalent value that is not justified.

We have lived through a period of depravity and insanity and finally of numbness and insensitivity. Out of the memories of wars, atomic explosions, atrocities, and race riots—out of a heritage of absurdity—a direct action movement has grown. We have taken the initiative from the adult spokesmen and leadership, setting the pace and policy as our actions evolve their own dynamic. Pessimism and cynicism have given way to direct action.

There are many factors which have translated our actions into a movement. For the first time in memory students have found a sympathetic press to publicize their actions. Perhaps it is a press gloating over the extra-legal, the deviant and the irresponsible, picking up an isolated instance of student rascality, giving it national attention and soon finding it repeated on half a dozen campuses. And, even so, there are many "major" papers that have taken little note of student action.

The University Press Service of NSA, the press work of CORE, the NAACP and other adult groups, and the public relations skills of the student activists themselves have combined to tell the world about student actions, and so to spread the movement.

The growing consciousness of the power of student movements abroad has also encouraged us; we see what they have done and we see that they are looking at us. There is nothing we would rather be than a student movement in European terms, and while we know that we are not, that our press makes the too facile analogy between our uprising and that of the Koreans or Japanese further encourages us.

But we must not be led into the popular characterizations of our activity as a "spontaneous new mass movement." In many of the protests—civil defense, capital punishment, the Uphaus conviction—what students did was to translate the undramatic campaigns of various adult organizations into dramatic student demonstrations. The direct action of the great peace movement has been similarly under adult auspices: the Committee for Nonviolent Action, the War Resisters' League, and the American Friends Service Committee. These movements were thus neither spontaneous nor strictly a student movement; the new thing is that students are involved at all.

Our enthusiasm for the expressions of student radicalism must be tempered when we look at the student leaders. Many are graduate students no longer in school at all. They have participated in radical or liberal activities throughout their college careers and are not strangers to firmly established liberal-left associations. It is this "radical fringe" that is providing the leadership, the organizational skills, and the articulation of the movement. The novelty and the great hope is that other students—undergraduates and those not involved with the liberal movement since childhood—are becoming involved and assuming leadership positions.

It must be borne in mind that comparatively few students are involved in any form of activity and [that] student action has been restricted to relatively few campuses. Much of the activity is disorganized, a great number of the projects never get off the ground or have to be abandoned for lack of support, and little has penetrated the mainstream of campus life. The student action groups have been afflicted with the usual petty politics and internal power struggles, producing a negative reaction among many students who had often been associated with liberal causes. This picture, when seen in the light of the large press, the dramatic techniques and the organizational support, must persuade us to a fairly modest view of the success of the movement.

These are not things to be lightly dismissed. The issues for which we have been fighting are so clear and so right, and the commitment we demand so slight, that we should expect much greater success. It is indicative of how far out of step we are with student thinking that our action can be so little regarded. The direct action technique, of course, scares off many, but its radical flavor is more often used to equivocate commitment and procrastinate action. It forces people to acknowledge that the implementation of principle involves change and that change involves resistance and conflict. College students are very happy to assent to principles, but they don't want to make anyone unhappy. The campus debate, accordingly, rarely focuses on the central moral issues of the movement; rather it is shifted to a multitude of peripheral questions that make it unnecessary even to confront the issue: Do we have enough information? Have all other channels of action been tried? Will we not do more harm than good? And, as a last recourse, is this . . . matter within our province and do we have the authority to take a stand? Such are the questions which students and student leaders present to us. Many of them are important questions, but none are excuses for inaction. And yet the degree to which they are used for inaction indicates that we do not have even the initial concensus from American students that something needs to be done and that all must be involved in the doing. Whatever may be our desires for a radical movement, we barely have . . . a beginning.

These remarks are not, however, addressed to the sit-in movement in the South—though they can be extended to the sympathy effort in the North. Southern students are calling for an immediate and fundamental change in social relations. They have the power in the technique of direct action and the inspiration of nonviolence to press their demands with success. They have organization and community support—support of the Negro community that is—and, in contrast to the North, they [the Southern students] have large parts of their student bodies and a great number of schools participating. And, if nothing else, their increasing tally of victories must persuade us that the sit-ins are indeed a mass movement. Whether they will be as effective in dealing with employment discrimination, housing patterns, or [the] . . . franchise, remains to be seen. They do not yet strike at the fundamentals of the social system when they act against Jim Crow, but they have an experienced and disciplined leadership, a method that can be and is being adapted to many other problems, and they see that their struggle does not end with the lunch counter or the library. Perhaps most important, they dramatize convincingly that Negroes—young and old—can and must take the leadership in this struggle. This is one of the chief factors which sets the sit-ins off from the rest of the year's student activity. The sit-ins operate in a community context; they call on the members of that community and they eventually involve the resources, organizations, and manpower of the community in their success. They overcome the traditional barriers of age and interest that separate town and gown, and they overcome the parochial appeal of the traditional forms of radical dissent, protest, or outrage. The justice that these students—and their elders—demand is a justice for themselves; it is not for some martyr or abstract cause, . . . or even for an oppressed brother. It is for themselves. This alone insures, in one form or another, the continuity of the movement.

There is also in the sit-in movement—with its Judeo-Christian orientation and its close connection whith the Negro Church—a dimension of radicalism little appreciated and often disdained by the North. The lunch counter as the object of the movement is of little intrinsic importance. The demand, however, is not for equal rights or constitutional guarantees, or protection of the laws; it is for a personal equality and dignity that has nothing to do with race. The demand is not to be treated equally but to be perceived equally: It is in this that the students have left many of their elders behind them. It is here that they are least able to communicate with their parents, and it is here that the South and North are most out of phase. The movement is in their own hands, and their own lives provide the continual measure of its success.

This immediate and personal involvement is not a claim Northern students can offer. The North offers an adaptation of the direct action method to a wide range of problems. It remains a method, and we don't see it as a positive interpersonal dynamic, for we are not close enough to the issues.

Nonetheless, the movement in the North has been remarkable. There has been hardly a national or international issue on which students have not been heard. And if in absolute terms whole student bodies have not been mobilized, the participation has offered a startling contrast to the dreary campus scene of recent years.

The factors which produced this renascence are not simple, and campus situations are too various and the participants too heterogeneous to yield any formula. A few generalizations might, however, yield a cautious perspective.

First, we should note that the campus hasn't been so quiet in the last few years—it just hasn't been so loud. For some campuses, the returning Korean veterans brought activity and controversy, for others young faculty members and outspoken graduate students. But what activity there was received little attention. The leaders of the earlier activity realized the necessity of creating a new group of leaders in social protest—and their efforts have paid off, because it is this new leadership, in the making for several years, which has taken the initiative in 1960.

The "beat" group has also provided initiative. The term "beat" has come to characterize all those who have deviated from the traditional college patterns. They are variously professional students, bohemians, political types, and non-students who still seem to be around. They are generally out of sympathy with what is going on in the world: Their reaction is often cynical detachment. The movement has drawn heavily, if not always reliably, on this group. They are responsible for the issue of dress standards which split many a picket line and still is the focus of controversy in striking a balance between the public image of the movement and the very importance of this group (which is, by definition, out of the main line of campus life). That fact indicates the exceedingly limited appeal of the movement. This group in time of dissension and irresolution, acts, and in so doing, takes the first step toward radicalism; the participation crystallizes commitment.

Other factors are operative: a reaction against the McCarthy suppression leading sometimes to a playful fraternization with radicals, the publicity given to fadism on the campus, the fund of the participation itself, or simply how easy the action is. There is nothing easier than picketing, marching, standing in a crowd. And finally there is the reaction to the constant pressure to be aware and get active and stop being apathetic.

In its early stages, student activity is neither very radical nor a very profound social protest. It generally does not go beyond a single issue, or see issues as inter-related, or stress that involvement in one issue necessarily leads to others. It does not, in short, seek root causes. In effect, a minimum commitment is sought. The continually expressed fear is that someone might be kept away because he doesn't like what the group thinks on "unrelated" issues: Therefore, the group doesn't think on unrelated issues and this often means that it doesn't think at all.

A direct consequence is the non-political nature of the movement. True, the participants would almost all fall to the left of the Republican Party and most to the left of the Democratic Party. It is non-political largely because of a lack of faith in the political process or in the established instrumentalities of change, but to these it offers no alternative beyond direct action. It operates first on the assumption that whether we are heard or not, the issues demand that we speak, and second that if we speak loud enough and in sufficient numbers, "something will happen." There is no recognition that the various objects of protest are not *sui generis* but are symptomatic of institutional forces with which the movement must ultimately deal. Direct action is not seen as a lever in the total process of social change. We call for disarmament, but we say nothing of what to do with the manpower, resources, industrial plant, and capital equipment that are tied up in the military machine. Problems of poverty, health care, wasted agricultural and natural resources, meaningless work—these issues arouse students neither to demonstration nor to discussion. Even in respect to civil rights, we do not speak to the essentials of social equality.

This failure to look beyond our own moral position is symptomatic of a protest, in contrast to a radical, movement. The movement only rarely goes beyond the store front. Attention to community relations—to say nothing of student relations—is minimal. If we provide the initiative and manpower, our appeal is none-the-less to the community, and yet we make little effort to bring massive community involvement in the movement.

These indications of isolation, narrowness, and shallowness

are nevertheless signs of a vigorous protest movement. It is a movement lacking in perspective, and little oriented to successful social change. It does, however, have the appeal, publicity value, manpower, and organizational resources to serve as a foundation for a movement of more fundamental protest and more positive radical direction.

A requisite for this deepening of the movement is participation as a continuing educational process. Specifically we should give attention to the following:

1. Direct action on a specific issue must serve as a channel to more generalized and articulated concerns. There may be some strategic value in local action groups themselves shying away from discussion, research, and debate, but they should insure that their members do undertake a deeper appraisal of social problems. This may be done through ties with other campus groups or with a national body that will provide the necessary informational and organizational resources.

2. There must be greater contact, communication and cooperation between the various specific action groups—locally and nationally. This would, of course, mean communication between groups acting on the same issue as well as between groups acting on different issues. Recognizing the value of single issue recruitment and limiting action to one issue deprives the student movement of a flexibility of manpower and artificially limits the perspectives of the participants. Recruiting for any action must be from the campus at large, not alone from those already deeply committed. This means an active campus relations and publicity program and a continuing sensitivity to campus opinion and reaction.

3. There must be continuity of leadership. This requires sharing and training of leadership and an attempt to broaden the base of campus involvement. It also means gaining the assistance, cooperation, and participation of adults and established national organizations. Their resources, staff, and often money, help a group to survive a period lacking in or divided in leadership.

4. Concern for coordinated programming, national planning,

and communications must not channel energies away from dynamic planning on local issues. Organization is not a substitute for action. The vitality of a local group comes from independence of programming and responsiveness to local democratic control. The role of centralized planning is to provide assistance in the form of newsletters, conferences, and coordination of occasional national activities. But these should be in response to local needs and at the behest of local leadership. This is necessary to insure the development of new leadership, enable local recruitment to proceed, and maintain flexibility.

In conclusion, it must be said that America is not fertile ground for radical or particularly deep social protest, and the average American student has neither the background nor the interests to lead him far away from the status quo or the complacent acceptance of directionless leadership in public affairs. The activities of this year have marked an initial but significant step away from social irresponsibility. The challenge ahead is to appraise and evolve radical alternatives to the inadequate society of today, and to develop an institutionalized communications system that will give perspective to our immediate actions. We then will have the groundwork for a radical student movement in America.

Robert Allan Haber is a past president of the Students for a Democratic Society. "From Protest to Radicalism" originally appeared in Venture, *an SDS publication in the fall of 1960.*

2. Race and Poverty in American Politics

But there is more of the past in the present than philosophy. There are also the music and the rhythm and the words, the songs people sing and the way they sing them and the meaning behind them, the unfathomable simplicity and the sly pun, the inexhaustible patience and the unflagging purpose, songs of King Jesus and the weary blues, the imagery and rhetoric of the speeches and the shouted response of the audience. To hear Mahalia Jackson sing, or Fannie Lou Hamer speak, or Martin Luther King preach is to be overwhelmed with the elemental impact of the past on the present. Cut these people off from the past and they would be struck mute.

C. VANN WOODWARD
(Commentary, *May 1965*)

THE QUIET WAR

by Bruce Payne

The quiet war in Mississippi appears in the national press as little more than a pattern of brutal and vicious incidents directed at Negroes and their friends in the civil rights movement. I know now that what is happening in Mississippi is more than a pattern of incidents, that the Negro half of that state faces a well-organized, coordinated, powerful, and intransigent foe. Black Mississippi faces not a pattern of brutality, but a plan of terror.

The terms of the battle in Mississippi are superlatively unfair, but in a sense, the sides are evenly matched. On their side, the white supremacists have the guns and the clubs, and the full legal power of the state, and an unequalled tradition of articulate bigotry. The civil rights workers, on their side, have dedication and unmatched courage, as well as the hope that the Federal Government, or perhaps even the national conscience, can be stirred to something more than a passing interest in their plight.

Yale students were invited to work in Mississippi on the Freedom Ballot campaign because we could direct national attention to it, and because we could help to show the Mississippi Negroes some of the concern that many whites share with them. These aims were partly accomplished, and now it remains for us to tell our stories and try to explain to at least some of our friends what is happening in Mississippi.

My story is not as interesting as those that should be told. The students who are working full-time in Mississippi face danger and imprisonment daily, and what they can report of brutality and injustice is far more shocking and disturbing. But part of the reason we went to Mississippi was to be able to give a personal and direct account of the civil rights movement in Mississippi to our own friends outside the South.

The Freedom Ballot campaign had the support of all the major civil rights groups in the state, but it was run by the Student Nonviolent Coordinating Committee, SNCC. Forty members of this group, white and Negro, are working full-time in Mississippi, directing their efforts at registering Negro voters. More than forty Yale students, along with about fifteen Stanford students, worked with the SNCC workers during the two weeks before the Mississippi gubernatorial election.

Police harassment is a constant factor in all Mississippi civil rights work, and I went into the state fully expecting to be arrested. Instead, I was beaten up and shot at, though I spent a fair amount of time in the lobby of the Natchez jail getting my co-workers released. This is not to say that the Natchez police ignored my activities. I was threatened by them and followed by them, and not arrested, it seems, only because they believed that local farmers could deal with me in a more effective and less official way.

I arrived in Natchez on the 29th of October, with Nicholas Bosanquet, a graduate of Cambridge and an Englishman now studying at Yale. The town is on the Mississippi River, about a two-hour drive from Jackson. Nearly half of the 30,000 residents of the town are Negroes; schools, churches, and public accommodations are almost entirely segregated. We had been told that Natchez had been a fairly quiet town in terms of civil rights, and that a number of Negroes had been registered voters for a good many years.

In Natchez, Bosanquet and I worked with George Greene, a SNCC worker, about twenty years old, from a Greenwood, Mississippi, Negro family. By the time we arrived in Natchez, George was already well known to the police. The driver of the bus he had taken from Jackson had reported him to the authorities for riding in front of the bus. (The victories in bus integration have so far been legal and formal ones, and Negroes seldom dare to make use of their newly affirmed rights).

Tuesday afternoon, while George conferred with the police about what sorts of activity for the Freedom Ballot would be legal in Natchez, Bosanquet and I spoke with Father William Morrissey, of the Holy Family Church and School. The Josephite fathers are a small order that has worked with Negroes in the South since 1893, and we found Father Morrissey and his fellow priests to be helpful and sympathetic to our work.

As we explained to Father Morrissey, the purpose of the Freedom Ballot campaign was two-fold. We were attempting to interest Negroes in voting for Aaron Henry (a Negro pharmacist from Clarksdale) for Governor, and Ed King (the white chaplain of Tougaloo College) for Lieutenant Governor, as write-in candidates in the Mississippi election. More important, we were organizing the Freedom Ballot itself, a mock election open to all Negroes over 21. The Freedom Ballot was conceived as a means of demonstrating the magnitude of the denial of Negro voting rights in the state and proving that large numbers of Mississippi Negroes actually wanted to vote.

The campaign was largely successful, in spite of an extreme amount of police harassment. But of the more than 80,000 votes cast in the mock election, very few came from Natchez. In the little time we were able to spend actually working with the Negroes of Natchez, we found many of them to be frightened and unwilling to make public their support of the campaign. Their fears were not unfounded, as we discovered in our experiences with the Natchez police and with whites from the outlying areas.

Around dinner time on Tuesday, George, Nick, and I passed out leaflets in the main Negro business district of Natchez. After dinner, we drove to Natchez College (a Negro Baptist institution) and spoke with its president. When we asked him if he would support the campaign, I saw beads of sweat break out on his forehead. To hide his fear, he soon became angry, forbidding us to speak with any of his students and ordering us off the grounds of the college. His problem was obvious: an insecure position of some status, that he was not willing to endanger. After we left, he called the police.

That night we stayed in George's room at a Negro rooming house. We could see police cars passing by on the street for a while, and we noticed the intermittent glow of a cigarette in a police car parked a little way up the street.

About 10:30 P.M. George went out, planning to drive to some of the Negro lodge halls and speak with their leaders about the campaign. He was arrested less than a block from the house, and charged with running a red light which existed only in the imagination of the policeman. He was further charged with the theft of the car which we had brought from Connecticut. I was informed by our Jackson office of his arrest shortly after midnight.

The next morning I appeared at the police station and was told that no one could do anything about George except the chief, who unfortunately was not in. While I waited for him, the captain accused me of being a Communist dupe and of looking like Bobby Kennedy, while the other officers tried to think of more original insults.

Chief J. T. Robinson had a lot to say when he finally saw me shortly after noon. He demanded a telegram from the owner of the car and warned me that the local people around Natchez would not stand for our activities. "They'll tear your head off," he said cheerfully. He also went on to warn me that if the Negroes ever demonstrate in Natchez and so much as one stone is thrown, "there'll be some slow walkin' and some sad singin'," and added, "My men have guns, and I've told them what to do with them."

By the time I got back to the rooming house, after having called New Haven for the telegram, I found that Nicholas had been arrested. Back at the station I agreed with the chief to get Nicholas out of town in exchange for the dismissal of vagrancy charges against him. I was worried about the problems he might face as an alien.

The telegram soon came, and George, Nicholas, and I were escorted out of town by a cavalcade of police cars. We drove to Vicksburg to put Nicholas on the bus, and then George and I returned to Natchez. At the airport, we picked up Ella Baker, a longtime civil rights worker and friend of SNCC who came to speak to some of the leaders of the Negro community with us.

While we met that evening with a few whites and Negroes at the rectory of the Holy Family Church, the engine of our car, parked down the street, was filled with sand and gravel. I don't think it was the police; they'd had plenty of time to tell others where we were. The meeting won little support from the Negro leadership for the campaign, although they admitted that the younger Negroes would probably be in favor of it, as we already had discovered. Father Morrissey bravely offered the use of his parish hall as a polling place.

I spent the next morning, Thursday, repairing the car, after staying the night at the rectory. The manager of the rooming house where George was staying had been told by the police not to let any more white people stay there. Around three o'clock I drove the two blocks to the rooming house and was followed by two men in a car that had been waiting across the street. One of them approached me as I walked toward the rooming house, saying, "Come here, buddy," but he was unwilling to follow me into the rooming house.

George told me that the men in the car had been following him around town that day, and that two of their friends were in another car. The police continued their surveillance as the two cars passed up and down in front of the rooming house.

Ella was due in Port Gibson that evening, and around four o'clock we packed her bags in the car and drove out of town. The two cars followed us up U. S. Highway 61 for more than forty miles. When we pulled into a service station in the business district of Port Gibson and got out to ask directions, the four men followed us, got out of their cars, and walked toward us. One of them walked up to me, looked at me for a moment, and started swinging. Two of the others soon joined in.

I ducked (nonviolently) and except for a few kicks in the legs, I caught most of their blows on the top of my head and on my neck and shoulders. Occasionally they stopped swinging to tell me not to come back to Adams County again, and warned me that if I did, I'd get worse treatment. They threatened George and Ella as well, but didn't hit them. A number of bystanders watched, but no one seemed interested in doing anything about the situation. Soon the men stopped hitting me, walked back to their cars, and drove away.

I was surprised at how little I'd been hurt, and glad that they'd only been using their bare fists. George and I left Ella in Port Gibson, drove to Jackson to return the car, and agreed to return to Natchez the next day.

That evening in Jackson we went to the Negro Elks' Club for a late dinner. I sat for a while thinking about the situation in Natchez, knowing it was important to show both the whites and the Negroes that we were not going to be run out of town, but fearing the possible consequences just the same. Now I could understand more easily the mixture of humor and coolness that makes up the style of many SNCC workers. One has to find a means of facing danger without being immobilized by it.

On Friday afternoon we were back in Natchez. I spent most of my time working on posters, and Saturday morning I set up our polling place in the parish hall. Then George and I decided to work some of the outlying areas, using the rented car as a "votemobile" to collect ballots for the mock election. About 11:30 A.M. we left Natchez for Fayette, about twenty miles north. A couple of miles out of town we found that we were being followed by two of the men that had beaten me up two days earlier. They were driving a '64 Impala, and we were in a '63 Chevy.

At the airport turnoff we tried to circle back to town, but they prevented the necessary left turn by driving next to us for a while in the oncoming lane. We then drove faster, though as George quietly observed, we'd have to outdrive them.

The scenery swam past us as we raced up the road. Light green fields, darker short pine trees, blue sky, bright sun, floated up to the edges of the highway and then away. An open stretch of road, and the Impala sped around us, running us into the shoulder. By then we were driving around 95 m.p.h.—no match for their speed. George backed up quickly and turned our car around, pointing out to me meanwhile that their driver fortunately wasn't very good.

We drove only a few miles, and were again run off the road. Again we turned around and raced away. A few miles north they tried a new tactic, passing us and pulling ahead, intending to block the road. We made a U-turn and headed south.

They caught up with us again, and again ran us off the road. They backed toward us and stopped, and one of the two men started to get out. We backed up then, and turned north. Traffic in both north and south lanes slowed their pursuit of us, and they nearly caused a serious accident. The next time they caught us we were only about eight miles from Fayette.

It was a narrow stretch of highway, and when they ran us off the road they nearly overturned their own car. We were unable to turn around as they backed toward us and parked at an angle across our left front fender, nearly blocking our chance of escape. One of the two got out, pointed a revolver at us, and said, "Get out," motioning us to his car. As he reached for our car door, he lowered his revolver, and just as he found the door to be locked, George shifted into low and stepped on the gas. The man with the gun fired one shot directly through the fender into the left rear tire, and then missed it with two more shots that left bullet holes in the rear of the car. As we swerved around their car and drove off we could hear air escaping from the tire. Driving at 100 m.p.h. became more frightening.

They got off to a slow start, but by the time we reached Fayette, they were less than fifty yards from us. We passed cars to the right and left, and ran all three red lights in the town. They tried to follow, but the press of traffic stopped them behind the second traffic light. With about six cars between us and them and out of sight for a moment, we turned off on a side road and into a network of unpaved roads where we could change our nearly airless tire.

We took a different highway back to Jackson and spent the afternoon with Justice Department officials. They were concerned, but had only a little hope of doing anything. The relevant sheriffs, when called, expressed little interest.

We decided that no purpose would be served by returning to Natchez ourselves, but two SNCC workers who were familiar with the town went down the next day to continue our work quietly.

Newspaper clippings began to come in from around the country. The fact that I had been beaten and shot at, it appeared, was a newsworthy item. Certainly I looked at it that way. But I reflected that the experience was not a new one for George; it was the third time he had been shot at during the year. This, however, was the first time the papers had considered it news. The immediate reaction to this reflection is to wonder if the press does not have a sizable amount of prejudice: It is news when a beating or a shooting happens to a white, but not when it happens to a Negro. But on second thought, it becomes clear that the press simply knows its business. It is *not* news when a Negro is beaten, shot at, or terrorized in Mississippi; it is the normal course of day-to-day events and life. The very horror of Mississippi is that terror and violence have come to seem normal and natural, that they are no longer out of the ordinary enough to "make news." Men in Mississippi, the segregationists and the civil rights movement alike, are affected by that environment in which violence is the expected and decency is the exception. Their perspective is one not paralleled in human affairs except, perhaps, in the front lines of a war.

The war in Mississippi, however, is a quiet war, a war that has been fought so long that those who live it and those who observe it can no longer distinguish it from peace. The civil rights movement did not create the war. It has been fought since the first days of slavery, during and since the Reconstruction. It is a thing not of days, but of centuries. The weapons of the civil rights movement, and of SNCC in particular, are the weapons of peace and of decency. Those weapons may seem soft, but armed with them, it is possible to end the awful quiet that surrounds the war in Mississippi. Possible, that is, to call the attention of Americans to the conflict and combat in Mississippi, to replace the illusion of quiet with the explosions and the screaming, the "slow walkin' and sad singin'" that are the reality. And when the sounds of war are heard, it becomes possible that men will seek to still them.

Bruce Payne, a graduate of the University of California at Berkeley, teaches government at Stillman College in Tuscaloosa, Alabama. This article originally appeared in The Activist, *Vol. 4, 1964.*

SPIRITUAL AND MORAL ASPECTS OF THE STUDENT NONVIOLENT STRUGGLE IN THE SOUTH

by Charles McDew

One of the main tasks of the sit-in leaders was to explain and interpret their new movement before bewildered (and often hostile) audiences in the South and the North. The following is one such attempt, a speech given to the Antioch College Conference on Human Rights, in October 1960. The speaker, Charles McDew, has been an active leader of the Student Nonviolent Coordinating Committee in Mississippi. This article first appeared in printed form in The Activist, *Vol. 1, 1961.*

The Nature of Our Opposition

The system of Southern Tradition is a fabrication of wishful thinking, self-delusion, false values, outmoded beliefs, and pig-headed, deliberate ignorance. White supremacy is the foundation stone of the entire system. Our white supremacists forget that it was a doctrine of racial superiority that set off World War II, which killed more than 10,000,000, and from which many other millions will never recover. No doctrine of racial superiority will hold up in the court of modern world opinion.

I say that the system of Southern Tradition is fabricated upon wishful thinking and self-delusion because our detractors insist on believing that Negroes are satisfied with second-class citizenship and inadequate wages and education and opportunities. They say this even in the face of our demonstrations, our intelligent use of the franchise, and our evident love for democracy.

I say that the system of Southern Tradition is founded on pigheaded deliberate ignorance because they [the white supremacists] legislate their prejudices, prostitute justice—where Negroes and whites are involved—and will not even consider the idea that Negroes share the same quality of humanity which they possess. The educated and the unschooled cherish the same stereotyped notions about Negroes. This is one of the reasons our nonviolent sit-ins have left them, as we say, "all shook up." They think of us as ignorant—and we display a level of intelligence that few of them practice. They think of us as slovenly, unkempt, and boorish—and we march among them well-groomed and in quiet dignity. They think of us as irresponsible—and we show that we are willing to go to jail if we violate any laws in our campaign of civil disobedience.

You would be surprised at how far white Southerners are willing to go to preserve a system which is both un-Christian and undemocratic. I know school teachers who will not register to vote because they think their trustees might not like it. I know others who continue to patronize stores we are boycotting for fear the manager will call the trustees and report that certain teachers are supporting the student movement. In Orangeburg the white school property is valued at five and a half million dollars and the Negro school property is valued at five million—but the white schools have only 6,500 pupils, and the Negro schools have 13,500 pupils. This is what they call "separate but equal" schools. And the thinking is that Negroes don't need as much, because Negroes *aren't* as much, can't learn as much, and in the system of Southern Tradition will not be given the opportunity to use as much. So, in their thinking, the schools are really "separate but equal."

This is the nature of our opposition. Any tactics short of violence may be used to preserve the status quo. But the outlawing of violence is not based on their respect for human life and values, but, they say that if they commit violence it will be used as propaganda in the North and by the NAACP. In this, they do the right thing—for the wrong reason. In the September term of court in Orangeburg, a Negro was tried for killing another Negro. Shot him five times on a downtown street. A number of white people appeared in court on his behalf, and the presiding judge, T. B. Greneker, in his acquittal remarks, said: "When I see all of these white people appearing here on behalf of this boy, I wonder what all the demonstrations and things were about last spring? When white people are this good to Negroes, what else can they possibly want?" Now, the trial brought out that the man who got killed wasn't even armed. So it was murder. But it was only a Negro who was killed. So the murderer wasn't fined as much for murder as we students were for marching up Russell Street. One of the ironies of this incident is that the same judge is the one who must hear the appeals from our sit-in convictions. Frankly, I do not believe that a judge who believes as he does is capable of ruling impartially in our case, and he ought to disqualify himself.

This is the nature of our opposition. When an announcement says that something is open to the public, the word public does not include Negroes. When we were on trial in Orangeburg, the judge tried to segregate us in the courthouse. When we stop at a service station, we find one rest-room marked "White Ladies," one marked "White Men" and a third one marked "Colored," just as if Negro men and women are of the same sex, and it's perfectly natural to send them to the same public toilet.

In our section half-truth is taken as truth, patronage masquerades as friendship, chauvinism is called democracy, and God is thought of as a Southern white man.

This is the situation—the system which we feel obligated to correct not only because it disadvantages Negroes, but because it blights everything it touches; it stunts the growth of a third of the States of this nation; it prevents realization of the American dream for millions of our citizens; it jeopardizes the good name of America around the world; and it causes the Southern white man to lose his soul—for he says something bad about God.

What is the nature of our opposition? In the words of the Apostle Paul: "We wrestle not against flesh and blood, but against principalities, against powers, against the rulers of the darkness of this world; against spiritual wickedness in high places" (Ephesians 6:12).

Now this quotation brings us to our next major question:

What is the Nature of Our Fight?

It may be stated in many ways. Dr. Martin Luther King, Jr., . . . calls it "the withdrawal of support from evil." In other terms it is called "seizing the moral initiative," "The use of moral force against immoral force," and "The attempt to create the beloved community" or to "build the city of God." The organization called "The Fellowship of Reconciliation" refers to our process as introducing a redemptive element into an otherwise explosive or "intolerably immoral situation."

At this point I'm reminded that a minister friend told me recently that the "sit-in" dates at least as far back as the times of Christ, for, one day he sat down beside a well in Samaria and when a woman came to draw, he said: "Please give me a drink of water" and this simple request shook both her life and her society to the very foundations. "How is it that you, being a Jew, and a man, say to me, who am a Samaritan and a woman, 'Give me a drink.' Don't you know that Jews and Samaritans have no dealings?" And Jesus saw immediately the evil of this situation, and its potential explosiveness, and spoke these redeeming words: "If you knew the gift of God you could not feel this way." And what is this "gift of God?" The gift of eyes that see life as others see it. The gift of ears that hear the hidden rebuffs as the underprivileged hear it. The gift of heart that feels another's care. "If you knew the gift of God, you'd know that there is enough water in this well for both of us, and that God blesses us with blessings which would enrich us both if we shared them."

Jesus asked for a drink of water, and all the old antagonisms of the centuries came to the surface. Negro students in our South can walk into a drug store and ask for a cup of coffee—and the entire fabric of our Southern civilization trembles to the foundations.

Now, it is axiomatic that you cannot draw a man to you by striking him a blow. Neither a left uppercut nor a right cross nor even a haymaker can win a man's love or admiration or cooperation. On the other hand, we go along with the Book when it says, "A soft answer turneth away wrath; but grievous words stir up anger." The story is told of an officer who once faced a personal enemy who, in an impulsive moment of anger, spat in his face. . . . But instead of striking back, the officer calmly reached into his pocket for his handkerchief, wiped off the spittle, and said, "If I could wipe your blood off of my soul as easily as I can wipe your spit off my face, I'd kill you." The angry one repented and the two became fast friends. "A soft answer," indeed, "turneth away wrath," but a blow by the officer would have made them enemies for life.

Our fight is not against persons, but persons are involved in the promotion and perpetuation of the system we would revise. The present system is an affront to the Christian doctrine of man—or perhaps I should say "the Judeo-Christian doctrine of man." The affirmations that "God created man in his own image" as Genesis 1:27 says, and "The Lord God formed man of the dust of the earth, and breathed into his nostrils the breath of life; and man became a living soul" as Genesis 2:7 declares, are foundations of our belief in the dignity and worth of each man and all men. The Southern doctrine of white supremacy calls Genesis a lie, and the man who excludes me from his lunch counter says something bad about God, for he says that God created me unworthy to be with certain others of His creatures in the universal need to fill the stomach with food. The man is saying: "God shouldn't have made you that way. If He'd made you like me I'd let you in." No conscientious Christian can stand idly by and see God demeaned in such a way.

This mention of the dignity of man as conferred by God's creation reminds me of something a minister said at one of Dr. Martin King's meetings last year. This was not the most handsome man you ever saw, so it was very striking to see him stand until everyone was absolutely quiet, and then say in a booming voice: "I want you to know that when God made me, He was at His very best." Audience reaction was tremendous and prolonged. Now, this is just where we students stand! When God made us, He was at His level best. And we want to create a society which will both offer the best and bring out the best in us. We believe that a society that keeps us out of the best schools, hotels, culture centers, the best jobs, housing, hospitals, libraries and recreation places, churches, and organizations is one which does not deserve to live, for it dehumanizes us by such stupid discrimination.

Now let us turn to another facet of our struggle. We are often accused of engaging in a fad—like the hula-hoop craze, says Governor Hollings of South Carolina. But I have seen with my own eyes evidences that the spiritual roots are deep, and that young students are more sincere about the Christian faith than they have ever been before. When we marched on Orangeburg on March 15th some 800 strong, there were many students who felt that they were not well enough grounded in nonviolence; that they might fight back on provocation. What did these two or three hundred do while we marched? They went to the church across the street and held a prayer meeting. The ministerial alliance of our town says that this is the most hopeful thing they've ever seen—just as the nonviolent demonstration was the most inspiring experience of their lives.

It seems that the fell clutch of circumstance closes in upon the Negro family about the time a child learns that he is colored and that there is a certain limit to his freedoms imposed by the color of his skin. The parents' explanations are always a contradiction of precepts learned in church and in democratic family life. The child's idealism is shattered. His natural ambition becomes belligerence. His dream becomes a nightmare. And his budding Christian faith receives a serious jolt. This "killing of the dream," as Lillian Smith calls it, occurs in preadolescence. And by the time he comes to college, the Negro student is in dire need of a faith which he can practice as a part of his growth and his daily adventure. The sit-ins offered the students a chance for the "word to become flesh," as it were. The sit-ins have promoted a challenging philosophy—the philosophy of love overcoming hate, of nonviolence conquering violence, of offering oneself as a sacrifice for a valuable cause. The sit-ins, too, offer adventure and an opportunity to live out the demands of decency and dignity. And who knows but that these same sit-ins may be the means by which the walls of Southern Tradition shall crumble far sooner than most of us had imagined.

The sit-ins have inspired us to build a new image of ourselves in our own minds. And, instead of sitting idly by, taking the leavings excreted by a sick and decadent society, we have seized the initiative, and already the walls have begun to crumble.

The nonviolent approach is designed to leave our opponent a facesaving device so that there will be little bitterness when the fight is over.

The nonviolent struggle challenges us to live out the Golden Rule.

It has given us a new perspective and a new purpose—a sense of mission, as it were.

And I can promise you, in the name of the militant Negro students of the South, that we shall not be satisfied until every vestige of racial segregation and discrimination are erased from the face of the earth.

THE POLITICAL SIGNIFICANCE OF THE FREEDOM RIDES

by Thomas Kahn

I am supposed to talk about the Freedom Rides and the response to them, North and South. That's too broad a topic to be handled in depth in the short time I have. Since a good deal has already been said about the response of the enemy, I want to talk about the response of the liberal community.

The problem is: We are achieving the declared goals of liberalism but we are not doing it in the liberal way. Even more than the sit-ins, the Freedom Rides were disruptive of the conventional liberal mentality. On the emotional level, the explosive violence in Anniston and Birmingham, much more than the cumulative violence absorbed by sit-inners, deeply disquieted the world of liberal unviolence. I use the term unviolence, awkward as it sounds, to designate a prevalent opposition to uninstitutionalized domestic violence and an uneasy attitude toward even nonviolent actions which may "provoke" it. In a period when the struggle of the labor movement is rarely characterized by violent clashes on the picket line (indeed, a picket captain in a recent New York strike declared that his men would "pull the nonviolence resistance bit" to prevent scabs from crossing the picket line)—in such a period there has evolved a bland and blind faith that social change, at least in this country, can always find a path free from violent consequences. This faith, which, it must be stressed, applies only to uninstitutionalized domestic violence—not to the militaristic ethic, the arms race, "legal" police violence, etc.—this faith rests on the conviction that "the system contains all the machinery necessary to adjust the conflicting interests of all groups." When the machinery gets clogged up, as it has since the Reconstruction, then the problem is declared to be terribly complex and those who will not temporize the injustice are called "precipitous."

Yet it is difficult to apply such terms to the Freedom Rides. The machinery had been used before the Riders set out. Fifteen years had passed since the highest court in the land had declared segregation in interstate transportation unconstitutional. If moderates could delude themselves that the rate of school desegregation—one per cent per year—represented "all deliberate speed," a richly inventive imagination, or malicious intent, would be required to discern any progress in fifteen years of flagrant noncompliance with the "law of the land" as handed down in the Morgan case. Not only was there a Supreme Court decision, but there was enforcement machinery, in the form of the Interstate Commerce Commission. No legislative action was necessary. All that was needed was a "stroke of the pen." Of machinery there was enough. But machinery was not enough.

The issues posed by the Freedom Riders were not complex. They were absolutely clear. The question of "property rights"—that devilish phrase that lodges itself, like a thorn, in the side of the American dream and induces paralysis of the will—which trailed the sit-inners, was not the issue here. Federal regulation of interstate commerce has long been established. Finally, the cliché about "outsiders" was patently ridiculous. After all, who else would use the interstate transportation if not the people from out of state?

I say all this not to list the arguments in favor of the Freedom Rides but to establish the Freedom Rides as a kind of symbol, because they raise certain questions which lie at the bottom of our entire movement. For this reason the national reaction to this symbol is an index of just where we are and where we should be going.

On the strategic level, the Freedom Rides have provided the most clear-cut demonstration of the sterility of legalism that our generation has witnessed. By legalism I mean the view that social revolutions can be carried out in the courtrooms. Working through the courts is, of course, a proper and necessary part of the struggle against injustice. The gains we win must be recorded, and precedents must be set. Like all effects, court victories can in turn become causes, helping to set the stage for new advances. Thus, the 1946 decision afforded a legal and moral basis for the Freedom Rides. It is also true that the 1954 school desegregation decision helped create an atmosphere and a certain confidence conducive to Freedom Riding. But it cannot be said that the 1947 decision actually integrated the bus terminals, any more than it can be said that the 1954 decision is really integrating the schools, or any more than it can be said that it was the courts and not the Montgomery Bus Protest that integrated the busses. That's a little like saying it was the Emancipation Proclamation that freed the slaves without mentioning Abolitionist agitation and the exigencies of the Civil War.

I think that we have to recognize that the Freedom Rides were a fluke—a bomb whose fuse we never lit. When it exploded, the noise was louder than anyone had expected. We owe the impact of the rides not to their intrinsic importance so much as to the irrationality of the segregationist officials. Had they not been so insane as to permit and encourage mob violence and bus-burning, it is likely that the Freedom Rides would have been just another direct action project.

This, it seems to me, is the most obvious weakness of the Rides.

Of course, I don't mean that they should never have taken place. I mean only that a project whose significance and impact are attributable to circumstances controlled by an irrational enemy should be recognized for the peripheral undertaking it is and not be made the center of our grand strategy.

A second weakness is more important. We should not be fooled by our own propaganda. For purposes of argumentation we may choose not to recognize differences between "insiders" and "outsiders." In this we are quite correct. On moral grounds we may argue, in the best tradition, that wherever there is injustice our own rights are not secure. On patriotic grounds we may argue that the barbaric racist system of the South imperils our national security and diminishes our national prestige, thus handicapping us in the face of expanding totalitarianism abroad. As taxpayers, we may insist that the quaint racial customs of Dixie are costing us money. We may use any combination of these and other arguments, and they are all quite sound and all quite helpful in combating, on an idealistic level, artificial notions of states' rights and in advancing the conception of the essential unity of the human family.

But this ideal will never be achieved through much argumentation, but only through a vital mass movement that systematically and relentlessly destroys the social institutions that stand in the way of the ideal. The building of such a mass movement, of which we now have but an embryo, depends in large measure on our having a strategy that does recognize the distinction between "insiders" and "outsiders," not so that the "outsiders" can be eliminated, but so that we keep ever before us the yardstick by which we can measure the value of their role: What did the "outsiders" leave behind them when they went home? Did they spark an indigenous popular movement with solid local leadership prepared to move aggressively into the vacuum created by their disruption and departure? Or did they derail the local movement and leave it demoralized, incapable of defense against retaliation and indisposed to future action?

I certainly don't mean to suggest that the Freedom Rides had this second, negative effect. On the other hand, I don't think that the Rides, in their very conception, were calculated to stimulate grass-roots movement on the local level. Unless I am mistaken, the masses of Southern Negroes are but slightly affected by segregation on interstate busses. Every victory over Jim Crow is to be hailed, but how the victory is achieved is also important. Recent reports indicate that throughout the Deep South Negroes rarely use the newly integrated terminal facilities. This is perfectly understandable and in no way supports the segregationists' contention that the Negro really doesn't mind his subordinate status. We really can't expect that courageous specialists in nonviolent direct action will integrate interstate transportation facilities—especially such peripheral facilities—and that immediately the black man in the street will feel free nonchalantly to walk in and demand service. Granted, this will take time. But how long it takes will be determined by whether the existing civil rights organizations can reach down to the black man in the street and, by dealing with his day-to-day problems, build for themselves a conscious mass base that will not permit a vacuum to develop.

Easier said than done. But until it is done, liberal America won't find it too hard, however conscience-stricken, to get off the hook. The Freedom Rides sent a sudden shock wave through the country. But material support was shamefully inadequate. At the height of the Freedom Rides financial contributions from trade unions had not exceeded $20,000! Protestant, Catholic, and Jewish organizations together had not contributed more than $10,000! In terms of human bodies, we have to admit, now that the drama is over, that four hundred is not a very large figure, really. And even of this figure, how few represented the mainstream of American liberalism!

Some of the reasons for the feebleness of the liberal response have been scattered throughout my remarks. For one thing, as I have suggested, there is a kind of ideological factor, if you will. We are not doing things the liberal way. The Negro revolt has not yet hit the North—except as expressed in black nationalism, which is not a challenge but a withdrawal. There is no Northern liberal *movement* in the area of civil rights. It is not we Northerners who have agitated Southern Negroes, as the racists would have it. The Southern Negroes have been agitating us. But no movement can be built upon fund raising and upon expressions of support for some other movement. How many Freedom Riders from the North had ever been arrested at home as a result of direct action against segregation and discrimination in housing or employment?

Let there be no mistake. The struggle today is in the South, and the more of us who are willing to enter the furnace, the better. But the liberal community will not be worth much to the South until it is revived in the course of struggle in its own backyard. And, the fact is, however we chafe under it, that the American Negro can advance no farther than the liberal-labor movement is prepared to go. This hard fact, and not mere sentiment, dictates the nature of our relationship with that movement.

The American labor movement, compared with its counterparts elsewhere in the world, is conservative. Not only has it dragged its feet inexcusably so far as the Negro is concerned, but its white membership is declining as a result of its overall policies. I think we have to look, shrewdly, to the labor movement as an ally, not because we like George Meany— I don't—or because we like white Southern workers, but because I know of no other major American institution of which it can be said with certitude that, if it does not move radically on civil rights, it will unquestionably be destroyed in our lifetime. In personal relations we may choose our friends according to what they say or think about us. But in politics we must choose our friends according to whether they cannot get along without us, despite themselves. I'm not talking about sentimental idealism; I'm talking about economics. Despite all talk about progress, the plight of the mass of Negro workers, most of them unskilled or semi-skilled, is getting worse as a result of automation and discrimination in job apprenticeship and retraining processes. A large mass of unemployed Negroes willing to work at sub-union wages depresses the labor economy and eats away at the foundations of labor organization. If the labor movement does not deal with this problem by wiping out racism in its own ranks, by organizing the South, and by taking the lead in the fight for total racial equality, it will go down in history as the largest labor movement in the world ever to have committed suicide. This may happen. I don't think it will. In any case, I refuse even to contemplate the consequences of such a catastrophe as it would affect all democratic impulses in this country.

To say that we must look to the liberal-labor movement as an ally does not mean that we have to adopt its position or to compromise with it. It is not by embroiling ourselves in the intricacies of the labor movement or by "learning the rules of the legislative game," as someone else suggested, that we will succeed in creating the kind of militant alliances that our struggle requires. We shall succeed through force—through the exertion of such pressure as will force our reluctant allies to accommodate to us, in their own interest. It is not because we do not *know* enough that we have not achieved our goals. We have more than enough legal experts, political scientists, and professional lobbyists. What we lack is political power.

This brings me to my final point: the Kennedy Administration and our attitude toward it. The first thing to be said about the new administration is that it *is* different from its predecessor. It is more dangerous. And it is potentially more helpful. This paradox arises out of the monumental dilemma with which the Kennedys have confronted us. If we are not careful, we may end up, I am convinced, the victims of one of the cleverest political strategems in American history.

The dilemma consists in this: The Administration has advised us that our most important objective must be winning the ballot. To this all other direct action efforts are secondary. This position is disarmingly correct on the surface. In fact, it is more or less what we have been saying for some time.

But what motivates this new interest in Negro suffrage? Certainly, foreign policy factors figure. The Cold War integrationists are growing in influence. But, more than anything else, the Kennedy policy represents an attempt to capture the civil rights movement for the Democratic Party. In itself, there is nothing wrong with this. If our movement could become integrated into a national political party that genuinely had our interests at heart, then we could rejoice that we had found a political vehicle that would make our movement more powerful. But the Administration seeks to absorb us into the Democratic Party without fundamentally changing the bastard character of that party. The Administration wants to register a certain number of Southern Negroes—possibly as a bulwark against Goldwater Republicanism—but to do so in such a way as to create as little friction as possible with the Dixiecrats.

Bob Moses mentioned the fact that Justice Department voting suits have been aimed at areas where Negroes were in a minority and avoided areas where Negroes were in a majority. This should serve as a reminder that a numerical increase in Negro votes does not necessarily mean an increase in Negro political power. A mere increase in Negro votes does not fundamentally threaten the position of the Dixiecrats. Nor does a literacy test bill which does not take the administration of such tests out of the hands of the master class. Behind the scenes money is being offered to civil rights groups which will emphasize "education"—whatever that means—as opposed to direct action. And while the Administration proclaims its unswerving devotion to the right to vote, it continues the appointment of Eastland cronies, like Cox, to Federal judgeships in strategic areas.

Against this background, the Administration's efforts to veer the movement away from direct action and toward "political action" are suspect. They are the most sophisticated means yet devised for obtaining a "cooling-off" period. Because the motivations of the Administration are suspect does not mean, however, that we should cut our own throats by refusing to recognize that the crux of the problem *is* political and that our aim must be to achieve political power.

What is the role of the student movement in all of this? First of all, we must recognize our own limitations. We cannot *ourselves* achieve political power. I know of no student movement that ever did. Even the most politically conscious, not to say revolutionary, student movements of our generation—in Korea, Cuba, Hungary, Turkey, Poland, and Spain—played two roles: They *sparked* activity by mass adult groups, and, especially in the earlier stages, they molded the ideology of the movement. When the students have failed in their objectives, it has usually been because the adult movements were unprepared to follow up or were helpless against the power of the opposition.

Returning to the United States, we find that while the students have sparked the voter registration drive and remain in the forefront of it, they cannot themselves carry out the ballot revolution. For one thing, except in Georgia, we are mostly too young to vote ourselves. In addition, the student movement is, by definition, cyclical and unstable. The sophomores who pioneered in the 1960 sit-ins are graduating. We lack the organizational base, the financial resources, and the stability of leadership required for the kind of massive assault that alone can demolish the political structure upon which the Southern oligarchy is perched. If only we had the resources! If only others had our will!

Given these limitations, what can we do? First, I would say, we should actively conceive of ourselves as the radical wing of the civil rights movement. This is the traditional role of students in all broad struggles. Relatively free of vested interests, of family obligations, and decisive economic ties, we can experiment with new techniques (always in the hope that they will later be adopted by those stronger than ourselves). We are in a better position to speak out against unprincipled or fruitless compromises. We are less susceptible to temptation than many of our older colleagues. In short, we are more strongly committed to the distribution of the status quo.

Second, we must give the movement its ideology, to the extent that we can make ourselves heard. This, it seems to me, means the concept of political realignment. This concept is all the more important in view of the present crisis of direction confronting civil rights forces. It is the only alternative to our being captured by the Democratic Party and eventually smothered under a blanket of political deals overlaid with tokenism and false rhetoric.

The term "political realignment" has been tossed around a good deal. I am not sure that is really understood. It does not mean supporting the Democratic Party. It means nothing less than a full-scale political revolution in this country—its vortex in the South. We tend to use the word "revolution" loosely. I am trying hard to be precise. The strategy of political realignment aims at the overthrow of a political class that presently rules the South and that, through its coalition with conservative Republicans, has maintained effective control over the reins of national power for decades. I think that's fairly precise.

The Southerners derive their power from two sources: on the local level, from disfranchisement of Negroes (and, to a lesser extent, poor whites), and, on the national level, from membership in the Democratic Party, generally acknowledged to be the majority party. As senior members of the majority party, they are assured of control of the most important Congressional committees. At the same time, they vote with the conservative Republicans 40 per cent of the time. Now, a lot of political scientists tell us that it's "healthy" to have a "margin of disagreement" within our parties. In fact, Arthur Schlesinger, Jr., tells us that one of the reasons America is great is that we are so "flexible" and "pragmatic." But I think you will agree that 40 per cent is kind of high as "margins" go, especially when you consider the questions on which there is disagreement, and especially when you consider that the figure would be even higher were it not for the various forms of cloakroom chicanery and log-rolling—involving, say, defense contracts and jobs in the bureaucracy—that go by the name of "liberal pressures" these days.

On the whole, the liberal and labor movements are also in the Democratic Party, although a few are scattered in the Republican ranks. It is for this reason that we have to focus special attention on the Democratic Party. The conflicts that exist in the Republican Party are not so thoroughgoing and are much more personality-centered than are those in the Democratic Party.

To focus special attention on does not mean to support. I personally did not support Kennedy in 1960, or the Democratic slate as a whole. On the other hand, there are some reform candidates in New York, like Mark Lane, the Freedom Rider, whom I would support, even if it meant registering as a Democrat, because he favors kicking the Dixiecrats out of the Democratic Party.

And that, at least superficially, is what realignment means: kicking the Dixiecrats out of the Democratic Party, so that they lose their majority-party privileges and have to shift for themselves or make their common-law marriage with Goldwater official. That would leave the Democratic Party pretty much in the hands of the liberal and labor forces.

Now, I don't think this brings the millenium. We have had too much experience with the official liberal and labor community to be exactly delirious in our enthusiasm for our reluctant allies. I personally see the necessity for economic and social changes in this country which are more fundamental than what these allies are on record for. But that is not the immediate question. The point is that a new Democratic Party—if it keeps that name—would give us for the first time since 1877 a national political vehicle that had no vested interest in the political, economic, and social subjugation of the Negro. Such a party would have more to do than make platform declarations about voter registration. It would actually have to conduct Negro voting campaigns in order to build a counter-base to the Dixiecrats. The present Democratic Party already has the South sewn up, and the Republicans enjoy too much Dixiecrat support to bother with seriously building an independent Southern constituency.

I think that it is within this context that we can see the meaning of what Rev. Smith is doing in Mississippi. With the help of SNCC, he and the other Negro candidates who have sprung up throughout the South have initiated the political revolution I have been talking about. For the first time since Reconstruction a real challenge has gone out to the Dixiecrats. It does not now seem likely that Rev. Smith will win, but this trend is unmistakable. And the Dixiecrats know it.

It is the job of the student movement to keep that trend going and to push it in a radical direction. It is no mystery that Kennedy has refrained from endorsing these Negro candidates, while he simultaneously calls for an increase in Negro voting. We must insist that the registration of a limited number of Negro voters diffused throughout white-dominated Southern counties is no substitute for rightful political power. There are still over a hundred Black Belt counties in the South. We must demand the right of Negroes to represent themselves. We must demand that Kennedy and his followers endorse Rev. Smith and the others, and let the

Dixiecrats do as they please.

If the Southern student movement is to be effective, it will have to build a base for itself, on the campus and in the community. But it will also need a vision, an enthusiasm, a direction. There is a great deal of talk about the Negro as the "soul of America." I confess I don't always know what this means. In the mouths of some it sounds mystical and other-worldly. In the mouths of others it is a hypostrophe to the twist. Maybe there's something in both notions. But my own feeling is that if there is any merit in the phrase, it has to do with a vision of freedom. And freedom is not an abstraction. It cannot be separated from the concrete day-to-day conditions that determine the quality of our lives. That quality, for our generation, has already been perceptibly elevated by what began in Greensboro. I don't know Rev. Smith personally. I don't really know what kind of man he is. But I strongly suspect that should the day ever come when he occupies Senator Eastland's seat, all of our lives, in a thousand pervasive ways, will be changed. Politics can do that. To spark that change is not a goal unworthy of our government.

At the time this article was written, Thomas Kahn was a student at Howard University and a member of the executive board of the Young Peoples' Socialist League. He is presently Executive Secretary of the League for Industrial Democracy. "The Political Significance of the Freedom Rides" was an address given at the SDS Conference on Race and Politics, University of North Carolina, in 1962.

SNCC IN ACTION: DIGNITY FOR THE ENSLAVED AND FOR US ALL

by Thomas Hayden

On September 5th, fear became terror throughout the region as a result of the beating of Travis Britt in Liberty. He and [Bob]

Moses accompanied four Negroes to the registrar's office. Let Britt's words tell the story.

"There was a clerk directly across the hall who came rushing out while we were waiting, and ordered us to leave the hallway. He said he didn't want a bunch of people congregating in the hall. So we left and walked around the building to the court house, near the registrar's window. By the time we reached the back of the building a group of white men had filed into the hall, in about the same spot we'd been 'congregating' in. They were talking belligerently. Finally one of the white men came to the end of the hall as if looking for someone. He asked us if we knew Mr. Brown. We said 'no.' He said, 'You boys must not be from around here'. We said he was correct. This conversation was interrupted by another white man who approached Bob Moses and started preaching to him: how he should be ashamed coming down here from New York stirring up trouble, causing poor innocent people to lose their homes and jobs, and how he (Bob) was lower than dirt on the ground for doing such a thing, and how he should get down on his knees and ask God forgiveness for every sin of his lifetime. Bob asked him why the people should lose their homes just because they wanted to register and vote. The white gentleman did not answer the question, but continued to preach. He said that the Negro men were raping the white women up North, and that he didn't want and wouldn't allow such a thing to start down here in Mississippi. He went on to say that the Negro in New York was not allowed to own homes or establish businesses so why didn't we go the hell back home and straighten out New York instead of trying to straighten out Mississippi. At this point Bob turned away and sat on the stoop of the courthouse porch, and the man talking to him took a squatting position. Nobody was saying anything. I reached in my pocket and took out a cigarette. A tall white man, about middle-aged, wearing a khaki shirt and pants stepped up to me and asked 'Boy, what's your business?'—at which point I knew I was in trouble. [Recall: Moses had already been beaten earlier, had filed charges, had called Washington, and was much less 'open game' than Britt at this point. T.H.] The clerk from the hallway came to the back door leading to the courthouse with a smile on his face and called to the white man, 'Wait a minute; wait a minute!' At this point, the white man, whom they called Bryant, hit me in my right eye. Then I saw this clerk motion his head as if to call the rest of the whites. They came and all circled around me, and this fellow that was called Bryant hit me on my jaw, then on my chin. Then he slammed me down; instead of falling, I stumbled onto the courthouse lawn. The crowd (about fifteen, I think) followed, making comments. He was holding me so tight around the collar; I put my hands on the collar to ease the choking. The clerk hollered 'Why don't you hit him back?' This set off a reaction of punches from this fellow they called Bryant; I counted fifteen; he just kept hitting and shouting, 'Yes, why don't you hit me, nigger? Yes, why don't you hit me nigger?' I was beaten into a semi-conscious state. My vision was blurred by the punch in the eye. I heard Bob tell me to cover my head to avoid any further blows to the face. I told Bryant if he was through beating me, I was ready to go. The clerk said, yes, I should go. Then this guy they called Bryant yelled, 'Brothers, shall we kill him here?' I was extremely frightened by the sincere way he said it. No one in the crowd answered the question, and Bryant (I found out his last name was Jones) released me. Moses then took me by the arm and took me to the street, walking cautiously to avoid any further kicks or blows. The Negro fellow that had been taking the registration test gave up in the excitement, and we saw him in his truck. The white men advised him to get the hell out of town, saying they were surprised that he was associating with our kind." Charges were not pressed.

On September 7th, John Hardy accompanied two persons to the registrar's office at Tylertown. The two were informed by the registrar that he didn't want to have anything to do with them because he was already involved in a suit with the Federal Government. Says Hardy: "I entered the office to ask why. The registrar, John Woods, had seen me on one other occasion, the 30th. After I told him my name, he came out very insultingly and boisterously questioning my motives and reasons for being in Mississippi and said I had no right to mess in the niggers' business and why didn't I go back where I came from. He reached into his desk drawer and ordered me out at gunpoint. As I turned to leave he struck me over the head with the pistol. I left his office and walked about a block. I decided to go to the sheriff's office to report the assault and possibly make charges. But this was not necessary because the sheriff found me. He told me to come with him or he would beat me 'within an inch of your life.' After being put in jail (the charge was resisting arrest and inciting a riot, and later disorderly conduct) I was interrogated at length by a city attorney and later by the district attorney. About 7:30 I was taken to Magnolia jail for 'your own protection.' I was in jail until the following night."

The Hardy case deserves more than outrage. It holds the possibility of legal response which might form a precedent against the state's using its official machinery to interfere with civil rights. John Doar of the U.S. Justice Department, Civil Rights Division, charged that if Hardy were tried and convicted, Negroes would be discouraged from attempting to vote (an action constituting a violation of the Civil Rights Act), and irreparable damage would be done the nation. Subsequently, the Federal Government has been striving to prevent Hardy's trial. On September 20th, the Justice Department, filing its complaint before U.S. District Judge Harold Cox in Meridian, Mississippi, asked for court orders forbidding intimidation or coercion of Negroes seeking to vote in Walthall and appealed for prevention of the Hardy trial.

On September 21st, Judge Cox declined to stop the state court trial. Among his remarks, as quoted by the Associated Press: "It is difficult to conceive how the United States can possibly be irreparably damaged by this criminal case down in Walthall County, Mississippi . . . While it must be presumed that John Hardy is guilty of everything with which he is charged, it must likewise be presumed that justice will be done in the trial of the case . . . This incident occurred September 7th and the government waited until September 20th to ask for instant relief. It looks like the government has a self-made emergency . . . [It would be improper] for me to permit a clash of the sovereignty of the state and Federal governments on such a case."

The Federal Government announced it would next appeal to the 5th Circuit Court of Appeals, in Montgomery, Alabama. On

October 4th, Assistant Attorney General Burke Marshall argued before the Montgomery Court that Walthall is a place of "near lawlessness." He accused Mississippi of a "trumped-up charge" in the Hardy case, which was "an attempt to intimidate them to prevent them from registering to vote." A Mississippi assistant attorney general, Edward Cates, responded (according to the AP) that the Federal Government is seeking to "condemn a whole state without evidence," that Federal lawyers have presented no proof that Negroes in Walthall are afraid to try to register following Hardy's arrest. A three-member tribunal is presently (October 13th) considering the case, with no outcome yet announced. [Editor's Note: The Justice Department suit has been successful.]

A little over two weeks after the Hardy beating, Mississippi terrorism reached a peak in the killing of a 52-year-old Negro, Herbert Lee. (The following information has been obtained from several private sources.) Lee was a member of the Amite NAACP. When SNCC came to Mississippi, Lee became an active, dedicated worker, assisting Moses in meeting people and arranging get-togethers. He lived on a farm just outside of Liberty, near the Louisiana line. On the morning of September 25th, he arose early, prepared to go to Liberty to gin cotton. As Lee drove his truck into Liberty, he was followed by Mississippi State Representative Eugene Hurst. Hurst and Lee had known each other for quite some time. Lee's brother, Frank, had apparently once purchased some of Hurst's land in Louisiana. In 1956 Hurst helped Lee get a cut in the cost of some land which Lee wanted to purchase. (The reduction was from $9,000 to $7,000.) Lee in turn promised Hurst a "tip" of some $500 upon completion of Lee's payments on his land. On September 25th, Lee had paid more than $6,500 on the land and was carrying a total of $287 in his pocket.

There had reportedly been a recent economic crackdown in the whole area. The white community was circulating a list of names of those Negroes seriously involved in the voter registration or NAACP "movements." Many were being cut off from basic commodities. Mr. Steptoe, the NAACP head in Amite, received a letter, for instance, telling him to pay off his debts. . . . Such was the situation that morning in Liberty, Mississippi. When Lee stopped his truck this morning, Hurst, who is the father-in-law of Billy Jack Caston, did the same. Hurst got out of his truck, and approached Lee, carrying a .38 in his hand. Lee remained in the cab of his truck. An argument ensued, partly about debts owed, partly about the .38, and partly about a tire tool Lee was alleged to be holding in the cab. Apparently the two challenged each other to put down their respective weapons. Hurst put his gun inside his belt. Lee edged across the seat, attempting to get out on the far side of the truck, which caused Hurst to run around the front of the truck. There Hurst is alleged to have said, "You didn't use the tire tool when you had it, and you're not going to use it now." Two motions followed, both by Hurst. The second motion was a downward thrust of the arm, a shot, and Lee was on his stomach with a .38 bullet in his brain. Hurst left the scene. Lee was left on the ground fully two hours before he was taken to the Negro coroner in McComb. A tire tool was near his body. A coroner's jury, after hearing whites but no Negro witnesses, ruled that the killing was in self-defense, and thereby a justifiable homicide. Hurst was never booked, charged, or tried.

In a county such as Amite, its caste system uninfluenced by the movement of ideas in the rest of the United States and the world, the tradition identified in 1937 by John Dollard (*Caste and Class in a Southern Town*) is still relevant: "One of the best ways for a politician to get notoriety was to kill a Negro; such an act would speed him on the way to getting office and reveal that his sentiments on the race question were sound." When appraising the effect of the Lee killing, it is well to bear in mind that it happened at a moment when the Negro's hope of gaining the vote was rising once again, that it was executed with apparently the full support of the white caste's law enforcement agency, legal system, and public opinion, that the privileged assailant is himself a symbol of the enthroned political power which the Negro vote would presumably seek to undercut, and that he is a symbol connected with a historic pattern of killing for political reputation. All of these factors influence the effect of the slaying regardless of whether or not Hurst actually killed Lee deliberately for his part in voter registration.

A week later a little scrawled but mimeographed sign went out:

Bulletin
Mass Meeting for Voter Registration
Oct. 2nd, Tuesday
Guest Speaker
Rev. Charles Jones
From Charlotte, N.C.
Masonic Hall 630 Warren
7:30
Collection will be taken for the
wife and ten children of
Mr. Herbert Lee.

The Pike County Non-Violent Movement, perhaps the youngest and most challenged in the South, was resuming operation. The five sit-inners had returned to jail. On October 3rd, the mass meeting was held. Parents attended and spoke. People stressed that the corrupt governments which permitted Lee's death could only be eliminated if Negroes registered. A total of $81 was collected for Lee's wife and ten children. An unarticulated decision was made: If Brenda Travis and Ike Travis were not re-admitted to Burgland High School, the students would protest. On the next day, the Negro high school principal, Commodore Dewey Higgins, ruled that the two would not be re-admitted to Burgland High School. For personal reasons, Lewis, 20 years old, had decided not to return to school. Brenda, however, had demanded entrance.

The Student Walkout

Chaos. . .during the previous day Martin Luther King sent an open telegram to President Kennedy protesting a "reign of terror" in McComb, and calling the Executive's attention to recent beatings. Several new SNCC people, returning from a successful national trip in quest of funds for bond for the sit-inners, had arrived in McComb on the morning of the 4th. Among those arriving was

Robert Zellner, a white man from Alabama who, as a white, was even more susceptible to mob hostility than a Negro, though in no sense could the Negro SNCC representatives feel secure.

The students—remember, one hundred under eighteen years of age—spent the mid-day preparing signs, and at about 2:30 P.M., they started to march downtown. Never before in McComb—never before in an area so rural, so violent—never before *anywhere in the South* with students so very young. One of them, thirteen years old, has been charged with "assault with intent to kill" because she ran over the foot of a white woman in a supermarket with a push-cart, and, subsequently, the two slapped each other. That is simply an example. The others, while a little older, suffer the same system and are moved by the same courage. And so they went downtown—with 119 in all, including nineteen students over age eighteen—and Bob Moses, Charles McDew and Robert Zellner. They walked through the Negro neighborhoods where families watched from the windows and steps and yards, through the downtown business district, down to the edge of McComb, and back up to City Hall. There the march halted. Elmer Haynes, one of the original McComb sit-inners, began to pray on the steps. Three times the police asked him to move on. He refused and was arrested. Then it was Lewis, Talbert, and sixteen year-old Brenda, in order, all arrested—Brenda violating juvenile parole. Each individual in the march stood quietly, waiting to be arrested. Moments before, a white man had tried to run over them with his automobile; now there were whites on foot, yelling, cursing. And each of the 114 left was quietly standing. Too much time was being taken up, so the police blew their whistles and pronounced everyone under arrest.

The whole march started up the stairs, on its way to be booked. As they did, a local white citizen reached out for Zellner and began to beat him. Hurting Zellner with the first punch, the man then grabbed him around the neck and began choking him and gouging his eyes. Then Bob Moses and Charles McDew were there, one holding the white's wrists, one clasping Zellner in protection. Moses and McDew were struck and dragged into the station by police, who then pulled in Zellner. The first statement inside the

Police Chief's office, according to Zellner, was, "Ought to leave you out there." Everyone was arrested and placed in jail. The nineteen over 18 years of age were arraigned on October 5th, after a night in Pike County Jail. Before Judge Robert W. Brumfield of McComb's Police Court, they pled innocent to charges of disturbing the peace; bond was $100 each. Nine also pled innocent to the charge of contributing to delinquency of minors; bond was $200 each. Trial was set for 9 A.M., October 23rd.

The nine charged on both counts were:

Curtis E. Hayes	Robert Moses
Isaac Lewis	Charles McDew
Stephen Ashley	Donald Gadson
Hollis Watkins	(John) Robert Zellner
Robert Talbert	

The high school students, meanwhile, refused to compromise their stand, as announced in the statement which they distributed:

> We the Negro youth of Pike County, feel that Brenda Travis and Ike Lewis should not be barred from acquiring an education for protesting an injustice. We feel that as members of Burgland High School, they have fought this battle for us. To prove that we appreciate their having done this, we will suffer any punishment they have to take with them.
>
> In the schools we are taught democracy, but the rights offered by democracy have been denied us by our oppressors; we have not had a balanced school system; we have not had an opportunity to participate in any of the branches of our local, state, and federal government; however, we are children of God who makes our fellowmen to love rather than hate, to build rather than tear down, to bind our nation with love and justice without regard to race, color, or creed.

Why only 100 students in a school of 600? A few of the others perhaps were opposed to change in the community. Many more, however, were clearly sympathetic with the revolt but either afraid or in conflict with parents, or tied economically to the white system.

And as for those who went to jail? "You get kind of hard," said McDew, "after two of three days without eating, lying on the floor with the window busted out. It is cold in McComb at night." Beyond the question of physical health hazards, the crucial problem was the threats on the lives of McDew, Moses and Zellner. By this time, everyone in the city knew them; they'd been photographed, facial close-ups appearing in the *Enterprise-Journal*, and now, in jail over the night, not far from the area where Charles Mack Parker was emasculated and lynched two years ago, they sat in their cells, confronted for four hours by a steady run of staring, muttering white visitors. "Do you believe in Jesus Christ?" was the question of a hostile local minister. "Do you believe that God is love?" was the question in return. "You don't believe in Jesus Christ, do you, you son-of-a-bitch; you'll go to hell and I'm going to see you get there soon." Four hours of threats and hatred.

The night passed, without death. The SNCC members were released on bond, and the next day the students solidified their commitment.

Brenda Travis, having broken parole by committing an offense within 30 days of her last one, is sentenced to one year in Colored Girls Industrial School, a detention home near Oakley, Mississippi. Until she is re-admitted, the students claim, they will not re-enter high school.

First they were told to return to school—after signing the following affadavit:

This is to advise that I am aware of the regulation of the McComb School Board concerning student walkouts in the McComb school system. This is to further advise that I have participated in such a walkout and am now asking for re-admission on probation. I also acknowledge that should I participate in a second school walkout that I shall be automatically expelled for the next school year.

They refused. They were a little scared; they felt odd without any history of Negro protest with which to identify because the sovereign state of their birth does not tell history honestly. They were almost all without planned futures. They were even giggling like kids that age do in Northern suburbs, but they refused—again and again.

On October 12th, Moses and McDew taught them classes in

their new "non-violent high school," the Negro Masonic Temple. The next week SNCC people taught other subjects: history, for example which the Mississippi school system presents in a thick book with a Confederate flag on one cover and the capitol of Mississippi on the other, and which tells of the "War of Northern Aggression," the positive aspects of slavery, and the heroism of the Ku Klux Klan in the South's series of crises.

The high school administration has declared that any student who has not signed the affadavit is thereby expelled for the rest of the year. Unless I miss my guess, most will not sign those slips. They'll take classes from SNCC or go to school elsewhere, and perhaps they'll petition the white school for admittance, and they'll take it to the courts, and someday they will win.

Perhaps this situation cannot be adequately conveyed. Does it become more real in noting that a white man connected with the broadcasting system there sees the solution to the problem in "throwing those little niggers in one bag, castrating them, and dropping the bag in the river?" Does it become more real in visualizing Herbert Lee lying on his face for two hours? Does it become real in recognizing that those Negroes are down there, digging in, and in more danger than nearly any student in this American generation has faced? What does it take? When do we begin to see it all not as remote but as breathing urgency into our beings and meaning into our ideals? James Baldwin said last year that these kids are the only really free people in the country; perhaps he is right. They have decided not only to protest but to seek social transformation as well, and that is revolution. They have decided it is time right now—not in a minute, not after this one more committee meets, not after we have the legal defense and the court costs promised—to give blood and body if necessary for social justice, for freedom, for the common life, and for the creation of dignity for the enslaved, and thereby for us all.

Thomas Hayden was president of SDS, 1962-63, and is presently a staff member of the Newark Community Union Project (ERAP) in Newark, New Jersey. The present article is part of a larger pamphlet, "Revolution in Mississippi," published by SDS in the fall of 1961. At that time Mr. Hayden had just graduated from the University of Michigan, and was working out of Atlanta as an SDS field secretary.

SNCC: AN OVERVIEW TWO YEARS LATER

by Bruce Payne

Bruce Payne worked for the Student Nonviolent Coordinating Committee in Mississippi in the summer of 1963. That experience formed the basis for an article, "The Quiet War in Mississippi," published in The Activist, *winter 1963. The following article is an overview, based on observation of and experience with SNCC during the two years that followed, and attempts a critical analysis of some of SNCC's ideas about democracy and political organization.*

The "new left" style in American politics, in its various manifestations, seems to be calling forth critics and advocates in the press at a truly alarming rate. At least part of the lesson should be obvious: The claim not to have an ideology, or the refusal to articulate one, draws both critics and supporters eager to manufacture one for purposes of either advocacy or attack. But the debate on the new left and its ideas, continuing for whatever reasons, underscores the feeling that something new is needed in American politics; and the vehemence of the critics often reflects a deep disappointment that the new left doesn't seem to have an answer.

I am afraid I share in the disappointment. The analysis of certain aspects of the work and ideas of the Student Nonviolent Coordinating Committee presented below is not an entirely favorable one. The aims of participatory democracy and "consensus politics" seem to me largely wrong-headed and doomed to failure, and I see a certain sort of inevitability in the destructive clashes occurring within the civil rights movement. Nevertheless, Mississippi SNCC people have taught much that is right about freedom and, consequently, about the "new" American society.

Both the virtues and the defects of Mississippi SNCC, as I conceive them, drive me to enter again into a controversy which I would rather avoid. What follows can only alienate some SNCC people still further, although it is hardly likely to win friends among the "liberal establishment," since it bears the clear implication that the liberal vision is an inadequate one for the future of America. But I hope that what I have to say is at least enlightening, if not convincing, to my friends and fellow workers on both sides.

What follows is a description of and commentary on some ideas that are a part of what might be called a "Mississippi SNCC ideology" (Mississippi because I know too little about SNCC in other states to speak confidently about it). More precisely, it is a discussion of a number of ideas that were widely shared by many workers in the Council of Federated Organizations in 1963 and 1964. (COFO was theoretically a coalition of SNCC, CORE, SCLC and the NAACP, but it was staffed primarily by SNCC people and a few CORE workers. By the fall of 1964 it had been largely superseded by the Mississippi Freedom Democratic Party.) The history of the activities of SNCC, COFO, and the MFDP in Mississippi is intimately connected with the growth of many of the ideas discussed below, but to present that history fairly and adequately is a much greater task than that which I have set for myself here.

It seems wise to begin the survey by noting that SNCC people generally refer to themselves and their organizations as "non-ideological." By this they mean that they do not have any *total* view of political and social life that enables them to offer a blueprint for the kind of society they would like to see in the future. They also mean that they are not committed to the views of any existing political organization—that they are not Marxists, Socialists, or Democrats.

The absence of a full-scale social program has as its concomitant an emphasis on immediate action. Direct action is not so divisive or significant for the Freedom Movement as it was for

Labor in the past. Partly because it has succeeded, and partly because the Supreme Court is tolerant, most people within the movement accept it. But direct action has always had supreme appeal to SNCC people, for whom indignation at injustice is a more compelling force than is social vision. The fact that voter registration (*i.e.*, political action) has been the leading tactic in Mississippi probably reflects the fact that voter registration there has involved great numbers of people in immediate participation and dramatic confrontation with danger.

The emphasis on action rather than ideology should not obscure the fact that SNCC people do have definite ideas about the future of their society, inside Mississippi and elsewhere. In examining these ideas, I have chosen eight topics for separate discussion: freedom, brotherhood, nonviolence, the power structure, middle-class values, the vote, leadership and consensus, and participatory democracy. These are followed by some general conclusions of my own.

Freedom

"*The newspapers and other outsiders call it civil rights and we call it FREEDOM.*" (*1964 summer volunteer in* Letters From Mississippi)

"*Over my head, I see Freedom in the air.*" (SNCC song)

People in the movement, and Negroes generally, react to the word freedom differently from the way they react to other words, like civil rights, or voting, or democracy. Freedom implies these things, and it includes most of the goals of the movement, but it is also something else. Freedom has a personal content as well: it is something worth living and dying for; it is something that relates directly to one's deepest hopes and desires.

Among the meanings of freedom that SNCC shares widely with orthodox American political ideology are the notions of freedom from unjust government, and freedom of opportunity. Of the four posters used by COFO in the 1963 Freedom Ballot, two concerned police brutality, and the other two opportunities for Negroes. Freedom from want is an obvious aim in a society where Negroes live in the direst poverty; so is freedom from fear and arbitrary power in a society in which violence against Negroes is encouraged, organized, and carried out by state and local officials.

Another meaning of freedom may be indicated by the following statements:

One sees freedom here that is so much more than the ironical fact that enslaved people are, at least relatively, the liberated ones. Some white people sit at their feet wondering at this sorrow freed and made beautiful, sensing dimly in themselves a similar pain. (*Letters from Mississippi*, p. 16)

And it is very ironic that segregation, in a very real sense, freed the Negro from a society which enslaves the self. (Jane Stembridge)

These two statements, the first from a 1964 summer volunteer, and the second from a girl who has been with SNCC since its beginning, evidence a conception of freedom that is attractive to many of the SNCC people who are in conflict with the values and beliefs of their middle-class families. This desire for freedom from guilt and a sense of sin—for psychological freedom—is, however, probably of concern for only a minority of SNCC workers.

Freedom of action—to do, say, and move as one pleases, without much restraint—is, on the other hand, a notion on which most SNCC people act fairly consistently. Good discipline exists within the organization in crisis situations, but only for the duration of the crisis. This conception of freedom is often directed against parents, teachers, and other authorities, and it sometimes comes into conflict with the political requirements of holding a group together. As a part of a group or personal ideology, this sort of freedom can and does provide a rationalization for numerous antisocial and selfish actions.

SNCC workers differ in their definitions of freedom, but all exhibit a uniformly intense commitment to the ideal:

Before I'll be a slave, I'll be buried in my grave,
and go home to my Lord and be free.

It has been SNCC's unique role to teach and show this kind of freedom and this kind of intensity to the rest of America.

Brotherhood

George Green, a Mississippi Negro SNCC worker, told me in the fall of 1963 why SNCC was able to keep working in Mississippi: "We're brothers. If anything happens to one of us, two more will take his place. We'll never turn back because each one of us is a brother to every other one." This sense of brotherhood is widespread within the organization, and George was right about the degree to which it has been responsible for SNCC's success in Mississippi.

It is probably also accurate to say that the conditions of work in Mississippi have reinforced SNCC's bond of brotherhood. Faced with great hostility from the whites, and a fear-ridden apathy from the Negroes, SNCC was more isolated and alone than most organizations, and its members naturally grew very close. To say more about what brotherhood means to SNCC is extremely difficult. And to know what *sort* of brotherhood, community, or solidarity really exists is almost impossible for one who, like myself, is an outsider.

Singing is the most usual expression of group solidarity in SNCC, and songs like *We Shall Overcome* and *We'll Never Turn Back* make the fraternal ideal explicit. Songs like the following may help to give a more adequate perspective on what sort of solidarity exists in SNCC:

> We are soldiers in the army
> We've got to fight.
> Although we have to cry
> We've got to hold up the freedom banner
> We've got to hold it up until we die.

This is the brotherhood of the trenches, and it depends to some extent on the existence of a common foe, and on common hardships and defeats.

The very intensity of the ties among SNCC's members is a source of considerable instability and stress within the organization. Animosities between individuals are likely to be as fierce as friendships are strong, while the real or imagined betrayal of deeply grounded loyalties can do irreparable harm to the social and working relations of the membership.

SNCC is likely to express considerable love toward the society they are trying to change and the people with whom they work. The staff refused to "tolerate" the summer volunteers at the orientation session in Ohio, asserting instead, "We love you." Toward the end of the summer of 1964, a volunteer described "what we are for" as follows:

> ...to build a society where the problems of the individual can never be forgotten, a world where understanding and love are the keys to success. (*Letters from Mississippi*, p. 203).)

On the other hand, SNCC is capable of heaping great abuse upon, and treating as its greatest enemies, those with whom it is in only minor disagreement.

This ambiguity in SNCC's vision of love, as I saw and heard it in Mississippi, is reflected in the personal lives of a number of SNCC workers who are more bitter and less loving toward disapproving families than their situations seem to me to require. This is to suggest that while most SNCC workers can meet love with love, and trust with trust, many meet partial love and trust with suspicion, and sometimes meet enmity with hatred.

One loyal friend of the movement and of SNCC commented despairingly that "The attitude among many hard and willing strugglers is that nothing less than a Kamikaze attitude is acceptable." Or, as a SNCC song says, "99½ Won't Do."

Nonviolence

SNCC's commitment to nonviolence has been consistently maintained, but for many it is a tactical commitment rather than a first principle. During the orientation program for the 1964 summer project, one volunteer wrote about the argument by Stokely

Carmichael (an influential SNCC staff member who differs from many SNCC workers on a variety of issues). Stokely argued that nonviolence worked for a long time because it was new and because it reached the press, and that as demands for jobs and voting threatened more important aspects of the status quo it would become less effective.

Stokely does not advocate violence. No SNCC workers are armed, nor are there guns in any SNCC office. What he is saying is that love and moral confrontations have no place in front of a brute who beats you till you cry Nigger.

My feelings, and I think these are common, are that nonviolence is a perverted way of life, but a necessary tactic and technique. It is harmful to the human person to feel that he must love a man who has a foot in his face. The only reason I will not hit back is because I will be in the hospital two weeks instead of one, and will be useless during that extra week. . . . (*Letters from Mississippi*, p. 30.)

Another volunteer took a different view on the basis of other SNCC workers' arguments.

When I came I thought Martin Luther King and his "love your enemy" was a lot of Christian mysticism. Now I can see it as a force and support, helping those who understand it. (*Ibid.*)

It is difficult to judge accurately what proportions of the SNCC staff share these views, but an increasing number, perhaps a majority, are in agreement with Stokely.

Southern Negroes would be at an even greater disadvantage in violent confrontations if the whites were not somewhat restrained by their fear of losing the monopoly on violence. Making this point in a recent review, C. Vann Woodward states a view of nonviolence that exhibits a historical dimension usually absent in SNCC ideology. The points he makes would be a valuable corrective to some ideas on the subject I've heard expressed in Mississippi.

Nonviolence is not an invention of white intellectuals, or whites of any sort, nor was it borrowed from India. It was born out of the anguish of an encounter with the white man through the centuries of his greatest power and arrogance. It saw the Negro through slavery, Civil War, and Reconstruction, in all of which he rejected the bloody tactics urged by well-wishers. And his steadfast adherence to the wisdom of his historic experience explains in large part why he, and not the red Indian, is the center of attention today. (*Commentary*, May 1965, p. 63.)*

SNCC's approach to history strikes me as wildly schizophrenic. Their passion for reading and talking about Southern history is equal to their opponents' passion for exaggerating it. On the other hand, they are sympathetic to Howard Zinn's attack on the "tyranny of history," the subject of much of Woodward's review. SNCC—if it has a single attitude toward history—sees it as being of value only if it is politically useful. "History" is the history one wants. SNCC's schizophrenia toward the past is vaguely reminiscent of *1984*: History, if it is not useful, must be altered (*e.g.*, "slave revolts" must be elevated to the status of incipient revolutions). But to alter history is to admit that it is not, in fact, useful; it is to recognize that our past accuses us. The psychological reaction of "doublethink" then becomes necessary: We change our history while insisting—and believing—that it could never have been otherwise.

The Power Structure

The "power structure" in Mississippi makes its presence painfully obvious, and SNCC people recognize that its members often act together in a concerted effort to maintain the status quo, or even to make the situation more intolerable for the Negroes. Yet

* The next paragraph in Woodward's review is also worth notice:
But there is more of the past in the present than philosophy. There are also the music and the rhythm and the words, the songs the people sing and the way they sing them and the meaning behind them, the unfathomable simplicity and the sly pun, the inexhaustible patience and the unflagging purpose, songs of King Jesus and the weary blues, the imagery and rhetoric of the speeches and the shouted response of the audience. To hear Mahalia Jackson sing, or Fannie Lou Hamer speak, or Martin Luther King preach is to be overwhelmed with the elemental impact of the past on the present. Cut these people off from the past and they would be struck mute.

the comments that are made and the songs that are sung indicate a belief in a similar *national* power structure, extant throughout the country, even, perhaps, continuous with that of Mississippi. The notion is not merely that there are a few people in the states and the nation that hold the bulk of economic and political power, but also that they act together to maintain their power and to increase their wealth.

It is possible to defend C. Wright Mills' "power elite" thesis as an honest radical perspective on the existing social order; the forces of which he speaks could and would act collusively against any attempts to alter the entire social structure. But the SNCC argument lacks the important conditional implied by Mills. The power structure, in the SNCC view, acts collusively, conspiratorially, on its own behalf and against the poor *whether or not* there is any present threat to the order. Moreover, the ranks of this monolithic elite include liberal as well as conservative groups and individuals. Stokely Carmichael's comment in the fall of 1964 that the refusal to seat the MFDP at Atlantic City proved that there was no difference between the liberals and the Goldwaterites was enthusiastically repeated by a number of SNCC people throughout the state.

Middle-Class Values

. . .we crap on the clean antiseptic decent middle-class image. It is that decency we want to change, to "overcome." (*Letters from Mississippi.*)

The constant attack on middle-class values by the entire "new left" derives at least some of its force from the fact that many of its members have only recently, and only temporarily, escaped from middle-class backgrounds. In Mississippi, antipathy to the values of the middle class is compounded by conflicts between SNCC and the organizations dominated by the Negro middle class, the NAACP, the business leagues, and many churches and fraternal organizations.

The problem of middle-class values takes many different forms.

Tactically, SNCC faces middle-class fears that civil rights activity will endanger the economic security of successful Negroes. In the long run, however, SNCC and the rest of the "new left" faces the problem that the values which they denounce are likely to be those that will be pursued by anyone liberated from poverty, indeed, that they may *already* be the values which the poor aspire to.*

Thus, SNCC workers seem to be less and less interested in individual progress toward better jobs or housing. The community is the critical factor, and building ties among its members by community organization is the main task if people are to be free to develop new values.

One Man, One Vote

SNCC's conception of equality differs from that of many Americans in the extent to which SNCC is willing to put it into practice. In voter registration work it has, at least, the U.S. Constitution on its side, if not the Supreme Court and the Justice Department. But many in SNCC are suspicious of voting as a universal panacea. SNCC members speak of the "irrelevancy of the vote" and by the middle of the 1964 summer project, some volunteers shared their view.

> . . .the vision of the North they brought with them, the Canaan where everybody can vote. You wonder, is freeing the Negroes for that end desirable? Is "freeing" them at all? And the problem becomes insupportably large because you realize that the character of an entire nation must be changed. (*Letters from Mississippi.*)

At present the proposition is that votes are not enough. The utility of voter registration for community organization work, and

* Another tactical problem, interesting in itself though without great importance in a study of SNCC ideology, is that of conformity to the values of the community within which SNCC workers are operating. The question of whether the battle for a new order should be waged on all fronts at once is seldom decisively answered, but SNCC projects have often insisted on conformity to the local mores, which resemble in many cases those of the middle class, *e.g.*, in matters such as sexual relations.

the hope that far-reaching change can be accomplished in one way or another through the electoral process, is likely to maintain SNCC's commitment to "one man, one vote" for some time. But a distrust of the normal procedures of American government is growing, and the question, "after the vote, what?" is being asked all across the south.

Leadership and Consensus

When an MFDP member stopped a vote at a meeting in Jackson with "We don't vote no more, we 'census," he was reflecting an attitude that was very much in evidence during the fall of 1964. Jack Newfield, in a recent article on the student left, says that

> . . .within SNCC—which has no membership, only staff—a Quaker style of consent has evolved, whereby decisions are delayed until the dissenting minority is won over. Occasionally this method causes observers to despair of SNCC's anarchy and confusion (*The Nation*, May 10, 1965, p. 493).

Newfield, however, is ignoring the structural battle that nearly tore SNCC to pieces at Atlanta in the early part of 1965. A memorandum issued after this meeting stated in part:

> The internal composition of the Student Nonviolent Coordinating Committee has been radically altered. The entire staff is now a part of the Coordinating Committee. We have established a Call Committee which invites as voting delegates the members of student and community groups across the South, including representatives of the Friends of the Student Nonviolent Coordinating Committee. . . . To assist in the day-to-day running of the organization, the concept of the secretariat was introduced. . . .

But the generally hostile stance of SNCC people toward leadership in American society has been maintained. Indeed, many of the Mississippi staff were opposed to the Atlanta decision, and most of the SNCC people in the state still argue against leadership in the movement and, by extension, in society. Bob Parris (formerly Bob Moses) says:

The people on the bottom don't need leaders at all. What they need is the confidence in their own worth and identity to make decisions about their own lives (*The Nation*, *ibid.*).

An article by Jimmy Garett in the SNCC newsletter sounds much the same:

We are taught that it takes qualifications like college education, or "proper English" or "proper dress" to lead people. These leaders can go before the press and project a "good image" to the nation and to the world. But after a while the leaders can only talk to the press and not with the people. They can only talk about problems as they see them—not as the people see them. And they can't see the problems any more because they are always in news conferences, "high level" meetings or negotiations. So leaders speak on issues many times which do not relate to the needs of the people (quoted in *The Nation*, *ibid.*).

Bob Parris, who was the most significant figure in Mississippi SNCC, has left the state (though not the movement). His reluctance to lead was always evident, but crisis conditions in '63 and '64 often called for immediate decisions, and Bob was the closest thing there was to a general. But on policy issues, he often left his position purposely vague, in order to let the staff have a free hand in choosing between the alternatives.

Bob's case illustrates one of the real problems of the anti-leader style of political organization. His opinion was eagerly sought because of his experience and the faith people had in his ability and knowledge. When he refused to give it, knowing that it would carry considerable authority, the group was deprived of some valuable counsel and sometimes spent great amounts of time trying to figure out what Bob really wanted, since he refused to say.

Participatory Democracy

Participatory democracy is the great hope of SNCC and the new left (especially Students for a Democratic Society, SDS). The style of community organization pursued by members of SNCC aims at a politics of consensus, with neighbors and friends meeting together to talk over common problems, in relatively unstructured and unorganized meetings. SNCC workers encourage these people to arrive at "group decisions," whether about protests, freedom schools, or projects for the good of their local areas.

The depth of the new left's reaction against political leadership is typified by the actions of a SNCC-organized neighborhood group in Vicksburg. After meeting at some length to discuss their feelings about the city, they made an appointment for *all* of the members to meet together with the mayor. Like a similar SDS group in Newark organized by Tom Hayden and others, these people were unwilling to be merely "represented" by a small group of leaders in discussions with the city "power structure."

While there is disagreement about how effective participatory democracy might be in solving national problems, there is widespread conviction that it is the best available hope. Though it may not be a panacea, SNCC members are willing to argue that it would have saved (and might still save) the labor movement from the conservatism of "labor leaders." Similar hopes are held out for other social institutions.

To the objection that various groups in a city or state, operating according to the terms of participatory democracy, might come to conflicting, and even evil conclusions, SNCC workers can point to contrary evidence from Mississippi. But the usual reply is that when freed from the false ideas imposed on them by the middle class and given a chance to work things out for themselves, "the people" can make the right decisions. The charitable view of human nature which this formulation seems to imply is not extended to white liberals, members of the establishment, or people in the Mississippi power structure, although it applies equally to the white and black poor. Other groups are not necessarily evil: The logical conclusion of the argument, often stated openly, is that, given relatively open minds, participatory democracy could solve the problems of any organization and, presumably, the political structure as a whole.

Another idea cautiously advanced by a number of Mississippi SNCC workers is relevant here: SNCC has regularly rejected the notion of an all-black movement (though not without considerable soul-searching). But in community organization work, with its concentration on building a community that is self-confident and able to act for itself, there is a definite bias against coalition with others outside the group, and against attempts at individual betterment that do not involve the community as a whole. In Mississippi and in the North, community organization and participatory democracy seem to be taking precedence in the thought of the new left, prior to jobs, housing, school desegregation, or voting.

Conclusions

As far as I can tell, the "new left" ideas of Mississippi SNCC bear a curiously symbiotic relation to the liberal vision. Like the traditional American reformers, SNCC is convinced that the solutions to the problems of the age have very much to do with the *procedures* by which we operate. The cure for democracy is more democracy. But while liberals opt for perfecting the system of parliamentary democracy, the new left chooses the democracy of consensus.

I have three major criticisms of participatory democracy as a substitute for traditional American political practices. They are the following.

1. That participatory democracy can only be maintained on the basis of continuing crisis; that without such a condition, no institutions can be designed that can maintain the intensity necessary to support them.

2. That participatory democracy offers no solution to the major problems of governing a large country, state, or even a large city.

3. That participatory democracy tends to interfere with important freedoms.

The attractiveness of participatory democracy is great when one sees it operating in Mississippi. It is exciting to see people deeply involved in political activity, meeting together to discuss common problems, and making decisions as a group rather than delegating their authority to representatives. Yet the very intensity of this sort of political organization, demanding whole-hearted commitment and much time and emotion, makes it particularly unstable. If oppression is deeply felt, a common enemy may maintain the intensity and keep the group together, but a recurrent state of crisis is usually necessary.

Involved in this objection is an assumption that making political decisions is unlikely to be a sufficiently absorbing activity to maintain the support of large numbers of people over long periods of time. SNCC is right in assuming that most poor people have a pretty good idea of some of the things they want, but whether they are willing to work out the means to achieve their ends is another matter altogether, especially if it becomes apparent that they can be assisted by people more knowledgeable and experienced than themselves. Most people at most times are willing to delegate authority to someone who, they believe, shares their views, and who is competent at putting them into practice. The fact that we have often had irresponsible political leadership is not necessarily an adequate reason for attacking the idea of leadership itself.

The second objection is that participatory democracy is no solution for the problems of a large, complex society. Many problems undoubtedly admit of subdivision. But some (*e.g.*, international relations) must be solved at a larger level. Democratic assemblies are particularly ill-equipped to receive and utilize complex information in an efficient or even useful way.

But my most serious quarrel with SNCC's notion of democracy is that it does not combine well with freedom or with a broader sense of fraternity. Primitive societies, tribal organizations, religious communities, and various other associations provide us with numerous examples of similar systems at work. And among those groups practicing some form of participatory democracy, the common denominator seems to be a high degree of agreement on many issues, and a hostility to unorthodox opinions. Socrates was, after all, condemned by a vote of the Athenian assembly.

Representative government, whatever its failings, provides a more secure protection for free thought and speech than direct democracy. It is no surprise that the major attacks on civil liberties in the United States have been able to enlist at least as much support from the masses as from the power elite. (Indeed, the American Right, too, finds its enemies in the "liberal establishment" and the "Eastern power elite.") McCarthyism was a popular movement, though strongly supported by some in powerful positions. If it was tolerated for too long by too many political leaders, fear of its popularity was at least one of their reasons.

I do not doubt that political participation by more citizens would provide a better support for civil liberties, but not by means of the equal participation of all in the decision-making process. The security would come rather from the increasing sophistication of those willing to devote adequate thought and time to political questions—*i.e.*, those willing to become more knowledgeable on political subjects than the rest of the community.

The argument that the present American political system fails to meet the needs of the people, and the suggestion that the new left vision of freedom and brotherhood is the crucial aspect of a new politics, seems to me of considerably greater force than the notions discussed in the paragraphs above. There is no denying that the status quo is desperately inadequate, or that a just and brotherly society should be desired by all. My fear is that the new left may be wrong in some of the changes it seeks in the social order, and in some of the methods it uses to achieve them.

In the earlier discussions I outlined a few of the problems in SNCC's view of freedom. More criticisms are suggested by the comment of a summer volunteer (already quoted above) that Negroes may be freer because of their oppression. It strikes me that this volunteer was right about the Negroes being, relatively, the liberated ones. And this suggests that if one is concerned about building a whole and healthy and free society, it is time to start worrying about liberating the southern (and, perhaps, the northern) white from his fierce and destructive hatred. There is a common failing among SNCC workers and others in the "new left": They often behave toward their opponents in such a way as to suggest that they could never share in the new order. A constant hope for the redemption of opponents and lukewarm supporters need not blunt the force of direct action. Getting the power to make the institutional changes, however, will do less good and more harm if the struggle *prevents* the changes of heart and mind that the institutions are designed to produce. Unarmed love may be inadequate; but it is also true that loveless power is a blunt and dangerous instrument.

It should not be forgotten after the foregoing that the faults of SNCC's ideology, as it is espoused in varying degrees, are largely caused by the overwhelming quantities of terror and injustice SNCC has faced in Mississippi. The credit, on the other hand, for the accuracy of many SNCC ideas must go largely to the workers, whose magnificent conceptions of freedom and brotherhood, and whose indignation at injustice, gave many of the rest of us a chance to face some of the realities of American life. The sign in the COFO offices bears an unmistakable, unavoidable message:

> There is a street in Itta Bena called Freedom.
> There is a town in Mississippi called Liberty.
> There is a Department in Washington called Justice.

Many things must happen to this country if its citizens are to find justice and happiness; one can still hope for the creation of a social movement that will be closer to what we need. My own hopes center around the attempts to restore state and local politics, developing more political participation and responsive political leadership at all levels. Community organization, aimed at building groups of people able to trust each other and act together, is certainly an important goal. But community organization must produce able leaders and an ability to join with other groups.

Community organizers need to take even more seriously the new left dictum that one should try to live now as if the good society were already here—to show by example the style and quality of life for which we are working. This may mean laughter and creativity, as well as indignation and sorrow. It certainly means that, as SNCC has demonstrated, freedom schools and political organizations go hand in hand. And real freedom schools need to teach painting and singing and literature, as well as politics and Negro history.

Finally, those who want to work for the new society will do well to look at what SNCC has done in Mississippi. Among its most important accomplishments has been its steadfast refusal to be beaten, no matter what the odds: a crucial ingredient in the great, though partial, victory that has already been won. "No Compromise" is a tactic that has worked well not only in Mississippi but in every town where a recalcitrant power structure could be moved only by direct action and constant insistence.

The inflexibility needs now to be turned inward, on ourselves. "No compromise, we'll never turn back" should be for us both a feeling and a proposition about how to live. And it means, or ought to mean, more about our own commitment than about our tactics in dealing with others.

It means this: We won't *settle for* anything less than everything we think is right and necessary. It may mean, we won't *settle for* anything—*i.e.*, we won't stop working for a better world for human beings; we are not going to be satisfied with a few reforms. We want nothing short of changed people, men in the fullest sense, who are as loving as they are free, who are as just as they are equal, and who from love and justice can appreciate actions of nobility.

Mr. Payne teaches government at Stillman College in Tuscaloosa, Alabama, and is a contributing editor for The Activist. *This article originally appeared in that journal's November 1965 issue.*

THE VINE CITY PROJECT PAPER ON "WHITES IN THE MOVEMENT"

This paper, written just prior to SNCC's formal commitment to Black Power, was prepared by the Vine City Project, a SNCC-affiliated community organizing project centered in the Vine City area of the Negro section of Atlanta. The paper is not "official" policy of SNCC, but represents the thinking of most individuals on the Atlanta project and many other individuals in the civil rights movement, north as well as south.

Preface

In attempting to analyze where the movement is going, certain questions have arisen as to the future roles played by white personnel. In order to make this issue clearer, we have written a few paragraphs, stemming from our observations and experiences, which serve as a preview to a broader study on the subject.

The answers to these questions lead us to believe that the form of white participation, as practiced in the past, is now obsolete. Some of the reasons are as follows:

The inability of whites to relate to the cultural aspects of Black society; attitudes that whites, consciously or unconsciously, bring to Black communities about themselves (western superiority) and about Black people (paternalism); inability to shatter white-sponsored community myths of Black inferiority and self-negation; inability to combat the views of the Black community that white organizers, being "white," control Black organizers as puppets; insensitivity of both Black and white workers towards the hostility of the Black community on the issue of interracial "relationships" (sex); the unwillingness of whites to deal with the *roots* of racism which lie within the white community; whites, though individual "liberals," are symbols of oppression to the Black community—due to the *collective* power that whites have over Black lives.

Because of these reasons, which force us to view America

through the eyes of victims, we advocate a conscious change in the role of whites, which will be in tune with the developing self-consciousness and self-assertion of the Afro-American people.

In concluding, we state that our position does *not* stem from "hatred" or "racism" against white people, but from a conscientious effort to develop the best methods of solving our national problem.

I

The myth that the Negro is somehow incapable of liberating himself, is lazy, etc. came out of the American experience. In the books that children read whites are always "good" (good symbols are white), Blacks are "evil," are seen as "savages" in movies, their language is referred to as a "dialect," and Black people in this country are supposedly descended from savages.

Any white person who comes into the Movement has these concepts in his mind about Black people, if only subconsciously. He cannot escape them because the whole society has geared his subconscious in that direction.

Miss America coming from Mississippi has a chance to represent all of America, but a Black person from neither Mississippi nor New York will ever represent America. So that white people coming into the Movement cannot relate to the "Nitty-Gritty," cannot relate to the experience that brought such a word into being, cannot relate to chitterlings, hog's head cheese, pig feet, ham hocks, and cannot relate to slavery, because these things are not a part of their experience. They also cannot relate to the Black religious experience, nor to the Black church unless, of course, this church has taken on white manifestations.

Negroes in this country have never been allowed to organize themselves because of white interference. As a result of this, the stereotype has been reinforced that Blacks cannot organize themselves. The white psychology that Blacks have to be watched, also reinforces this stereotype. Blacks, in fact, feel intimidated by the presence of whites, because of their knowledge of the power that whites have over their lives. One white person can come into a meeting of Black people and change the complexion of that meeting, whereas one Black person would not change the complexion of that meeting unless he was an obvious Uncle Tom. People would immediately start talking about "brotherhood," "love," etc.; race would not be discussed.

If people must express themselves freely, there has to be a climate in which they can do this. If Blacks feel intimidated by whites, then they are not liable to vent the rage that they feel about whites in the presence of whites—not that one is anti-white, but because the efforts that one is trying to achieve cannot succeed because whites have an intimidating effect in direct proportion to the amount of degradation that Black people have suffered at the hands of white people.

It must be offered that white people who desire change in this country should go where that problem (of racism) is most manifest. That problem is not in the Black community. The white people should go into white communities where the whites have created power for the express purpose of denying Blacks human dignity and self-determination. Whites who come into the Black community with ideas of change seem to want to absolve the power structure of its responsibility for what it is doing, and to say that change can only come through Black unity, which is only the worst kind of paternalism. This is not to say that whites have not had an important role in the Movement. In the case of Mississippi, their role was very key in that they helped give Blacks the right to organize, but that role is now over, and it should be. People now have the right to picket, the right to give out leaflets, the right to vote, the right to demonstrate, the right to print.

These things which revolve around the right to organize have been accomplished mainly because of the entrance of white people into Mississippi, in the summer of '64. Since these goals have now been accomplished, their (whites') role in the Movement has now ended. What does it mean if Black people, once having the right to organize, are not allowed to organize themselves? It means that Blacks' ideas about inferiority are being reinforced. Shouldn't people be able to organize themselves? Blacks should be given this right. Further [white participation] means in the eyes of the Black community that whites are the "brains" behind the Movement and Blacks cannot function without whites. This only serves to perpetuate existing attitudes within the existing society, i.e., Blacks are "dumb," "unable to take care of business," etc. Whites are "smart," the "brains" behind everything.

How do Blacks relate to other Blacks as such? How do we react to Willie Mays as against Mickey Mantle? What is our response to Mays hitting a home run against Mantle performing the same deed? Is our interest in baseball ordered by our appreciation of the artistry of the game, or is it ordered by the participation of Negroes in baseball? One has to come to the conclusion that it is because of Black participation in baseball. Negroes still identify with the Dodgers because of Jackie Robinson's efforts with the Dodgers. Negroes would instinctively champion all-Black teams if they opposed all-white or predominately white teams. The same principle operates for the Movement as it does for baseball: A mystique must be created whereby Negroes can identify with the Movement.

Thus an all-Black project is needed in order for the people to free themselves. This has to exist from the beginning. This relates to what can be called "coalition politics." There is no doubt in our minds that some whites are just as disgusted with this system as we are. But it is meaningless to talk about coalition if there is no one to align ourselves with, because of the lack of organization in the white communities. There can be no talk of "hooking-up" unless Black people organize Blacks and white people organize whites. If these conditions are met, then perhaps at some later date —and if we are going in the same direction—talks about exchange of personnel, coalition, and other meaningful alliances can be discussed.

In the beginning of the Movement, we had fallen into a trap whereby we thought that our problems revolved around the right to eat at certain lunch counters, or the right to vote, or to organize our communities. We have seen, however, that the problem is much deeper. The problem of this country, as we had seen it, concerned old Blacks and old whites [and therefore] if decisions were left to the young people, then solutions would be arrived at. But this negates the history of Black people and whites. We have dealt stringently with the problem of "Uncle Tom," but we have not yet gotten around to Simon Legree. We must ask ourselves who is the real villian? Uncle Tom or Simon Legree? Everybody knows Uncle Tom, but who knows Simon Legree?

So what we have now [in SNCC] is a closed society. A clique. Black people cannot relate to SNCC, because of its unrealistic, non-racial atmosphere; denying their experiences of America as a racist society. In contrast, SCLC has a staff that at least maintains a Black facade. The front office is virtually all Black, but nobody accuses SCLC of being "racist."

If we are to proceed towards true liberation, we must cut ourselves off from white people. . . . We must form our own institutions, credit unions, co-ops, political parties, write our own histories. One illustrating example, is the SNCC "Freedom Primer." Blacks cannot relate to that book psychologically, because white people wrote it and, therefore, it presents a white viewpoint.

To proceed further, let us make some comparisons between the Black Movement of the (early) 1900's and the Movement of the 1960's—the NAACP with SNCC. Whites subverted the Niagra Movement which, at the outset, was an all Black Movement. The name of the new organization was also very revealing, in that it presupposed that Blacks have to be advanced to the level of whites. We are now aware that the NAACP has grown reactionary, is controlled by the power structure itself, and stands as one of the main roadblocks to Black freedom. SNCC, by allowing the whites to remain in the organization, can have its efforts subverted in the same manner, i.e., through having them play important roles such as community organizers, etc. Indigenous leadership cannot be built with whites in the positions they now hold.

These facts do not mean that whites cannot help. They can participate on a voluntary basis. We can contract work out to them, but in no way can they participate on a policy-making level.

The charge may be made that we are "racists," but whites who are sensitive to our problems will realize that we must determine our own destiny. We, as Black people, must re-evaluate our history, our ideas of self, the world, Africa and her contributions to mankind. We must take the credit for our contributions to this society and to the world. Credit will be given to white people where it is due, but surely our contributions must be given credit. These myths (of inferiority and "savagery") must be broken by Black people, so that no mistake can be made about who is accomplishing what for whom. This is one way to break the myths.

As to the charge of "Black racism," as against white supremacy: we can say that the racial makeup of any organization does not make it racist, i.e., supreme court makeup of all white judges, Black churches and Black businesses being all Black.

The naming of the newspaper, "Nitty-Gritty," which served to polarize the feeling of race, illustrated in a very graphic manner the attitudes that whites have towards cultural aspects of our society. The whites were opposed to the name and Blacks were affirmative on the issue. The alternative was the "Atlanta Voice" —surely such a name could not speak to the needs of grass-roots Black people.

Black people can say to the "Nitty-Gritty": I can see myself there. Can say to Mays hitting a home run: I see myself there. Can say to the Atlanta Project: I see myself there!

II

In an attempt to resolve an internal crisis that is now confronting SNCC, the Black-White issue (which is causing eruptions that are seriously hampering our struggle for self-determination) must now be dealt with.

In an analysis of our history in this country, we have been forced to come to the conclusion that 400 years of oppression and slavery suffered in this country by our Black forebears parallels in a very graphic way the oppression and colonization suffered by the African people. The questions can be rightfully asked, what part did the white colonizers play in the liberation of independent African nations; who were the agitators for African independence? Answers to those questions compel us to believe that our struggle for liberation and self-determination can only be carried out effectively by Black people.

The necessity of dealing with the question of identity is of prime importance in our own struggle. The systematic destruction of our links to Africa, the cultural cut-off of Blacks in this country from Blacks in Africa are not situations that conscious Black people in this country are willing to accept. Nor are conscious Black people in this country willing to accept an educational system that teaches all aspects of western civilization and dismisses our Afro-American contribution with one week of inadequate information (Negro History Week) and deals with Africa not at all. Black people are not willing to align themselves with a western culture that daily emasculates our beauty, our pride, and our manhood. It follows that white people, being part of western civilization in a way that Black people could never be, are totally inadequate to deal with Black identity which is key to our struggle for self-determination.

When it comes to the question of organizing Black people, we must insist that the people who come in contact with the Black masses are not white people because no matter what their liberal leanings are, they are not equipped to dispel the myths of western superiority. White people only serve to perpetuate these myths; rather, organizing must be done by Black people who are able to see the beauty of themselves, are able to see the important cultural contributions of Afro-Americans, are able to see that this country was built upon the blood and backs of our Black ancestors.

In an attempt to find a solution to our dilemma, we propose that our organization (SNCC) should be Black staffed, Black controlled and Black financed. We do not want to fall into a dilemma similar to that of other civil rights organizations. If we continue to rely upon white financial support we will find ourselves entwined in the tentacles of the white power complex that controls this country. It is also important that a Black organization (devoid of cultism) be projected to our people so that it can be demonstrated that such organizations are viable.

More and more we see Black people in this country being used as a tool of the white liberal establishment. Liberal whites have not begun to address themselves to the real problems of Black people in this country; witness their bewilderment, fear, and anxiety when Nationalism is mentioned concerning Black people. An analysis of their (white liberal) reaction to the word alone (Nationalism) reveals a very meaningful attitude of whites of any ideological persuasion towards Blacks in this country. It means that previous solutions to Black problems in this country have been made in the interests of those whites dealing with those problems and not in the best interests of Black people in this country. Whites can only subvert our true search and struggle for self-determination, self-identification, and liberation in this country. Re-evaluation of the white and Black roles must NOW take place so that whites no longer designate roles that Black people play but rather Black people define white people's roles.

Too long have we allowed white people to interpret the importance and meaning of the cultural aspects of our society. We have allowed them to tell us what was good about our Afro-American music, art, and literature. How many Black critics do we have on the "jazz" scene? How can a white person who is not a part of the Black psyche (except in the oppressor's role) interpret the meaning of the Blues to us who are manifestations of the songs themselves?

It must also be pointed out that on whatever level of contact Blacks and whites come together, that meeting or confrontation is not on the level of the Blacks but always on the level of whites. This only means that our everyday contact with whites is a reinforcement of the myth of white supremacy. Whites are the ones who must try to raise themselves to our humanistic level. We are not, after all, the ones who are responsible for a genocidal war in Vietnam; we are not the ones who are responsible for Neo-Colonialism in Africa and Latin America; we are not the ones who held a people in animalistic bondage over 400 years.

We reject the American Dream as defined by white people and must work to construct an American reality defined by Afro-Americans.

III

One point we would like to emphasize is the failure on the part of conscious whites and Blacks in dealing with the American reality in terms of differences. We are beginning to emphasize the analysis of the differences between Black and white people.

There has been an escapist attitude on the part of SNCC of looking at the problem as if race did not matter. This negates the special history of Black people in this country, mainly the slavery period and the inhuman forms of segregation we have been forced to suffer. Another important point is that most Blacks and whites tend to view Blacks in the light of the myth that the power structure has created and perpetrated in this country. Black people are considered as "citizens" along the same lines as white people in this country, when in reality, Black people are a semi-colonialized people, victims of a domestic colonialism. Our introduction into this country occurred during the same time as the partition of Africa and Asia by the European powers, so that the American institution of slavery was, too, a form of Western Colonialism. Therefore Black people in this country react in the same way as do other colonial peoples to their environment and experience; but the myths of America label them citizens, which is an unreal attitude.

Also, one of the main blocks in terms of Black self-recognition and self-identification in this country has been interference from the dominant white society. From the 1900's to the present time Afro-American writers and thinkers have had to contend with the encroachment of white intellectuals upon their culture and upon their thoughts. Not only did the white intellectuals encroach upon their thought and culture but they brought to it their whole American background of racism and paternalism so that Black culture was portrayed as something being base, second-rate, or below the culture of the United States, which was considered "serious" or "real." One graphic example of this is modern Afro-American music. This music which is rooted in the whole experience of our people in this country was not even named by Black people. Modern Afro-American music is named "jazz," which is a term that is derived from white American society. It is white slang for sexual intercourse; so that our music which may be called the mainstream of our culture was looked upon as being base and second-rate or dirty and containing sensuousness, sexuality, and other eroticisms. This, however, says more about the white American psyche than it does about aspects of Afro-American culture.

One of the criticisms of white militants and radicals is that when we view the masses of white people we view the overall reality of America. We view the racism, the bigotry, and distortion of personality; we view man's inhumanity to man; we view in reality 180 million racists. The sensitive white intellectual and radical who is fighting to bring about change is conscious of this fact, but does not have the courage to admit this. When he admits this reality, then he must also admit his involvement because he is a part of the collective white America. It is only to the extent that he recognizes this that he will be able to change this reality. Another concern is how does the white radical view the Black Community and how does he view the poor white community in terms of organizing. So far, we have found that most white radicals have sought to escape the horrible reality of America by going into the Black Community and attempting to organize Black people while neglecting the organization of their own people's racist communities. How can one clean up someone else's yard when one's own yard is untidy? Again we feel that SNCC and the civil rights movement in general is in many aspects similar to the anti-colonial situations in the African and Asian countries. We have the whites in the Movement corresponding to the white civil servants and missionaries in the colonial countries who have worked with the colonial people for a long period of time and have developed a paternalistic attitude toward them. The reality of the colonial people's taking over their own lives and controlling their own destiny must be faced. Having to move aside and letting this natural process of growth and development take place must be faced. These views should not be equated with outside influence or outside agitation but should be viewed as the natural process of growth and development within a movement; so that the move by the Black militants in SNCC in this direction should be viewed as a turn towards self-determination.

It is very ironic and curious how aware whites in this country can champion anti-colonialism in other countries in Africa, Asia, and Latin America, but when Black people move towards similar goals of self-determination in this country they are viewed as racists and anti-white by these same progressive whites. In proceeding further, it can be said that this attitude derives from the overall point of view of the white psyche as it concerns the Black people. This attitude stems from the era of the slave revolts when every white man was a potential deputy or sheriff or guardian of the State. Because when Black people got together among themselves to work out their problems, it became a threat to white people, because such meetings were potential slave revolts. It can be maintained that this attitude or way of thinking has perpetuated itself to this current period and that it is part of the psyche of white people in this country whatever their political persuasion might be. It is part of the white fear-guilt complex resulting from the slave revolts. There have been examples of whites who stated that they can deal with Black fellows on an individual basis but become threatened or menaced by the presence of groups of Blacks. It can be maintained that this attitude is held by the majority of progressive whites in this country.

It is a very grave error to mistake Black self-assertion for racism or Black supremacy. Black people in this country, more so than the colonial peoples of the world, know what it means to be victims of racism, bigotry, and slavery. Realizing our predicament from these inhuman attitudes it would be ridiculous for us to turn around and perpetuate the same reactionary outlook on other people. We more than anyone else realize the importance of achieving the type of society, the type of world, whereby people can be viewed as human beings. The means of reaching these goals must be, however, from the point of view of respecting the differences between peoples and cultures and not pretending that everyone is the same. The refusal to respect differences is one of the reasons that the world is exploding today. Also expanding upon the differences among peoples and the respect it should be accorded: if one looks at "integration" as progress then one is really perpetuating the myth of white supremacy. One is saying that Blacks have nothing to contribute, and should be willing to assimilate into the mainstream of great white civilization, i.e., the West.

A thorough re-examination must be made by Black people concerning the contributions that we have made in shaping this country. If this re-examination and re-evaluation is not made, and Black people are not given their proper due and respect, then the antagonisms and contradictions are going to become more and more glaring, more and more intense until a national explosion may result.

When people attempt to move from these conclusions it would be faulty reasoning to say they are ordered by racism, because, in this country and in the West, racism has functioned as a type of white nationalism when dealing with Black people. We all know the havoc that this has created throughout the world and particularly among nonwhite people in this country.

Therefore any re-evaluation that we must make will, for the most part, deal with identification. Who are Black people; what are Black people; what is their relationship to America and the world?

It must be repeated that the whole myth of "Negro Citizenship," perpetuated by the White Power Elite, has confused the thinking of radical and progressive Blacks and whites in this country. The broad masses of Black people react to American society in the same manner as colonial peoples react to the West in Africa and Latin America, and have the same relationship—that of the colonized towards the colonizer.

WHAT WE WANT

by Stokely Carmichael

One of the tragedies of the struggle against racism is that up to now there has been no national organization which could speak to the growing militancy of young black people in the urban ghetto. There has been only a civil rights movement, whose tone of voice was adapted to an audience of liberal whites. It served as a sort of buffer zone between them and angry young blacks. None of its so-called leaders could go into a rioting community and be listened to. In a sense, I blame ourselves—together with the mass media—for what has happened in Watts, Harlem, Chicago, Cleveland, Omaha. Each time the people in those cities saw Martin Luther King get slapped, they became angry; when they saw four little back girls bombed to death, they were angrier; and when nothing happened, they were steaming. We had nothing to offer that they could see, except to go out and be beaten again. We helped to build their frustration.

For too many years, black Americans marched and had their heads broken and got shot. They were saying to the country, "Look, you guys are supposed to be nice guys and we are only going to do what we are supposed to do—why do you beat us up, why don't you give us what we ask, why don't you straighten yourselves out?" After years of this, we are at almost the same point—because we demonstrated from a position of weakness. We cannot be expected any longer to march and have our heads broken in order to say to whites: Come on, you're nice guys. For you are not nice guys. We have found you out.

An organization which claims to speak for the needs of a community—as does the Student Nonviolent Coordinating Committee—must speak in the tone of that community, not as somebody else's buffer zone. This is the significance of black power as a slogan. For once, black people are going to use the words they want to use—not just the words whites want to hear. And they will do this no matter how often the press tries to stop the use of the slogan by equating it with racism or separatism.

An organization which claims to be working for the needs of a community—as SNCC does—must work to provide that community with a position of strength from which to make its voice heard. This is the significance of black power beyond the slogan.

Black power can be clearly defined for those who do not attach the fears of white America to their questions about it. We should begin with the basic fact that black Americans have two problems: they are poor and they are black. All other problems arise from this two-sided reality: lack of education, the so-called apathy of black men. Any program to end racism must address itself to that double reality.

Almost from its beginning, SNCC sought to address itself to both conditions with a program aimed at winning political power for impoverished Southern blacks. We had to begin with politics because black Americans are a propertyless people in a country where property is valued above all. We had to work for power, because this country does not function by morality, love, and nonviolence, but by power. Thus we determined to win political power, with the idea of moving on from there into activity that would have economic effects. With power, the masses could *make or participate in making* the decisions which govern their destinies, and thus create basic change in their day-to-day lives.

But if political power seemed to be the key to self-determination, it was also obvious that the key had been thrown down a deep well many years earlier. Disenfranchisement, maintained by racist terror, made it impossible to talk about organizing for political power in 1960. The right to vote had to be won, and SNCC workers devoted their energies to this from 1961 to 1965. They set up voter registration drives in the Deep South. They created pressure for the vote by holding mock elections in Mississippi in 1963 and by helping to establish the Mississippi Freedom Democratic Party (MFDP) in 1964. That struggle was eased, though not won, with the passage of the 1965 Voting Rights Act. SNCC workers could then address themselves to the question: "Who can we vote for, to have our needs met—how do we make our vote meaningful?"

SNCC had already gone to Atlantic City for recognition of the Mississippi Freedom Democratic Party by the Democratic convention and been rejected; it had gone with the MFDP to Washington for recognition by Congress and been rejected. In Arkansas, SNCC helped thirty Negroes to run for School Board elections; all but one were defeated, and there was evidence of fraud and intimidation sufficient to cause their defeat. In Atlanta, Julian Bond ran for the state legislature and was elected—twice—and unseated—twice. In several states, black farmers ran in elections for agricultural committees which make crucial decisions concerning land use, loans, etc. Although they won places on a number of committees, they never gained the majorities needed to control them.

All of the efforts were attempts to win black power. Then, in Alabama, the opportunity came to see how blacks could be organized on an independent party basis. An unusual Alabama law provides that any group of citizens can nominate candidates for county office and, if they win 20 per cent of the vote, may be recognized as a county political party. The same then applies on a state level. SNCC went to organize in several counties such as Lowndes, where black people—who form 80 per cent of the population and have an average annual income of $943—felt they could accomplish nothing with the framework of the Alabama Democratic Party because of its racism and because the qualifying fee for this year's elections was raised from $50 to $500 in order to prevent most Negroes from becoming candidates. On May 3, five new county "freedom organizations" convened and nominated candidates for the offices of sheriff, tax assessor, members of the school boards. These men and women are up for election in November—if they live until then. Their ballot symbol is the black panther: a bold, beautiful animal, representing the strength and dignity of black demands today. A man needs a black panther on his side when he and his family must endure—as hundreds of Alabamians have endured—loss of job, eviction, starvation, and sometimes death, for political activity. He may also need a gun, and SNCC reaffirms the right of black men everywhere to defend themselves when threatened or attacked. As for initiating the use of violence, we hope that such programs as ours will make that unnecessary; but it is not for us to tell black communities whether they can or cannot use any particular form of action to resolve their problems. Responsibility for the use of violence by black men, whether in self-defense or initiated by them, lies with the white community.

This is the specific historical experience from which SNCC's call for "black power" emerged on the Mississippi march last July. But the concept of "black power" is not a recent or isolated phenomenon: It has grown out of the ferment of agitation and activity by different people and organizations in many black communities over the years. Our last year of work in Alabama added a new concrete possibility. In Lowndes county, for example, black power will mean that if a Negro is elected sheriff, he can end police brutality. If a black man is elected tax assessor, he can collect and channel funds for the building of better roads and schools serving black people—thus advancing the move from political power into the economic arena. In such areas as Lowndes, where black men have a majority, they will attempt to use it to exercise control. This is what they seek: control. Where Negroes lack a majority, black power means proper representation and sharing of control. It means the creation of power bases from which black people can work to change statewide or nationwide patterns of oppression through pressure from strength—instead of weakness. Politically, black power means what it has always meant to SNCC: the coming-together of black people to elect representatives and *to force those representatives to speak to their needs.* It does not mean merely putting black faces into office. A man or woman who is black and from the slums cannot be automatically expected to speak to the needs of black people. Most of the black politicians we see around the country today are not what SNCC means by black power. The power must be that of a community, and emanate from there.

SNCC today is working in both North and South on programs of voter registration and independent political organizing. In some places, such as Alabama, Los Angeles, New York, Philadelphia, and New Jersey, independent organizing under the black panther symbol is in progress. The creation of a national "black panther party" must come about; it will take time to build, and it is much too early to predict its success. We have no infallible master plan and we make no claim to exclusive knowledge of how to end racism; different groups will work in their own different ways. SNCC cannot spell out the full logistics of self-determination but it can address itself to the problem by helping black communities define their needs, realize their strength, and go into action along a variety of lines which they must choose for themselves. Without knowing all the answers, it can address itself to the basic problem of poverty; to the fact that in Lowndes County, 86 white families own 90 per cent of the land. What are black people in that county going to do for jobs, where are they going to get money? There must be reallocation of land, of money.

Ultimately, the economic foundations of this country must be shaken if black people are to control their lives. The colonies of the United States—and this includes the black ghettoes within its borders, north and south—must be liberated. For a century, this nation has been like an octopus of exploitation, its tentacles stretching from Mississippi and Harlem to South America, the Middle East, southern Africa, and Vietnam; the form of exploitation varies from area to area but the essential result has been the same—a powerful few have been maintained and enriched at the expense of the poor and voiceless colored masses. This pattern must be broken. As its grip loosens here and there around the world, the hopes of black Americans become more realistic. For racism to die, a totally different America must be born.

This is what the white society does not wish to face; this is why that society prefers to talk about integration. But integration speaks not at all to the problem of poverty, only to the problem of blackness. Integration today means the man who "makes it," leaving his black brothers behind in the ghetto as fast as his new sports car will take him. It has no relevance to the Harlem wino or to the cottonpicker making three dollars a day. As a lady I know in Alabama once said, "The food that Ralph Bunche eats doesn't fill my stomach."

Integration, moreover, speaks to the problem of blackness in a despicable way. As a goal, it has been based on complete acceptance of the fact that *in order to have* a decent house or education, blacks must move into a white neighborhood or send their children to a white school. This reinforces, among both black and white, the idea that "white" is automatically better and "black" is by definition inferior. This is why integration is a subterfuge for the maintenance of white supremacy. It allows the nation to focus on a handful of Southern children who get into white schools, at great price, and to ignore the 94 per cent who are left behind in unimproved all-black schools. Such situations will not change until black people have power—to control their own school boards, in this case. Then Negroes become equal in a way that means something, and integration ceases to be a one-way street. Then integration doesn't mean draining skills and energies from the ghetto into white neighborhoods; then it can mean white people moving from Beverly Hills into Watts, white people joining the Lowndes County Freedom Organization. Then integration becomes relevant.

Last April, before the furor over black power, Christopher Jencks wrote in a *New Republic* article on white Mississippi's manipulation of the antipoverty program:

> The war on poverty has been predicated on the notion that there is such a thing as *a community* which can be defined geographically and mobilized for a collective effort to help the poor. This theory has no relationship to reality in the Deep South. In every Mississippi county there are *two* communities. Despite all the pious platitudes of the moderates on both sides, these two communities habitually see their interests in terms of conflict rather than cooperation. Only when the Negro community can muster enough political, economic, and professional strength to compete on somewhat equal terms, will Negroes believe in the possibility of true cooperation and whites accept its necessity. En route to integration, the Negro community needs to develop greater independence—a chance to run its own affairs and not cave in whenever "the man" barks. . . . Or so it seems to me, and to most of the knowledgeable

people with whom I talked in Mississippi. To OEO, this judgment may sound like black nationalism....

Mr. Jencks, a white reporter, perceived the reason why America's antipoverty program has been a sick farce in both North and South. In the South, it is clearly racism which prevents the poor from running their own programs; in the North, it more often seems to be politicking and bureaucracy. But the results are not so different: In the North, non-whites make up 42 per cent of all families in metropolitan "poverty areas" and only 6 per cent of families in areas classified as not poor. SNCC has been working with local residents in Arkansas, Alabama, and Mississippi to achieve control by the poor of the program and its funds; it has also been working with groups in the North, and the struggle is no less difficult. Behind it all is a federal government which cares far more about winning the war on the Vietnamese than the war on poverty; which has put the poverty program in the hands of self-serving politicians and bureaucrats rather than the poor themselves; which is unwilling to curb the misuse of white power but quick to condemn black power.

To most whites, black power seems to mean that the Mau Mau are coming to the suburbs at night. The Mau Mau are coming, and whites must stop them. Articles appear about plots to "get Whitey," creating an atmosphere in which "law and order must be maintained." Once again, responsibility is shifted from the oppressor to the oppressed. Other whites chide, "Don't forget—you're only 10 per cent of the population; if you get too smart, we'll wipe you out." If they are liberals, they complain, "What about me?—don't you want my help any more?" These are people supposedly concerned about black Americans, but today they think first of themselves, of their feelings of rejection. Or they admonish, "you can't get anywhere without coalitions," when there is in fact no group at present with whom to form a coalition in which blacks will not be absorbed and betrayed. Or they accuse us of "polarizing the races" by our calls for black unity, when the true responsibility for polarization lies with whites who will not accept their responsibility as the majority power for making the democratic process work.

White America will not face the problem of color, the reality of it. The well-intended say: "We're all human, everybody is really decent, we must forget color." But color cannot be "forgotten" until its weight is recognized and dealt with. White America will not acknowledge that the ways in which this country sees itself are contradicted by being black—and always have been. Whereas most of the people who settled this country came here for freedom or for economic opportunity, blacks were brought here to be slaves. When the Lowndes County Freedom Organization chose the black panther as its symbol, it was christened by the press "the Black Panther Party"—but the Alabama Democratic Party, whose symbol is a rooster, has never been called the White Cock Party. No one ever talked about "white power" because power in this country *is* white. All this adds up to more than merely identifying a group phenomenon by some catchy name or adjective. The furor over that black panther reveals the problems that white America has with color and sex; the furor over "black power" reveals how deep racism runs and the great fear which is attached to it.

Whites will not see that I, for example, as a person oppressed because of my blackness, have common cause with other blacks who are oppressed because of blackness. This is not to say that there are no white people who see things as I do, but that it is black people I must speak to first. It must be the oppressed to whom SNCC addresses itself primarily, not to friends from the oppressing group.

From birth, black people are told a set of lies about themselves. We are told that we are lazy—yet I drive through the Delta area of Mississippi and watch black people picking cotton in the hot sun for fourteen hours. We are told, "If you work hard, you'll succeed"—but if that were true, black people would own this country. We are oppressed because we are black—not because we are ignorant, not because we are lazy, not because we're stupid (and got good rhythm), but because we're black.

I remember that when I was a boy, I used to go to see Tarzan movies on Saturday. White Tarzan used to beat up the black natives. I would sit there yelling, "Kill the beasts, kill the savages, kill 'em!" I was saying: Kill *me*. It was as if a Jewish boy watched Nazis taking Jews off to concentration camps and cheered them on. Today, I want the chief to beat hell out of Tarzan and send him back to Europe. But it takes time to become free of the lies and their shaming effect on black minds. It takes time to reject the most important lie: that black people inherently can't do the same things white people can do, unless white people help them.

The need for psychological equality is the reason why SNCC today believes that blacks must organize in the black community. Only black people can convey the revolutionary idea that black people are able to do things themselves. Only they can help create in the community an aroused and continuing black consciousness that will provide the basis for political strength. In the past, white allies have furthered white supremacy without the whites involved realizing it—or wanting it, I think. Black people must do things for themselves; they must get poverty money they will control and spend themselves, they must conduct tutorial programs themselves so that black children can identify with black people. This is one reason Africa has such importance: The reality of black men ruling their own nations gives blacks elsewhere a sense of possibility, of power, which they do not now have.

This does not mean we don't welcome help, or friends. But we want the right to decide whether anyone is, in fact, our friend. In the past, black Americans have been almost the only people whom everybody and his momma could jump up and call their friends. We have been tokens, symbols, objects—as I was in high school to many young whites, who liked having "a Negro friend." We want to decide who is our friend, and we will not accept someone who comes to us and says: "If you do X, Y, and Z, then I'll help you." We will not be told whom we should choose as allies. We will not be isolated from any group or nation except by our own choice. We cannot have the oppressors telling the oppressed how to rid themselves of the oppressor.

I have said that most liberal whites react to "black power"

with the question "What about me?" rather than saying: "Tell me what you want me to do and I'll see if I can do it." There are answers to the right question. One of the most disturbing things about almost all white supporters of the movement has been that they are afraid to go into their own communities—which is where the racism exists—and work to get rid of it. They want to run from Berkeley to tell us what to do in Mississippi; let them look instead at Berkeley. They admonish blacks to be nonviolent; let them preach nonviolence in the white community. They come to teach me Negro history; let them go to the suburbs and open up freedom schools for whites. Let them work to stop America's racist foreign policy; let them press this government to cease supporting the economy of South Africa.

There is a vital job to be done among poor whites. We hope to see, eventually, a coalition between poor blacks and poor whites. That is the only coalition which seems acceptable to us, and we see such a coalition as the major internal instrument of change in American society. SNCC has tried several times to organize poor whites; we are trying again now, with an initial training program in Tennessee. It is purely academic today to talk about bringing poor blacks and whites together, but the job of creating a poor-white power bloc must be attempted. The main responsibility for it falls upon whites. Black and white can work together in the white community where possible; it is not possible, however, to go into a poor Southern town and talk about integration. Poor whites everywhere are becoming more hostile—not less—partly because they see the nation's attention focused on black poverty and nobody coming to them. Too many young middle-class Americans, like some sort of Pepsi generation, have wanted to come alive through the black community; they've wanted to be where the action is—and the action has been in the black community.

Black people do not want to "take over" this country. They don't want to "get Whitey"; they just want to get him off their backs, as the saying goes. It was, for example, the exploitation by Jewish landlords and merchants which first created black resentment toward Jews—not Judaism. The white man is irrelevant to blacks, except as an oppressive force. Blacks want to be in his place, yes, but not in order to terrorize and lynch and starve him. They want to be in his place because that is where a decent life can be had.

But our vision is not merely of a society in which all black men have enough to buy the good things of life. When we urge that black money go into black pockets, we mean the communal pocket. We want to see money go back into the community and used to benefit it. We want to see the cooperative concept applied in business and banking. We want to see black ghetto residents demand that an exploiting landlord or store keeper sell them, at minimal cost, a building or a shop that they will own and improve cooperatively; they can back their demand with a rent strike, or a boycott, and a community so unified behind them that no one else will move into the building or buy at the store. The society we seek to build among black people, then, is not a capitalist one. It is a society in which the spirit of community and humanistic love prevail. The word love is suspect; black expectations of what it might produce have been betrayed too often. But those were expectations of a response from the white community, which failed us. The love we seek to encourage is within the black community, the only American community where men call each other "brother" when they meet. We can build a community of love only where we have the ability and power to do so; among blacks.

As for white America, perhaps it can stop crying out against "black supremacy," "black nationalism," "racism in reverse," and begin facing reality. The reality is that this nation, from top to bottom, is racist; that racism is not primarily a problem of "human relations" but of an exploitation maintained—either actively or through silence—by the society as a whole. Camus and Sartre have asked, can a man condemn himself? Can whites, particularly liberal whites, condemn themselves? Can they stop blaming us, and blame their own system? Are they capable of the shame which might become a revolutionary emotion?

We have found that they usually cannot condemn themselves, and so we have done it. But the rebuilding of this society, if at all possible, is basically the responsibility of whites—not blacks. We won't fight to save the present society, in Vietnam or anywhere else. We are just going to work, in the way *we* see fit, and on goals *we* define, not for civil rights but for all our human rights.

Stokely Carmichael is chairman of the Student Nonviolent Coordinating Committee. This article appeared in The New York Review of Books, *September 26, 1966.*

ONLY CONNECT: REFLECTIONS ON THE REVOLUTION

by Jonathan Eisen

The recent apparent upsurge of racism in Northern communities—the "counter revolution" as it is termed in certain circles—has prompted a far-reaching reaction among student civil rights proponents. This, combined with the threat of proliferating violence, is prodding discussion and debate which is no longer concerned with theoretical or even moral considerations.

Two years ago, student leaders were still talking in terms of equal rights, race and racism in American politics, and civil disobedience. Major debates were held within the student movement over violence versus nonviolence. Eliminating segregation in lunch counters, beaches, libraries, and parks preoccupied many groups.

Although these issues still command attention, recent considerations—from the effects of the March on Washington to the recent Wisconsin primary—are pointing to an emphasis on problems of the economy as they relate to human rights over a broad social spectrum. Attention is being given to what are increasingly viewed as "economic root causes" of discrimination, and poverty itself is now being regarded as inseparable from some of the deeper forms of racism in our society.

Led by the Students for a Democratic Society and the Northern Student Movement, a conference was held recently at the University of Michigan both to search for new direction in political analysis and to explore the reasons for what student leaders view as the current stagnation of the civil rights movement.

The theme of the conference centered on the fact that society's denial of civil rights can no longer be divorced and treated separately from the other social and economic ills which beset this country. Connections were found and explored between poverty and discrimination, slums and police brutality, apathy (estrangement) and war, and in the last analysis, the contemporary "ruling class."

Within the realm of tactics, demonstrations of nearly every kind —including the more recent attempts at traffic-snarling, garbage-dumping, and the more tried and true methods of picketing and leafleting—were judged and found wanting. And for these young activists, the handwriting on the wall is clear. As one student from Swarthmore College described it, "We can demonstrate until we are all in jail, but neither the inconvenience we cause nor the moral witness we present will alter the situation. The trouble is, we just aren't reaching the centers of power."

Pressure is mounting, and not only from this type of frustration. What is now being acknowledged is that the civil rights movement is now, and probably has been for some time, out of control. The problem is no longer one of mobilization. The "masses" are there. However, difficulties are arising as interim successes serve only to generate more militant demands on a relatively unyielding structure. Caught on the horn of its own slogans of "Freedom Now!," the movement is generating resistance within its own ranks as the connection between action and the acquisition of freedom becomes suspect. The meaning of direct action (on which the movement *qua* movement is based) melts after the first, second, or even the fourteenth encounter with the local police doesn't seem to produce tangible results.

Hence, with an increased feeling of solidarity, there also has appeared increasing chaos as the movement batters itself against the passivity and resistance of society at large.

"We are faced by a society which refuses to yield, and we are without the necessary sanctions. We have demonstrated every night for two weeks against the conditions in our schools (Chester, Pa.), and yet the school board has even refused to meet to discuss the problem."

Compromise has therefore become an anathema to the new

leadership. Wary of every attempt to "buy us off," these young people see compromise as "taking too long" and doing too little. Basic change in social institutions is seen as an immediate imperative. The political order has served not as an institution in which to funnel social pressure, but as a sponge, soaking up the thrust of social change, and rendering progressive movements impotent. In this connection, wide and obvious reference was made on several occasions to the Populist movement of the 1880's and 90's. Determined, then, to have learned their lessons from the past, students are exploring the various avenues of organization designed to act effectively on the "roots" of social malaise.

One thing is certain: The crisis in tactics is viewed as concomitant with the "unrepresentativeness" of the present civil rights leadership. Although adult and student leadership have long been at serious odds over both strategy and ideology, current disagreement seems to have gone beyond the point of reconciliation. The vision of the student groups aims at "grass roots" democracy, a stressing of the broader issues in the economy, and an emphasis on transracial class solidarity. By contrast, adult leadership is viewed in many ways as "elitist," accommodating to the political status quo, and "middle class" both in background and tactics. "They accept the system," and thus are unwilling to incorporate in their purview the essential demands on the current system of economic organization. In order to obtain redress to their grievances against society, "the primacy of private property" must be discarded, and the political "slum landlords" replaced by men heedful of popular needs.

Neither the law, nor the courts, nor (implicitly) those civil rights organizations which base their plan of action on legal changes, is exempt from criticism. "The real fight for equality" will acknowledge that "the law has failed, and that new laws die because the social situation is the same as before. We must realize that the Supreme Court is no panacea."

"Acceptable channels of protest" are no longer tactically desirable or (as demonstrated above) seen as politically relevant. The need to "develop indigenous leadership" was strongly emphasized and grass roots participation in basic decision-making seen as the essential vehicle. Change itself would most likely arrive when the "power centers" like the banks were threatened. Jesse Gray, leader of the Harlem Rent Strike, called for an extension of the strike to a "national movement to withhold rent." The question of civil rights was posed as one which hinged on economy, and the economy fastened on the direct exploitation of the poor, and, finally, civil rights hinged on the abolition of poverty.

Roger Blough's statement of non-interference in Birmingham was read and enjoyed for its irony.

As the conference progressed, it became increasingly evident that hitherto propounded guidelines were in the process of drastic alteration; morality/immorality fell by the way.

"Americans must wake up and realize that some white people are just not salvageable," Bill Strickland, NSM head stated, "—something Negroes have known for quite a long time" (laughter, applause). Stress here was on finding a handle to approach the core economic issues which are "obviously national." Localism seems to have been relegated to the dim area of the past, as the discussion proceeded to the powers of the national government now blockaded and lying unused. "You cannot 'boycott' basic industries; you cannot 'boycott' basic institutions," Strickland went on. Racism, then, was considered too interwoven in society to be extricated by "selective buying."

But if the Negro community is encountering resistance and is moving in conflict and chaos, at least the basic "thrust" has been established from which a new departure can develop. Perhaps the thrust itself is one of the more important causes of the current dilemma. Without insurgency, there is no advance, and without advance, no resistance.

The white community, on the other hand, to which anxious glances are being directed by the Negro leadership, has received no such organizational stimuli to give it a sense of being upwardly mobile. Yet because of a shrinking labor market unskilled whites are fearful about the jobs they hold so tenuously, and more often than not they are coming to view not only the "Machine" but the Negro (who is caught in a similar situation) as the advancing enemy who must be stopped.

With this as background, Strickland and others see that "the burden of acceleration is now on the whites." To paraphrase, "We are moving ahead, but ultimately cannot succeed without you. We are developing our own (read Negro) leadership, so you (read white liberals) go back (read we don't need you any more and resent being led by whites) and take care of your own." Seen ahead is conflict between two groups which should be allies, and the very last thing anyone wants are race wars. It is thought that there will be blood enough this summer.

It is felt that the "white slums" are rapidly falling victim to virulent right wing racist propaganda; temerous allusions were made to the results of this activity on the electoral front.

Taking their cue from the various reports which are now serving to make the poor a bit less invisible, SDS has initiated a program (under the direction of the extremely able and articulate Rennie Davis, graduate student at the University of Michigan) to work with whites.

The purpose of the new group (Economic Research and Action Project, ERAP) is to move concerned students into Northern urban areas to organize the unemployed, with the ultimate aim of pressuring various communities around the issues of jobs, slums, schools. Reminiscent of the thirties, apple selling is again being pressed into service, as class lines are again stressed and the woeful state of our urban areas demonstrated.

"Program," a word and concept of organization being emphasized, now is beginning to include demands for a diversion of funds from military, space, and foreign aid (the balance of which is military) to help provide the jobs which can fulfill essential community needs not now being met. A desire to escape from corporate paternalism seems to undergird much of the thinking, and discussion proceeded in some cases to revolve around "seizing jobs" for work which is needed but isn't contracted because it is "unprofitable." The necessity for "democratic participation" was asserted here with the idea that society can and should be providing a minimum standard of living for its citizens. With this, it is felt that the racism which is given such a fertile ground in a society which seems to need large numbers of unemployed, will be greatly reduced.

What is more relevant, however, is the fact that the students are becoming more aware of their own limitations at the same time their intellectual and "programmatic" horizons are expanding. The "crisis in tactics" is a very real and honest admission that nobody seems to know where the movement is going or how to "catch up with it." The only sure thing is that society must be changed to allow equality.

Although old members of the left may choose to parallel student involvement today and their own of thirty years ago, there remain inescapable differences. If any "doctrine" can be found today, it is the logical *result* of the grouping of different strands of different movements, and not the genesis.

Like the Populism by which many of the new student leadership set their clocks (what is the story of the sons hating their fathers and embracing their grandfathers?), there is a conjoining, indeed a pluralistic cohesion reflecting the diversity of the new civil rights movement. And rather than focusing attention on specifics, these leaders are embracing the whole of society, trying to find some systematic coherence.

Jon Eisen, a former editor of The Activist, *is a graduate of Oberlin College and the University of Illinois Institute of Labor-Industrial Relations. He is presently studying at the University of Edinburgh in Scotland. "Reflections on the Revolution" is reprinted from* The Activist, *#10, spring 1964.*

THE BATTLEFIELDS AND THE WAR

by Todd Gitlin

The battlefields we have chosen as organizers, and organizers of organizers, are the communities of the under-America: cities and towns and rural spreads where people live materially deprived, politically alienated and used, and victimized by social and economic institutions beyond their comprehension and reach. This is entirely as it should be, since people strongly afflicted with the rottenness of our society are best capable of exorcising that rot. The process of social change must involve the movement of masses of people. Movement becomes meaningful when the people directly afflicted organize for change, for it is then that people are sensing their own possibilities as men, their power to make things happen. The poor know they are poor and don't like it; hence they can be organized to demand an end to poverty and the construction of a decent social order.

The problem is that needs immediately felt are not the only needs people have, and that the satisfaction of either set of needs is generally not possible unless certain things happen outside the given community....

Needs and "Needs"

One of the diabolical successes of this organized society is that it perverts people's notions about themselves into fantasies that perpetuate an unjust system. This is universally so, I think, but particularly true about the poor, the unemployed, the Negroes. If you can get to the suburbs you'll be green, safe, and happy.... Negroes are inferior....What you really need is Dial Soap and tailfins....If you get a Ph. D. you will be needed and happy....You are powerful because you can vote....and so on down the line. As Baldwin puts it, after a lifetime of brutalization, "you become a nigger": You act out the image that the Respectables have of you. Cultural and commercial pressures generate artificial "needs" that, in the minds of the victims, displace more genuine human needs.

That this process operates seems undeniable, but more than one conclusion can be drawn. One is that *everything* people say they want is the product of the process, and is therefore suspect; it is the product of distorted values that are in turn products of a distorted culture. The underlying premise here is that men are blank slates upon which the environment writes its will; there are no such things as basic "human needs." The conclusion is appealing for its "modern" relativism, its veneer of tolerance, but it is a blind alley; for if no needs are basic, then we cannot separate "true" from "false" needs, and we might just as well conclude that all expressed needs are "true." In other words, everything that is, is for some reason, and is good. The first conclusion degenerates into an involved rationalization for the status quo.

If we reject this approach, as I think we must, then we must decide for ourselves which expressed needs are genuine or "just," and which are artificial or wrong. That decision process is more than an abstract exercise in political philosophy, though, since it bears directly on some of the major organizing issues—what to do about racism in lower class white communities, or virulent anti-Communism, for example. No hard-and-fast rule can be laid down for dealing with expressed needs we consider wrong when we encounter them, and it is not the purpose of this working paper to pluck rules from the sky. What I want to emphasize is that the remedy for improper "needs" must be an *educational* one. Of course organizers are learners, but they must be educators as well. The opposite of constituent education is not "the free expression of human needs," but rather education carried out, day to day, by people and institutions other than ourselves—that is to say, by the corrupting and degrading organs of the cold war and corporatism. Education must be the third element, along with research and action, in any organizing project.

Real Needs and Levels of Explanation

Let us assume that organizers in a lower-class community have identified certain felt needs as basic. These may be elemental material needs—decent housing, jobs, income, no rats, food, playgrounds, etc. They will also include less tangible needs conducive to a sense of dignity, purpose, and human possibility—good education, participation in community and national decisions, participation in a movement that promises a new society, etc. These needs are near the surface; they can be organized into demands. This is a beginning state; it signals the congealing of individualized concerns into organized expression. The very process of massing into a movement contributes to a sense of personal power and thereby makes possible further steps in the *organizing* and *focus-*

ing of the resulting aggregate power.

At this early stage, preferably before, the organizers must acquaint themselves with various levels of explanation for the nonfulfillment of felt needs. For example, you are working among white unemployed in a Northern city. Why are these people unemployed? At one level, because certain plants have automated, or moved to regions with "better labor conditions," or been squeezed out of existence by corporate gigantism. At another level, because Federal funds that might produce jobs are fed into the defense budget. At still another level, because public and democratic planning to satisfy felt needs is prohibited by the corporate economy and the free-enterprise ethos.

People may or may not be aware of some of these varieties of explanation; this must be found out. All of them are true in one sense or another, but not all of them are relevant to remedying the condition of unemployment. Those plants have automated because it is profitable to do so; others have moved out of town because it is profitable to do so; then "more plants" is not the answer to the condition of unemployment. The fact of the matter is that the national job structure is in transition from a predominantly blue-collar to a predominantly white-collar one, and that the private economy nationally has stopped generating more new jobs than are being destroyed. No single plant is responsible for the general condition of joblessness, although obviously particular jobs have been destroyed by particular plants or plant departures. And the same processes that destroyed particular jobs will continue to destroy other jobs and to prohibit the massive job-creation necessary to eliminate unemployment.* Aside from temporary fluctuations in the employment level in a given community, the

* This is not to deny that in the short run unemployment may decrease. Industrial expansion will rise this year because of the tax cut. But not even government economists believe that this expansion will last more than two years, at most, and it may even accelerate the process of automation. Still, in the short run the "boom" may pose an obstacle to those organizing efforts oriented solely around the issue of unemployment. This is one strong argument for an organizing approach that encompasses a variety of issues. Although it is true that a higher *percentage* of the unemployed live in poverty, in terms of actual numbers, more of the employed than the unemployed live in the "Other America."

argument must be made that unemployment is chronic and that the private economy is not set up to eliminate the condition.

Levels of Target

An inventory must then be made of city financing and budgets. What amounts have been appropriated in the past for public construction—schools, parks, hospitals, low-cost housing, mass transit, etc? What training and apprenticeship programs exist for the resulting jobs? What public facilities of this nature are needed, and how many jobs could be created through their construction? The answers constitute ammunition.

In the first place, an effort can be made to exhaust city (including state-city and federal-city) construction and training projects by applying for positions in them. The results will be inadequate, of course, and this fact should be noted and made public. In the second place, direct action can employ such facts in a particularly damning fashion. The city and county governments must be pressed to appropriate funds requisite to the filling of community needs: in demonstrations, sit-ins, electoral campaigns. One rule of thumb here is that electoral campaigns are most effective when more direct means have (1) proved the limits of their effectiveness, and (2) further solidified the organization of the movement. But this is by no means a rule without exceptions, and the finger-to-the-wind approach is likely to prove more generally satisfactory. What is most important at this stage of the game is to make sure that successes (*e.g.*, the New York City rat elimination program) and failures are each fully understood throughout the movement and the larger community. Small successes are healthy and magnetic for any movement, but the limitations of these successes should be made clear. Roughly, the broader the program and the deeper its roots within the movement, the less will be the likelihood that the movement will be stymied by a limited success. Besides, we operate on the assumption that needs are deeply enough felt to transcend the satisfaction of minor surface symptoms. In any case, the city itself will be able to do very little. Since cities (and states) compete for private investment, any drastic increase in city tax rates will leave it disadvantaged in the game of grab. The tax base will not be sufficient for the magnitude of public investment required, whether for jobs themselves, or housing, or schools, or mass transit. Since this is equally true for the state, there is probably little success-mileage to be made from an assault on the state government, *unless the grievance chosen to be capitalized on involves the state directly*. (As in the case of the Illinois welfare-payment cut.) Moreover, with rare exceptions the state government is only marginally, if at all, a better target than the community; increasingly it is the pawn of the federal government in the realm of job- and service-creating appropriations, and its greater and more varied constituency makes it less susceptible than the city to community pressure.

Even in the absence of President Johnson's self-proclaimed "war on poverty," it would be increasingly obvious to the disadvantaged that only the Federal Government has the financial resources and the legitimacy to meet the spread of felt needs. The rhetoric of the "war," the fact that it is declared to be "unconditional," contributes the notion of federal *responsibility* to wage war on poverty. The diffuseness of the rhetoric means that within the broad limits "anything goes." Federal programs can usefully be matched against the rhetoric and found wanting; grass-roots programs, like that of the Chester Committee for Freedom Now, can be publicized as consistent with the announced intent of the "war." These two elements, federal *power* and federal *responsibility*, must be discussed, amplified, and elaborated within each movement.

The responsibility is easily established; it is part and parcel of the rhetoric, and moreover it is morally evident—the states' rights bugaboo should carry little weight among the exposed poor. The power, on the other hand, is less well understood. Perhaps it can best be explained in a negative fashion: That is, *who else but the federal government* has the power to create jobs, to raise income, and to build the schools and hospitals and other civic centers required for the age of decency? As Jack Minnis points out in his working paper, the moral and material defaults of localized industry are largely the defaults of centralized capitalism, and to attack the outpost, you must attack the central fortress. (The question of the most effective approach to that center, as Minnis also emphasizes, is an open one contingent on many particulars.) Similarly, the only organized power center in the country is the Federal Government. The precedent is there for federal job-creation (public works) and community need-fulfillment (Housing and Home Finance Agency, and many other programs). The funds are there—the majority of them are chucked into a sea of defense—but they are there nevertheless. And if power capable of countervailing corporate power is *not* there, then it is nowhere. Here again, any community movement faces an educational task of major proportions: to hammer away at the irresponsibility and needlessness of defense expenditures, to illuminate the changing nature of the Cold War, and to pose clear and democratically supported models of new communities within the power of the Federal Government to support and fund.

The defense budget will prove recalcitrant, with all the interests that are staked on it, but the demand for a reduction in expenditure is by no means a radical one at the present time. No less an eminence than former Assistant Secretary of Defense Roswell Gilpatrick has recently argued that a 25 per cent cut in the defense budget is likely by 1970. Sensing the heightening possibility of unmanageable domestic unrest, eager to expand the budding *detente* with the Soviet Union, the Administration will increasingly rationalize the defense budget and shave it, allocating one sector of the proceeds to minimal welfare expansion and the rest to tax deductions of one sort or another. Movement demands for domestic priorities must stay ahead of the Administration's attempts to undercut discontent with token defense reductions. Thus, movements must eventually articulate the demand for substantial defense cuts in order to keep the Administration on the defensive.

At the final level of explanation, that of corporate power, sweeping technological change, and ethical default, the target is still the Federal Government but the problem is qualitatively different. Research on the possibility of long-term full employment will continue and most likely will continue to produce nothing like a definite answer. Education must admit to the uncertainty but spell out both possibilities and their meanings. At some stage in the crystallization of a community movement, discussion should turn to the likelihood of the obsolescence of traditional conceptions of work, the exploration of newer conceptions, and the need for democratic, multi-level, participatory planning to ensure the utilization of an abundant technology to democratic rather than authoritarian ends. Here again, any proposed solution must be *national*—a constitutional amendment providing for guaranteed income and guaranteed education, a national planning structure—and will require Federal action.

The Development of Demands and the Role of Education

In the above two paragraphs, I have used the words "eventually" and "at some stage." They are intentionally vague. There can be no universally applicable timetable for the introduction of a sequence of demands. What seems clearer, though, is that education revolving around the next higher level of demand must precede action around that demand. The reasons are essentially two-fold:

(1) A each level of demand and target, both limited successes and failures will happen. Limited successes will be used to advantage—they will not weaken by virtue of cooptation—if they are seen in the perspective of the totality of demands. This totality is horizontal—the sum of a variety of demands—and thus prohibits satisfaction at the local level, as I've said above. It should also be vertical, ranging from higher welfare payments to completion of the welfare state to democratic national planning, since at the Federal level even a totality of separate welfare demands runs *some* chance of being provided for. Education must make clear in what way the horizontal aggregate depends on the vertical progression. In other words, movement participants must plumb the depths of their demands, to decide *what kind* of houses they want to live in, *what kind* of jobs they want to hold, *what kind* of physical arrangement they want for their communities. Education in this context should not mean something manipulative or superimposing; it should be catalytic, designed to bring to the

surface of the collective consciousness people's buried feelings about how they want to live. At some stage—here again, the timing should be flexible, to be judged by "feel"—radical city planners, teachers, and artists might be brought in as resources and participants. Different educational forms, from "Freedom Schools" for children to mass meetings to bull sessions, should be experimented with, and their utilities discussed and compared. Failures should also be discussed and their causes analyzed, so that the next strategy may be arrived at and its necessity democratically understood.

(2) If we believe in the possibility, however remote, of a new order of things, then the unfolding of a community movement must bear within it some seeds of that new order. Aside, then, from the strategic imperatives of discussion, education, and democratic decision-making, there is an added moral imperative. People must find their way out of the restricted perspectives imposed by their condition and toward the light of overview, of understanding of how things tick and why. Only then will they be able to make fulfilling use of new programs and new institutions. The alternative is the perpetuation—indeed, the technological strengthening—of minority rule and mass powerlessness.

It may be argued that the mass debate on program and strategy envisioned here is rendered impossible by the stultifying power of the mass media, the deadening torpor of poverty, and the rest. Maybe. The best we can say is that we don't know. Illiteracy and its concomitants are widespread in the communities in which we will be working. But American history offers an inspiring model, that of the Populist movement. Around 1890 there were well over a thousand Populist newspapers, with total circulation in the hundreds of thousands. Copies of books like Edward Bellamy's *Looking Backward* were sold in cheap editions in the hundreds of thousands. Speakers from the Farmers' Alliances toured local affiliates throughout the South and West. The result, as described by contemporary observers, looked and sounded like this:

People commenced to think who had never thought before, and people talked who had seldom spoken. On mild days they gathered on the street corners, on cold days they congregated in shops and offices. Everyone was talking and everyone was thinking.... Little by little they commenced to theorize upon their condition. Despite the poverty of the country, the books of Henry George, Bellamy, and other economic writers were bought as fast as the dealers could supply them. They were bought to be read greedily; and, nourished by the fascination of novelty and the zeal of enthusiasm, thoughts and theories sprouted like weeds after a May shower....They discussed income tax and single tax; they talked of government ownership and the abolition of private property; fiat money, and the unity of labor; ... and a thousand conflicting things....

Mary E. Lease, Jerry Simpson, ... and half a hundred others who lectured up and down the land, were not the only people who could talk on the issues of the day. The farmers, the country merchants, the cattleherders, they of the long chin-whiskers, and they of the broad-brimmed hats and heavy boots, had also heard the word and could preach the gospel of Populism. The dragon's teeth were sprouting in every nook and corner of the State. Women with skins tanned to parchment by the hot winds, with bony hands of toil and clad in faded calico, could talk in meeting, and could talk right straight to the point. [Quoted in John D. Hicks, *The Populist Revolt* (University of Minnesota Press, 1931), pp. 132, 159.]

Now the illiteracy rate in the Western states in 1880 ranged from only 3.6 per cent to 6.2 per cent, way below the national average; and although the rate in Southern states ranged up to 55 per cent, it remains true that illiteracy in central cities today is higher than in many of the states of Populist days. Still, it remains to be shown whether the difference is qualitative or simply quantitative. Widespread education and discussion comparable with that of seventy-five years ago as the links between varying levels of demands and analysis, between disparate demands emanating from different communities, may be possible even today, and we won't know until we try.

Tactics, Timing, and Theoretical Imperatives

The fact that solutions must be national and must involve

Federal action leaves a variety of tactical issues unresolved. There are still the very critical issues of timing and the expenditure of human and financial resources at any given time.

No general rule set down within the confines of an office could cover the multiplicity of situations organizers will confront. In Mississippi, for example, the limitations of local- and state-directed activity are clear, and the purpose of such activity is largely to demonstrate the entrenchment of obstacles and the immediate need for Federal intervention. (Even under the proposed Civil Rights Bill, the law requires that local movements "go through the motions" to demonstrate local illegalities and terrorisms.) In New York City, on the other hand, city and state governments may already have a good deal of discretion over housing and school construction and location. Here and elsewhere, the extent of localized power needs to be found out—budgets consulted and analyzed, local officials interviewed, tax structures understood—if only to document the extent of local impotence. Stages in the demand and target hierarchies can be skipped if the reasons are understood within the movement.

Massive gatherings of movements from many communities at the state and national levels pose special problems. A march on Washington for Jobs and Freedom, a demonstration at the Democratic Convention against the seating of the Dixiecrat Mississippi delegation, a demonstration of unemployed Kentucky miners in Washington, all involve the balancing of a number of factors. Such projects take movement participants and organizers away from their communities; they involve vast expenditures of money and time and energy; they may represent a least common denominator among demands. On the other hand, by their format and target they may illuminate an obstacle and point to the wielders of power; recruitment and publicity may contribute to the solidification and expansion of the movement in the community as well as to the appearance of new supportive groups. Before deciding on such a venture, participants should ask:

(1) What effect will it have on the solidification, crystallization, and dedication of purpose, and on the expansion of the local movement?

(2) What will its outcome teach about the nature of the national structure of power, the relations among issues, new strategies?

(3) Which community groupings might be forced closer to the movement if they were forced to take a stand on a large, public undertaking?

The answers must be weighed against the negative factors, and a balance struck. We know, for example, that the demonstration of the unemployed Hazard miners in Washington in January, 1964, gave a real boost to their organization. It would be useful to find out the effect of the August 1963 March on Washington on local movements. (To what extent, for example, did it generate the organization of the Chicago school boycotts?) Likewise, the effect of the Aaron Henry-for-Governor campaign in Mississippi. According to the second question, a demonstration against the seating of both the Alabama and Mississippi delegations at the Democratic Convention might be more fruitful than that against the Mississippi one alone, since it would illuminate the very well-knit connections between the Alabama economy and a number of national corporations. Not dogmatically, but as guidelines, these questions should be kept in mind and discussed when a massive, nationally-focused undertaking is proposed. Timing will always be a subtle issue, and an ear to the ground is the critical instrument.

Whatever the tactics and timing adopted, a national focus and a nationally coordinated strategy will be needed at some time in the future, for the issues of the economy, of public allocations, are national in scope and require national solutions. Local successes are important as morale builders and learning experiences, but their extent will be confined. At some point national power must be sought and this will require the adherence of groups not immediately affected by the conditions of poverty. Community movements should at some point in their development try to pick up the support of professional groups; they might consider joint programs, both demonstrative and educational. Some support may be expected to congeal around the movement in any case. Picking up this support does not necessarily require toning down movement demands, but it is likely to require *extending* demands and meshing educational processes. Again, where overlapping interests can be identified, education must be catalytic and exploratory, never imperious.

Whether the achievement of national power involves a third party or not is fiercely hard to know now. Earlier efforts—the Populists, Socialists, Communists, Progressives—can be studied with profit, but the answer is bound to be a new one; all the past can do is remind. Nor will it ever be easy to tell what is premature and what overdue, when "conditions are ripe" and when they are arid, or whether a given expenditure of resources is a wise one.

Todd Gitlin graduated from Harvard University in 1963. President of SDS, 1963-64, and coordinator of the Peace Research and Education Project (PREP) of SDS, Mr. Gitlin is now working on his M.A. in Political Science at the University of Michigan. He lives in Chicago, where he is engaged in writing a book on the lives of poor whites on Chicago's Northside. This article was originally published as an SDS working paper in April of 1964.

ORGANIZING THE UNEMPLOYED: THE CHICAGO PROJECT

by Richard Flacks

When SDS first decided to send organizers into cities as part of their ERAP project, they admitted to a certain amount of apprehension about the probable response the organizers would encounter. They expected to be surprised, and they were. What follows is a description, written in April 1964, of the beginning of the Chicago ERAP project (JOIN), and the responses of distrust, suspicion, interest, and, finally, tentative commitment on the part of the community.

The Politics of Unemployment

The most frightening symptom of America's social and economic stagnation is the rate of joblessness in our society. The unemployment rate is frightening because: (a) it remains high (hovering around 6 per cent for the last seven years); (b) it is relatively unaffected by periods of prosperity; (c) it affects certain groups in the society with special force (12 per cent of our youth are unemployed; Negro unemployment in the ghetto runs as high as 20 per cent for adults, 40-50 per cent for young Negroes); (d) it is likely to increase rapidly due to the simultaneous impact of the population explosion and automation. These aspects of modern unemployment reflect the low growth rate of our economy, the stagnation of the public sector, and the uncontrolled use of technology.

Unemployment is a political problem. Major centers of power in our society support policies which prevent full employment and actively favor a high rate of unemployment. Corporation managers favor a substantial pool of unemployment since this is an effective barrier to union organizing and pressures for higher wages. During the recent years of high unemployment, the rate of wage increases has been cut in half and the labor movement has been seriously weakened due to the unemployment of workers in manufacturing industries. The business community opposes an expansion of the public sector for a host of reasons. The defense corporations want public money channeled into weaponry since this is their sole means of profit maintenance. Corporate executives oppose government intervention and regulation of the automation process. Finally, the corporate economy flourishes best when production levels are below full capacity; this allows prices to remain high and profits to be maximized.

. . .

Given this structure of power in our society, there can be no possibility of a solution to the problem of modern unemployment. A necessary condition for the solution of the problem is the organization of centers of political and economic power which are capable of effectively challenging the dominating influence of the corporations. The major institution having this capability at the present time is the labor movement. But an outstanding tragedy of our time has been the labor movement's tendency to act to protect the jobs of those presently employed and presently unionized rather than acting decisively in behalf of those who are presently or potentially without jobs.

Many now recognize that the problem of unemployment will not be dealt with until the unemployed organize and act in their interest, until they themselves are represented in the political arena. But there is also a widespread belief that such organization is virtually impossible—that, for a variety of reasons, jobless men are incapable of sustained social action.

The civil rights movement has demonstrated that traditional beliefs about organizing the unemployed should now be drastically modified. For in Birmingham, in Brooklyn, and in many other places, unemployed Negroes in substantial numbers have participated actively in protest movements, and in many cases have organized directly to demand jobs.

But the civil rights movement *itself* cannot be regarded as an effective mechanism for representing the demands of the unemployed. This is true first of all because the demand for jobs for Negroes neglects the fact that jobs for everyone are scarce. Secondly, the demand for jobs for Negroes produces tremendous tensions and negative reactions among white workers and white unemployed.

From a theoretical point of view, then, the best way toward an effective movement of the unemployed would involve the organization of white as well as black jobless.

The Chicago Project: Beginnings

It was considerations such as these which prompted the Students for a Democratic Society to attempt to develop an organizing project among white unemployed. Through its Economic Research and Action Project, SDS hired Joe Chabot as its field worker. Chabot was a sophomore at the University of Michigan and had had a wide range of work and organizational experience. Chabot was sent to Chicago in September 1963. Chicago was selected for a number of reasons: its substantial rates of Negro and white unemployment, the varied nature of its work force, the extensive and diverse nature of its white slums, Chabot's familiarity with the city, etc. Chabot's initial assignment was to live in a white lower-class area and to attempt to make contact with white unemployed youth. The initial expectation was that unemployed young people would be the most "ready" for organizing initiatives since their problems were most severe (statistically) and the ingrained inhibitions against the system which exist among white adults would be less evident among youth.

Chabot spent his first six weeks on Chicago's Near Northside. He talked with young people in settlement houses and on the streets of the neighborhood. He also spent a great deal of time observing the established institutions of the community: The Northwest Community Organization, the settlement houses, churches, and political life of the neighborhood.

Chabot soon learned that his initial expectations about the organizational "readiness" of white unemployed youth were in many ways invalid:

They don't have jobs and most of them make or get what money they have from the old man or small criminal acts. They are in revolt and they are winning, although what they are winning isn't good. After about 15, most of the fellows look or act openly hostile toward do-gooders, church settlements, government, etc., and effectively break all ties with these institutions. School isn't liked and isn't seen as being too helpful . . . They don't like their teachers and their teachers probably don't like them . . . and when they have an older brother who graduated and he doesn't have a decent job either, then they see in fact that schools haven't helped him so why "put up with something I hate when it isn't helping me." They hate the police and the police are oppressive. They feel if anyone has anything to offer them it's because they're going to need you to screw someone else. I don't know whether they want jobs. I know they don't want jobs for less than 2 dollars/hour. Politics to them is knowing someone, and that's what it actually is. But what's worse is the prevalent feeling that *their bad state simply comes from being at the wrong place at the wrong time* and that if this hadn't been so they would have made it like the rest. . . . There is nothing to make them think socially at this time and nothing to give them confidence that in action their lives can improve. . . . At this point it is disenchanting to know that I've not met one fellow in the age group I would like to work in who is thinking socially. (Chabot, "Organizing Unemployed Whites:" an interim report).

An effort to develop protest activity among these youth could conceivably have been developed, but the task would have been a long and frustrating one, partially because of the attitudes of these boys, and partially because Chabot was a solitary individual, lacking any base or position within the community which would enable him to relate to the boys.

But while Chabot had been living in the Near Northwest he continued to expand his contacts and develop his store of information about Chicago—particularly about the political and economic institutions and organizations in the city. In the course of several months, he had attended dozens of meetings of neighborhood organizations, church groups, civil rights organizations, business groups, unions, etc. He gradually developed a rough picture of political life in Chicago. He also educated himself with respect to the economic statistics of the city and constructed maps of the city's population—ethnic distributions, employment figures by neighborhood, etc.

The most important contact which Chabot made at this time was with the leadership of the Packinghouse Workers Union in Chicago. The UPW, in August 1963, had received a rather enthusiastic response to some initial efforts to organize former members who had lost their jobs in the industry. A meeting called prior to the March on Washington drew 400 unemployed. The Union, however, was unwilling to commit major resources to an unemployed organizing effort—in large part because they did not see a way to organize white as well as Negro unemployed and felt that it would be unwise to build an unemployed organization solely of Negroes.

Chabot's arrival on the scene had a catalytic effect. Here was someone able to work full time on the task of organizing white unemployed, someone who was ready to begin and who had some organizational and financial resources to help initiate the project. Jesse Prosten and Leon Beverly of the UPW staff, and Jay Miller of the American Friends Service Committee then committed themselves to developing the structure for the organization of the unemployed.

JOIN—The Committee for Jobs Or Income Now

These people plus some other unionists and church people

formed a loose committee responsible for aiding and developing the organization. The group decided that the operation was to be called JOIN—the Committee for Jobs Or Income Now.

It is instructive to examine in detail and in rough chronological order the various problems and decisions which those involved in the organization have been facing. What follows is a case study of the early stages of a social movement which is developing virtually "from scratch."

Developing Mass Contacts

The first organizing problem to be faced was that of finding an effective means of making contact with unemployed workers and recruiting them into the organization. An initial thought was to find neighborhoods of high unemployment—both white and black—and establish storefront offices in the neighborhoods. But this proved to be a difficult task with respect to whites because very few neighborhoods existed in which the unemployment rate was dramatically high. A better opportunity presented itself: the discovery of a large unemployment compensation office on the Northside through which thousands of white jobless passed daily. The decision was made to establish a storefront office and meeting place several doors down from the UCO on North Kedzie. This was done in mid-February 1964. In March, Leon Beverly of the Packinghouse union established a JOIN office on the Southside for the purpose of recruiting Negro unemployed. SDS hired a second field worker, Dan Max, to work with Chabot in the Northside JOIN office.

Chabot and Max worked initially as follows: Each day Max would leaflet those entering and leaving the UCO, while Chabot remained at the office, prepared to talk to people who came in response to the leaflet, serving coffee, holding meetings, etc. Various unions and other organizations cooperated in preparing the leaflets, and new leaflets were prepared each week. In the first week, at least one hundred unemployed came into the JOIN office; in the six weeks since it has been opened some 400-500 men have participated in discussions at the office.

Setting up the Organization

In addition to the daily informal meetings at the JOIN office, an attempt has been made to establish an initial decision making structure. Several Thursday evening meetings have been held, and special efforts were made to have those unemployed who were most interested in JOIN attend. These meetings have drawn from 5-30 people. An informal steering committee has been established to plan an action program. In addition, a "grievance committee" was formed to assist people who have trouble with the bureaucracy of unemployment compensation. These two committees represent first steps in involving the unemployed in the development of the organization. Several of the men have volunteered to help leaflet the unemployment compensation office. The grievance committee has handled its first "case": A man whose compensation check was being withheld through entangled red tape approached JOIN with his problem. A delegation went with the man to talk to the UCO supervisor; within a week the man was receiving his checks again.

Thus, within six weeks, a foundation for an unemployed organization on the Northside has been laid. About 80 unemployed men have committed themselves to work for the organization and to participate in its action programs. About 10-15 of these are sufficiently committed to have attended meetings regularly and have begun to engage in organizational activity.

Building a Base of Support

As the organizing effort on the Northside proceeded, there was simultaneous development of the supporting structure of the organization. Such a development was imperative if the organization was to get off the ground. Initial financing for office rent and subsistence for Chabot and Max came from SDS. People in the neighborhood contributed furniture for the office. One unionist paid for the installation of a sink, another contributed a used mimeo machine, a third contributed the cost of a used car for Chabot and Max. These haphazard initial efforts to generate resources for the project were supremely gratifying but there was a need for more systematic means for supporting the operation.

Now a core group of advisors have begun to build a sponsor list of people committed to aiding JOIN. A union has promised to print a massive number of JOIN brochures.

Efforts are being made to enable JOIN representatives to speak and raise money at local union meetings and to make contact with church groups and other organizations in the city. The immediate goal is the establishment of a large and representative body of JOIN supporters to aid in fund raising and other problems, and to raise enough support to enable JOIN offices to function without major subsidy from outside organizations.

Thus, in approximately two months, the JOIN operation has won substantial commitment from a number of key people in established liberal organizations and institutions, and a definite mechanism creating a stable and self-sustaining organization has begun to emerge.

It is important to note, in addition, that although much of the building of support has been undertaken in a planned and systematic fashion, a number of important achievements have occurred spontaneously. For example:

—a student at the Chicago School of Social Work has decided to drop out of school to do full time volunteer work for Northside JOIN. His plan is to establish the grievance committee on a viable basis, and to develop a service operation—principally, a referral service for people who need the assistance of social agencies.

—a woman with skills in employment counselling—herself unemployed—is planning to establish a job referral service for JOIN.

—a high school teacher in the area—a person with a number of contacts in the community—has become extremely enthusiastic about the project, and is assisting JOIN in making contact with the community and with a group of low-income teenagers from a nearby high school. These teenagers potentially can assist in JOIN action programs; conceivably they can be stimulated toward developing their own action program.

—a trade unionist in the area of the office has taken a strong interest in the project and has played a highly supportive role in terms of community relations and other problems.

It is these and other self-generated contacts and events which represent the most accurate measures of the extent to which a project of this kind really represents the felt needs of the community and is really capable of becoming a self-sustaining organization.

THE PROBLEM OF RECRUITMENT

But of course the real test of the organization will be its ability to recruit unemployed workers, to mobilize them for action, to involve them in decision making and the life of the organization, and to enable unemployed to assume the leadership of the organization. The men who are presently being recruited are not typical, for the most part, of those who pass through unemployment compensation. Observations suggest that the initial recruits are generally older, less skilled, and less socially integrated than the average white on unemployment compensation. In part this is due to the fact that the skilled, or white collar, young white person does not at the moment face a severe problem of prolonged unemployment even though he may be temporarily out of a job. White unemployment rates in these categories are probably below the national average, and at the present time in Chicago, jobs are available for men with these characteristics. The problem is more acute for men in their fifties and sixties, and a large proportion of JOIN recruits are in this age bracket. Another factor leading to the recruitment of atypical unemployed is the probability that many of the men will (quite understandably) not take seriously a new and somewhat mysterious organization staffed by young fellows who seem a little wet behind the ears.

Thus, the temporary nature of much of the unemployment on the Northside, and the unwillingness of many of the unemployed to identify themselves as unemployed will probably set limits at least initially on the expansion of JOIN to include large masses of white unemployed. But much can be done to greatly increase the participation and the typicality of those who come to the compensation office.

One immediate next step is to involve those who are already

committed in the task of organizing. This involvement will go beyond just leafletting; JOIN members will be asked to "buttonhole" other unemployed and attempt to engage their interest directly. Experimentation with buttonholing indicates that this is extremely effective in bringing people into the JOIN office—far more so than just leafletting and displaying signs.

Toward Action

A second mechanism for recruitment will be the development of an action program. Up to now, recruitment has primarily been an attempt to involve people in an organization without a concrete focus for participation. The result of this is that there is a tendency for those who are most committed to be active because of personal needs to participate in an organization, and not simply because of their concerns about unemployment. This situation will change as concrete actions are agreed upon and people are asked to become involved in specific activities.

There is no doubt that a large number of those who have expressed interest in JOIN are waiting for such action before they more fully commit their time and energy to the organization.

The first visible public action planned by JOIN will take place on May 4. On that day, unemployed from both the North and South Sides will converge on the Loop for the purpose of leafletting and selling apples. The selling of apples will be a symbolic reminder to the public of the existence of mass unemployment in Chicago. . . .

Concrete plans for action beyond May 4 have not yet been formally made although a great many ideas for future action have been discussed.

Future actions which have been proposed include both activity directed at immediate problems and grievances of the unemployed, and actions designed to dramatize unemployment and generate pressures for jobs.

Action around Grievances

Many grievances of the unemployed have to do with the administration of unemployment compensation itself. Red tape and bureaucratic errors often create situations of deprivation and confusion for an unemployed person. Petty nastiness on the part of UCO "deputies" is a constant source of irritation and indignity. JOIN's newly formed grievance committee hopes to develop an action program around these kinds of problems focusing on specific instances of injustice which arise.

A second kind of grievance is connected to institutions such as finance companies who exacerbate the problems of the unemployed and generate further misery by taking back the family car and appliances and landlords who evict for non-payment of rent, and by such as loss of union membership, pension benefits, health insurance, and other fringe benefits. JOIN members have discussed the possibility for direct action against finance companies and similar kinds of activity designed to prevent or alleviate the vicious cycle of misery which prolonged unemployment can generate.

A final set of immediate problems has to do with the way in which society "provides" for those who are unemployed. Unemployment compensation payments are plainly inadequate; they ought to last for the duration of one's unemployment. In many cases, there is a need for additional welfare benefits. JOIN participants have discussed the possibility of increasing compensation to minimum wage levels, providing additional payments for dependents, and providing free health clinics and surplus food distribution.

Demanding Jobs

More important than action around specific grievances is the development of an action program around the demand for more jobs. The apple-selling demonstration would be the first step in such a program. Future actions which have been discussed include: delegations (to City Hall, to Springfield, to Senators Douglas and Dirksen, and to Washington) demanding jobs, picketing, mass demonstrations, symbolic actions such as apple-selling, and other forms of civil disobedience designed to dramatize unemployment (at key spots such as City Hall, corporation offices, shopping centers, etc.), street rallies and similar activity at all compensation offices in the area, and the like. The attempt will be made to plan a "trajectory" of action designed to involve an ever-increasing number of unemployed around a more and more specific and meaningful political program.

Toward a Political Program for Jobs

JOIN participants have already begun to discuss the kinds of political demands which need to be made. These include such proposals as: the diversion of space, defense, and foreign aid funds to job-creating public works programs; reduction of retirement age and increased social security and pension benefits; "jobs or income"—a guarantee of a decent standard of living for every citizen; adequate job training and adult education programs, and the like.

Hopefully, the pressures generated by an effective action program would lead others in the city to take up and work for the JOIN program. A key element in the JOIN strategy is a notion that the demand for a solution to the problem of unemployment can generate new political alignments which can have important effects on the structure of power in the city and nationally. We shall return to this point shortly.

Thus, JOIN is seen as moving from a situation in which a handful of individuals from various liberal organizations plus a couple of full time student organizers created a crude organizational mechanism for mobilizing the unemployed, to an organization with a developing action program around a worked-out series of demands both for the immediate alleviation of problems and a long-range attack on the job problem. The involvement of an increasing number of unemployed people in the organization's activity and development will be enhanced by demonstrating to these people that JOIN can be of direct benefit to them. This is why the organization is undertaking a series of service functions as an important aspect of its operation.

Education and Research

JOIN will have failed in its purpose if it does not rapidly develop an effective educational program for its members and others who come into contact with it. An extensive supply of literature on economic and social issues . . . needs to be created immediately. Some of this material can be obtained from trade unions, churches, and other organizations. But a great deal of it ought to be prepared by students connected to the project and by JOIN members themselves. Especially valuable would be one-page leaflets which, in simple terms, describe particular aspects of the JOIN program and provide the basic arguments for advocacy of particular policies. A . . . weekly newspaper could be issued by the JOIN offices and distributed at the UCO. In fact, the weekly leaflet already constitutes a basis for such a newspaper. Evening meetings with local speakers need to be held on a regular basis; also possible are street rallies during the summer months.

These educational activities are crucial parts of the JOIN program. For a major fact of our time is the inability of people to think clearly about the society in which they live. The unemployed who come to JOIN are no exception to this generalization. A high percentage of them are opposed to expansion of the public sector; most are revolted by the word "socialism" and claim to be strong supporters of free enterprise; many conceive of their jobless state as due to their own shortcomings, or perhaps to the fact that other people—Negroes, married women, young people—are moving in on their jobs. This is not to say that these people are incapable of realistic perception of their problems; it is rather to say that the picture they have received through the mass media continuously distorts their own experience. For example, a typical comment was made by a young fellow who suggests that the government is too "socialistic" and that unemployed workers should not depend on the government for aid but should organize and mobilize their own power. Many of those who come to JOIN readily assent to its program of direct action for jobs because this fits with what they have learned from their own experience. But their perception of the "enemy" is fuzzy or worse, because of the obfuscating effects of American mass culture. JOIN can make a significant contribution by fighting obfuscation in terms which poorly educated people can understand.

An extensive program of research is needed as JOIN activity develops. Such research would include economic analysis of the

Chicago area to determine in concrete detail the facts about unmet public needs and the kinds of public programs which would have to do with the effectiveness of government and private agency programs in dealing with the problems of the unemployed. Further, legal research and assistance need to be developed to cope with problems of unemployment compensation, finance company problems, and similar kinds of difficulties. Another class of research would be "action research"—through systematic participant observation to evaluate JOIN's organizing efforts and resolve organizational difficulties which arise. Another would be the development of community surveys as JOIN attempts to broaden its grassroots base to neighborhoods, youth groups, and the like. And still another example would be research on corporation practices with respect to automation and layoffs and means to expose and attack these practices.

The research and education adjuncts to JOIN provide an excellent means for developing new kinds of community contacts and support. A large number of people from the academic community—faculty and students—can be drawn into such research activities and into the development of educational programs. Similarly the intellectual skills of researchers and education people within established social action groups can be utilized. These skills are important in and of themselves; moreover, the involvement of these intellectuals is likely to generate debate and new kinds of activity in the communities from which these people are drawn. For example, a faculty member at a local college who becomes involved in JOIN activity may come to see the possibilities for new concepts of adult education on the college level—adult education for those who are unemployed or otherwise disadvantaged. He then becomes an activist for change within his own institution.

Broadening the Base of Support

This is one example of the many potential ways that JOIN can make connections with a variety of individuals, groups, and institutions in the city—connections which can strengthen the organization by providing intellectual, financial, and other resources, and by providing allies. We have already mentioned the strong possibilities for constructing a representative group of supporters. But potentially the base of support can be much broader than this immediate group.

Perhaps the most important potential source of support is employed workers. Efforts are now being made to gain access to local unions; teams of JOIN members will speak to local union meetings to tell about JOIN and to raise money. A more dramatic means of raising money will be leafleting and the sale of apples at plant gates on pay day. These will be effective ways of reminding employed workers of threats to their own job security, of arousing interest in JOIN, and of raising money. This effort will be considerably enhanced if local union leaders and shop stewards visibly assist the JOIN workers.

A second source of support is from liberal middle-class people. The Northside JOIN office is in a middle-class, primarily Jewish neighborhood. People from the community have already expressed interest; some have donated furniture and equipment to the office. JOIN speakers at local club, church, peace, PTA, and other community organization meetings can be an effective means of obtaining local aid.

Third, there is the possibility that the JOIN support advisory committee can become a kind of representative body of those forces and groups within the city which can be mobilized for effective political action. Thus the members of this group, although acting as individuals, become centers of initiative within their organizations and institutions. In this way, a city-wide political movement for full employment and a better Chicago may develop. Such a movement would be a necessary precondition if the demands of the unemployed are to be met. JOIN by itself cannot mobilize sufficient power to achieve social change; only a new alignment of forces in Chicago can bring this about.

Finally, there is a strong possibility that a number of unions and other organizations will commit major resources to the task of organizing the unemployed. Already, the International Union of Electrical Workers has announced such a program; it is very likely that the United Automobile Workers will follow suit. It is not clear whether such commitments would be made to JOIN, or whether the effort would take place, so to speak, "above" JOIN. In any event, should such a thing take place, the JOIN participants would then be confronted with the decision of merging with a more massive and more bureaucratic, effort or of retaining their own organizational identity. The paradox is that the more effective JOIN is, the more likely it is that such an attempt to organize from above will take place.

Broadening the Grassroots Base

In addition to expanding "at the top," JOIN has the capability of extending its contacts at the grassroots. There is now the possibility of reaching teenagers and involving them in JOIN activity by making contact with local teenage social groups in nearby high schools. There is also a plan to construct a map on which could be located the neighborhoods in which JOIN members are concentrated. This would open the possibility of establishing neighborhood JOIN clubs and ladies' auxiliaries. As these grassroots contacts are developed, the JOIN program would become increasingly diversified and multi-issued, and a fruitful basis for grassroots political action would be created.

Richard Flacks is an Assistant Professor of Sociology at the University of Chicago. At the time this article was written (April 1964) he was working on his doctorate at the University of Michigan, and was a Research Associate at the Center for Research on Conflict Resolution at the same university. This article was part of a report on the progress of the ERAP project in Chicago.

CAN THE POOR BE ORGANIZED?

by Kimberly Moody

One of the more significant debates among the activities of the student left revolves around the question of the "radical potential" of the poor. Can they be organized for constructive change? What types of organization work most effectively, and which groups among the poor are most receptive to community organization? Finally, the most important question of all, has the cycle of poverty destroyed the ability of the poverty-stricken city-dweller to see beyond his own, immediate neighborhood? The following is a contribution to this debate, submitted to community workers for the Economic Research and Action Project of SDS.

To a great extent the SDS analysis of American society *assumes* that those who are the most deprived are naturally those who will be the most anxious to change society in accordance with their own interests. Thus, in our analysis, the "disinherited" are seen as the primary agents of social change. A further assumption, of course, is that the "disinherited" are the most suitable for organization—after all, they have the most to gain and the least to lose. In my opinion, this view of social change is not borne out by the facts. It is my belief that it is not necessarily those who are in the *worst* straights who are the most likely to be effectively organized for purposes of social change.

First of all, it is not clear that the "disinherited" are homogeneous in any sense which is relevant to insurgent organization. While it is true that the poor Negro and the poor white have similar problems as far as their economic situation is concerned, it is not true that their problems end there. For instance, with the exception of a small and dispersed sector of whites, it is not true that whites and Negroes have the same housing problem. In urban areas, poor whites do have more mobility in housing than Negroes or Puerto Ricans. Generally, poor whites have better homes than their non-white counterparts. In Baltimore, at least, it is nearly impossible to find a significantly large and geographically centralized area of exceedingly bad white housing. There are such areas, but they are small and widely dispersed. There are also the questions of wage differentials which are manifested clearly in census data. Discrimination, whether or not its original cause is economic in nature, acts as an independent variable when it comes to questions of the homogeneity of the disinherited. Finally, of course, there is the fact that while in the Negro community racial consciousness tends to act as a force that favors organization for social change, in the white community the same factor operates as a distinctly regressive force when it exists. Thus, to a certain degree the issues that projects deal with in these two different communities—even though they are on the same economic level—will differ in form and even in content. This, in turn, has implications for the unification of such projects.

Secondly, it seems to me that when discussing social change it is necessary to view strata of society in terms of their function within society. Specifically, by this I mean, what the functional relationship of any given group is to the economy. For instance, is the situation of an unemployed worker the same as that of a miserably underpaid, but nonetheless employed, worker? Is it possible to organize short range programs that speak to each group with equal relevance? Also, is the position of the habitually unemployed person the same as that of a worker who is unemployed for the first time after years of work and relative security? If it is admitted that these people have somewhat different immediate interests, which group will be most open to organization for economic change? Or to put the same question another way: Historically, what sectors of our society have been most given to insurgent activity?

From an historical point of view, I believe it is fairly clear that it has *never* been the poorest sector of society that has rebelled. Rather, it has been that sector or those sectors that have been most pressed by the prevailing structural contradictions of the society at that time. Thus, the Populists rebelled against the burgeoning control of urban financial interests and railroad corporations that came into structural conflict with their interests. Likewise, the labor movement formed at the end of the nineteenth century in response to the structural development of industrial capitalism. Again, in the thirties labor reorganized itself in response to structural changes in industry. It is interesting to note that it was not the miserably poor that rebelled in the thirties, but primarily those who were employed. The Unemployed Councils formed by the Communists in the early thirties seem to have been short-lived (however, information on these Councils is very difficult to obtain). In fact, to my knowledge, major social upheavals in this country (or in any advanced capitalist country) have never been led by those who are essentially outside the economic processes of society. What does this mean today?

Before answering this question directly, it would be worthwhile to identify the various strata that exist within the overall category of the disinherited. First, there are those who are habitually unemployed. In many northern urban areas, these people are immigrants from the south who came north to escape habitual unemployment and hopeless poverty but who (as Harrington and others have pointed out) have only succeeded in transporting their hopelessness into their new area. Washington, Baltimore, and Detroit are overflowing with such people. This group is both black and white, but I shall deal primarily with those who are white, as this is the subject matter of this paper. To a great extent, these people are the hard core of what we call the poor whites. They are a homogeneous group with a common cultural heritage which, incidentally, is a nightmare for radical community organizers. This heritage is shot through with individualism (in the worst sense), anti-laborism, and racism. Interestingly enough, people from this culture ("crackers" and "hillbillies," in the vernacular of the put-down) become extremely class conscious and militant when organized into labor unions and, of course, employed on a regular basis, *whether or not they shed their racism*—witness the Florida railroad workers. This group of people present immense problems to community organizers. While they are unquestionably the most difficult people to organize, for many obvious reasons they are one of the groups that it is most important that we organize.

Secondly, there are the old poor. These are former immigrant groups, which tend to be closely knit and isolated from other poor groups (though this varies from city to city), and assorted less cohesive ethnic groups. Both of these groups ("hillbillies" and "ethnic" minorities) tend to be outside of the economy, traditionally. They do not have a feeling of having a "right" to a job, which the newly unemployed or occasionally unemployed have. They will accept incredibly bad jobs and be "happy" about their situation. Indeed, for these people, bad jobs are a real relief from constant misery.

A third group—and an extremely important group—is the rapidly growing young unemployed. Like the permanently unemployed, they are outside of the functioning of the economy and have little or no sense of having a right to a job and security. In the white community, they find that they can still live off their parents. At any rate, they know no other world than that of constant idleness. The situation and attitudes of these youths probably depend on what group their parents are in, but their plight is identical.

The next group is the newly unemployed. These are people who have had jobs and possibly even security but who, in the last few years, have become the victims of technological "progress." They are used to being part of society and to receiving at least some of its benefits. Many of them are stuck with debts (from buying "on time") that they acquired while working. Even those without debts, however, are truly socially dislocated. It is this group which is most clearly the immediate victim of the most recent structural change in our economy. Related to this group are those who are now decently employed but may soon join the newly unemployed—and who are to a growing extent conscious of this situation.

Lastly, there are those who are employed but are poor by virtue of the fact that they have bad jobs. These people are part of what Harrington calls the "economic underworld." They are the tail end of the working class and, when they are organized, of the trade union movement. Socially, they seem to be interspersed with most of the previously mentioned sectors.

Before continuing, let me say that I share the basic radical analysis that the *long-run* interests of all of these groups are identical. This analysis, however, is not very helpful when it comes to the question of where one *starts* to organize for the purpose of accomplishing this long-run goal. In order to approach the question of where we start when we attempt to organize "poor whites," we must see which sector of the poor has the most radical potential.

By radical potential, I mean the potential to have *conscious* disaffection from the *cause* of one's present misery. This seems to be asking too much, but I cannot see how anything less can serve as the *starting* point of the new insurgency—or any insurgency. By this I do not mean that our potential radical must have a sophisticated conception of the cause that can be identified. Obviously, this will be more difficult for different sectors of society. For instance, it is difficult for the *permanently* unemployed to perceive the cause of his misery because it lies in areas of knowledge with which he is unfamiliar. On the other hand, the newly unemployed worker can easily identify automation as the cause of his plight. It is a fact that the permanently unemployed (including youth) and those who are poorly employed perceive the cause of their problems to be personal in nature. This seems to stem from the fact that working class and poor people in general have a very local, often even a block, orientation and that they do not perceive any structural aspects of the economy as they have never really been a part of it. For the worker this localism (or neighborhoodism, to be more exact) is offset by the experience of the working place and in many cases by membership in a union—whether or not he actively identifies with his union. Thus, for the newly unemployed worker there is a conscious reaction to his *new* situation *in terms of his old one*. This conflict between the terms in which he thinks and the new situation in which he finds himself is the essence of social dislocation. The permanently poor are not dislocated; they are simply poor—there is no conflict within their own consciousness.

It is, therefore, my contention that the most fruitful area in which to *start* the organization of poor whites is *not* among those who are the poorest, but among those who are newly poor. It is this group which will respond most actively to new ideas and to organization. If organizations can be developed for this group, then the other groups, related to this group as they are through various primary and secondary groups, will respond. Seeing organized attempts to end the general causes of their misery and being presented with a causal explanation for it, they will respond to those aspects of the program that are directed toward them. Even here, however, it seems to me that there will be little response among the poorest sector until *some* results can be seen as stemming from this movement—for instance, a public works program that will employ them as well as the newly unemployed. There are also structural relationships between these various groups: trade unions, identical work places (such as between the occasionally unemployed and the poorly employed), family (especially relevant to youth unemployed), neighborhood, etc.

In specific programmatic terms, this means that I would prefer: Employment Referral Services (with an active propaganda program) in areas near both newly unemployed and permanently poor groupings, to neighborhood organization as such; initial stress on personal contact with the younger newly employed, to that with youth gangs (who will probably associate us with social workers, in whom they are already up to their necks); questions of unemployment compensation, to those on welfare in general; vocational retraining, to tutorials, etc. Of course, I am not proposing that we rigidly exclude these other things, but rather that when we have resource problems, we give priority to the first suggestions. Nor does this list exhaust the programmatic possibilities for the white community.

Finally, there is the extremely important question of how we handle the race problem in white projects. I think it extremely important that organizers in the white community make themselves clear on the race question immediately. Obviously, the goal of these projects is to develop an integrated movement of the poor. There is no area of organization where the race issue causes more antagonism than in that of employment. For this reason the necessity of integrating the racial aspects of unemployment into the program is important. Whites must be made to realize that they cannot win their demands at the expense of the Negro. Arguments for biracial unity will be most effective if they are economic in nature, *i.e.*, designed to appeal to the interests of the whites. Christian love has failed abysmally as a technique for the last 200 years, and there is no reason to think that such arguments will be effective now. The related question of at what point we actually attempt to integrate an unemployment movement (or whatever specific movement we start with) is less clear. It might be useful to experiment with biracial demonstrations or rallies, before integrating the organizations themselves. Incidently, most of these organizations will not be integrated at first for simple geographic reasons—*i.e.*, whites and Negroes often live separately, even when poor. Where you have an integrated area, however, it might be best to start right off with integrated organizations. It is hopeful that there is historical precedent for integrated movements about economic issues. Nonetheless, the movement we are looking forward to is different in that unlike most of these in the past this movement must have a set of demands and programs that are specifically Negro-oriented.

Kimberly Moody is a graduate of Johns Hopkins University. A member of the SDS National Council, he is one of the directors of the ERAP Community Council in Baltimore, Maryland. This article was originally distributed in mimeograph form by ERAP for its workers in various community projects around the country.

THE WAR ON POVERTY: NOTES ON INSURGENT RESPONSE

by Rennie Davis

There has been no shortage of writers to refute the claims of Johnson's War on Poverty. The liberal-radical publications have echoed each other in a long critique. Johnson's "total war on want" is predicated on the questionable assumptions that the economy is "sound" and that a few dollars and a few demonstrations will start a giant parade of poor people toward middle-income America. The official poverty program, as we have been told, does nothing to strike at economic stagnation or to reverse the generally regressive tax structure in the country. It will not rehabilitate the slums or build public homes or plan for human needs in any manner requiring basic changes in the status quo political economy.

Its belittlers say that the War on Poverty amounts to no more than a dramatic consolidation of existing service programs plus a new version of Roosevelt's CCC. The current debate is whether Johnson's battle cry is the rhetoric of a cruel politician after a few votes or a sincere search for temporary amelioratives to face the crisis of joblessness and youth delinquency. But the implications of the War on Poverty are more significant than the size of its first budget would imply.

The President's televised Poverty Message to Congress and the 1964 Economic Opportunity Act which followed it have brought a remarkable array of people from universities, private welfare and charitable organizations, foundations, and local governments vying for the poverty millions. The announced commitment to "total victory" has shaken funds loose from numerous private sources for research, air travel, conferences, publicity, and prospectuses related to poverty. Citizens' groups like the UAW-backed Crusade Against Poverty have been formed to supplement and keep a watch-eye on the program of Johnson. In city after city, Johnson's declared war has mobilized "poverty corporations" comprised of the city's political and business elite who are meeting to determine the size of their bid for the available poverty contracts. The magnitude of influential involvement in the "token" war on poverty is impressive and is a compelling reason for those of us who work *cooperatively* in a young movement of urban and rural poor to ask, on what side do we stand in this war on poverty?

Predecessors to the War on Poverty

Wherever SDS supports field organizers in poor communities, there is a local government making preparations for a war on poverty. None of these preparations shape up to be very big or show evidence that they could have any significant relation to the people with whom we work. However, each is potentially a copy of the dozen or so community action projects already in existence through which private and public agencies are implementing multi-purpose, heavily financed programs of social, legal, educational, and economic aid to poor people. Community action empires exist or are in advanced stages of planning in Boston, Charleston, Cleveland, Chicago, Detroit, Houston, Los Angeles, Lane County (Oregon), New Haven, Providence, Minneapolis, New York, North Carolina, Oakland, St. Louis, Syracuse, and Washington, D.C. If we are able to take the Washington officials at their word, it is these million dollar empires that are to be duplicated in the more advanced stages of the Johnson War on Poverty. They are the concrete examples behind the catchy war imagery of the new poverty outfit.

What significantly characterizes the largest and most "advanced" of these demonstration community organizations is their approach to poverty as a problem in logistics requiring professional planning and supervision for execution. One is struck by the fact that the military language used by Johnson has real significance for those who run these corporate giants. They have an approach to poverty that is distinctly military. And in defending civilian populations, like any army, they are apt to overpower the "enemy" while trampling the people.*

The Army Approach to Poverty

The individual who assumes that the solution to poverty is to help the poor secure more money without otherwise changing power relationships is one who may unknowingly lend time and talents toward increasing the dependency and powerlessness of the poor. The army approach to poverty, often the brainwork of most sincere men, works toward this end. Its strategy (based on an "objective" measure of community needs) is to blanket a "blighted" area, as efficiently as possible, with those services and improvements needed to fill individual and community deficiencies (training, slum clearance, clean-up, jobs, community centers, and so on). The army approach recognized that the miseries of forgotten people are the consequences of interrelated complex problems which require comprehensive rather than single-pronged solutions. But overall solutions and programs to implement them come from above, rather than below. Civilian acquiescence to a

* For another exposition of the military approach to poverty, see Edgar and Joan Cahn, 73 *Yale Law Journal* 1317.

"needed" poverty program is demanded; citizen planning and initiative are not. Wars are fought by trained professionals for the citizenry.

Central to the army approach is the mobilization of community power and expertise into a single, overall campaign. "Effectiveness" against poverty requires a coordination of established service agencies and the people who "can get things done": the available experience, knowledge, and resources of the non-poor community are brought together for an efficient and rational program of aid.

The consequence of federating *existing* community powers into the War on Poverty is to guarantee a program and a strategy which discourages local initiative and protest and opposes fundamental community change. With welfare and school boards, the mayor and businessmen, church, union, and charitable organizations contributing to the benevolent community drive, valuable services—some greatly needed—may be given away, but by the agencies and individuals from whom the poor should be free. In no case will the army approach encourage powerful initiative by the poor in their own behalf. The "best" community action organizations may stimulate indigenous community groups "to keep the city honest" or accept limited militant actions like rent strikes or civil rights demonstrations as "necessary." But none which are rooted in existing community power and dependent on large budgets and a good image for longevity will tolerate serious civilian uprisings as a consequence of their war on poverty.

The local community group that wants a welfare program fairly administered, or wants rats out of living quarters or wants a politician on city council who will represent the needs of the forgotten people may not "fit in" with the strategy of the army approach. An independent organization of poor people can deeply irritate a powerful welfare agency or slumlord or councilman—all of whom may be major backers to the local War on Poverty. They can be a powerful source of criticism and protest and agitation which can only impair the "overall" program.

If possible, ways will be found to stop an indigenous, dissident group—by buying off its leadership with jobs and status in the official program; by discrediting the organization of the community with smears of communist control; by cutting members off welfare. Experience has shown that the army approach to poverty can be used as a weapon to combat local protest movements.

A Strategy of Insurgent Response

Two assumptions are basic to our discussion: (1) Poverty in America can be eradicated, but not without a new political basis for public planning, guaranteed levels of human decency, and massive public programs to allow people to work at urgently needed, social tasks. (2) The seeds for a real war on poverty lie in the powerful Negro movement and the significant stirrings of poor whites now converging around the common problems of poverty.

The notes which follow are *for people who work on these assumptions*, who are anxious that Johnson's army approach to poverty not destroy a young movement only slightly aware of its own potential and who want to help find means for the poor to assume the initiative and control in any war on poverty.

A "strategy of insurgent response" begins by asking what is most worthwhile about Johnson's War on Poverty and in what ways we can encourage its better tendencies: The War on Poverty will dramatize for all the slums and shacks and prisons of poverty; it will provoke new consciousness among many deprived and alone people to see poverty in social rather than individual terms; it may legitimize the fight against poverty in the way churches made civil rights acceptable; and, in many instances, as local officials are being compelled to travel into poor lands to make new promises they cannot deliver, the basis will be laid for neighborhood struggles and new political action.

Our response to Johnson's War on Poverty should be to help it do all of these things better: by challenging the top-down approach of the city poverty warriors; by dramatizing the deeper nature of the economic crisis in our inner cities and rural "pockets;" by turning government services into the just victories of organized people rather than hand-outs to the weak and dependent; by converting the rhetoric of the official campaign into greater consciousness and articulate demands from the forgotten poor man.

Specific means for accomplishing these objectives will be called "insurgent response." It is not a phrase signifying fundamental opposition to the War on Poverty. Insurgency is conceived as a way to challenge the donor-donee relationship built into the army method of dispensing aid and as a set of tactics which help visibly to contrast the magnitude of poverty-related problems against Johnson's token poverty program.

Insurgency is not a general strategy, easily applied where there are wars on poverty, nor can it be until Johnson's own tactics are more clearly articulated and concretely applied. It can be illustrated only by examples responding to the specifics of the present legislation and the scattered efforts to implement it.

The Specifics of the Present War on Poverty

What is contained in the Equal Opportunity Act and what is the basis for insurgency? The relevant sections of the seven titles can be quickly summarized:

Title I. *Youth Programs*

$412.5 million is authorized for three programs: (a) "conservation camps" and residential training centers for approximately 40,000 youth this year and 100,000 next year to increase the employability of young people in a "Job Corps;" (b) $150 million to governments and private organizations to pay full or partial cost of employing young people to continue their education or to increase their chances of employment through work-training; (c) $72.5 million to allow 140,000 youth to enter or continue college by getting part-time employment through a federally supported work-study program.

Title II. *Urban and Rural Community Action Programs*

$340 million appropriated for (a) "stimulation and incentive for urban and rural communities to mobilize their resources to combat poverty through community action programs." Such programs should provide new employment opportunities, improve motivation, and better the conditions in the community and the work-place through a program "which is developed, conducted, and administered with the maximum feasible participation of residents of the areas;" (b) programs of basic education and literacy for adults; (c) information centers to encourage voluntary assistance for needy children.

TITLE III. *Special Programs to Combat Poverty in Rural Areas*

$35 million for (a) loans to improve farms and develop family cooperatives; (b) assistance to migrant families for education, sanitation, and housing; (c) indemnity payments to farmers for milk which had to be removed from the market because of pesticide contamination.

TITLE IV. *Employment and Investment Incentives*

No specific amount is authorized. Small business loans up to $25,000 are available for low interest, particularly to firms hiring long-term unemployed.

TITLE V. *Work Experience Programs*

$150 million to pay the costs of experimental or pilot projects designed to stimulate states to adopt programs providing constructive work experience or training for unemployed fathers and needy persons.

TITLE VI. *Administration and Coordination*

An office of Economic Opportunity is established to administer the Act and to work with other agencies and organizations in a "coordinated attack" on poverty. The Director is authorized to recruit and train "Volunteers in Service to America" (VISTA) who will work against poverty in local communities upon request of state or local agencies or private organizations. No volunteer can enter a state without the approval of the Governor.

TITLE VII. *Treatment of Income for Certain Public Assistance Purposes*

The first $85 plus one-half of any amount over $85 paid to a person under Title I or II in any month cannot be counted as income in determining a person's need for public assistance. No grant made to families under Title III shall be regarded as income in determining the need of any members of that family.

Title II is the critical provision, though it is not yet heavily funded. Federal agencies are specifically mandated (Sec. 612) to give preference to any application for assistance to a community action program. (Jack Conway is Director of Title II.) Without Title II, the Act is not a significant departure in government programming—some small loans to businessmen and farmers; training programs for a few; fix-up, paint-up, clean-up by college students in slum areas. Title II opens the door to an unlimited range of service and community organizing activities, with federal and local funds meeting the expenses. It will stimulate the formation of a new army of professionals and social workers, to whom, in some areas, may be granted the power and wealth to distribute valuable services to materially deprived citizens, but unfortunately, in a manner detrimental to individual dissent, community protest, or national political action from the poor.

It is on the probability that the army approach to poverty will dominate any escalation in Johnson's war that a list of responses is now proposed—tentative suggestions for compelling democratic alternatives for implementing a real war on poverty. The illustrations are brief and for discussion.

I—*Challenging the Unrepresentative Nature of the "Poverty Corporations"*

Sec. 202 of the Poverty Act provides for "maximum feasible participation" of the poor in developing, conducting, and administering the poverty program. Yet, in most cities, the mayor has already joined representatives of business, welfare, and school institutions into a Poverty Board or Corporation in which the poor hold no stock. Poverty Boards, meeting typically in secret session, have completed several hundred program prospectuses for consideration by the Office of Economic Opportunity. In all but one city where SDS has organizing projects, circulated copies of the draft program have been *exceedingly* scarce. Requests from indigenous organizations to participate in the deliberations of the Poverty Board have been denied. Not even the major civil rights, trade union, charitable, church, and other "substantial" liberal organizations have generally had a say in the city's plan or had access to draft copies of the anti-poverty plan.

While Johnson's program explicitly calls for representation of the poor, few cities or counties have made even token gestures in this direction. In Cleveland, Ohio, movement people have used this issue to call the hand of the local politicians behind the War on Poverty. SDS staff and representatives of four indigenous community organizations have joined church, university, and civil rights people in a Citizens' Committee for an Adequate Poverty Program in Cleveland. This city-wide coalition was formed to expose the Mayor's Poverty Board as a business and political enterprise of questionable motivation rather than a sincere program to help low-income people. Not one representative of the city's inner region—the hard core of Cleveland's poverty—is on the official Board. The current demand of the Citizen's Committee is to double the 22-man Board with additions to include persons at or below the poverty level, members of low-wage and Negro unions, clergy groups close to poor people, civic leaders from poverty areas, civil rights representatives, and social work and teaching groups. The "rebel groups," as one welfare mother describes them, have succeeded in getting Washington to postpone a grant to Cleveland until an investigation of the rebel charges can be held.

City-wide challenges of this sort may be generally feasible where established liberal groups have not been invited to the Poverty Corporation, though they have programs involving substantial members of low-income people. As in many cities, in Baltimore and Philadelphia the conditions for challenge exist and the idea is being considered seriously. Representatives of inner-city churches, trade unions, charitable organizations, and indigenous community organizations will form a coalition committee more representative of the poor than one Mayor's hand-picked Board. Their demands will be for Washington to recognize the citizens' group as the appropriate agency for preparing and executing the city's poverty program.

From the point of view of the organizer, the advantages of coalition challenges to the war on poverty are that they create a congenial forum for discussion of city politics and radical alternatives—with potential liberal allies; they provide a worthwhile experience of indigenous community leadership outside their own groups; and they publicly dramatize the top-down approach of the city poverty program.

The disadvantages, based on the experiences of the SDS Cleveland Community Project, are that liberals will talk about putting the poverty program into the hands of the poor, but not believe it possible; the local poor people, while benefiting from the discussions and getting a better understanding of differences in the liberal-radical end of the political spectrum, will not have a conception that they are in an organization belonging to them (which is correct); the staff organizers will have new pulls on their time and feel pressures which erode the psychological frame of mind needed to work steadily in the bars and the streets and the homes of the community (formal meeting, many phone calls, trips downtown, reversions to the "old rhetoric," etc.)

Challenges issued directly from the indigenous community groups to the elite Poverty Board may be a more effective and appropriate means of spotlighting an unrepresentative poverty army corps and will run fewer risks of co-option than would working through an essentially non-poor committee of liberals and radicals. Also, preparing for a grassroots challenge will be more consonant with organizational work in the community union than coalition building among people in all parts of the city.

II—The War on Poverty as a Basis for Community Organizing

In the towns and villages where deprivation is personal rather than organized resentment, can the war on poverty be an issue that will bring people together? Can it be a talking point on doorsteps and street corners—which people understand, are mad about, or would come to a meeting to learn more about? In ERAP, there is disagreement among organizers on these questions, with many insisting that the federal poverty program is complicated and difficult to explain and that there are deeper felt grievances than the government's fraudulent pledge to end want. But in Baltimore and Chicago JOIN projects (predominantly unemployed people) limited experience indicates the "poverty" issue raises fundamental questions which people quickly grasp: that the typical way programs to help the poor "never do any good;" that poverty means a lack of jobs and money and control in people's lives and Johnson's war isn't going to fill these lacks; that most of the money will be spent on fat salaries and new office space and won't get into the pockets that need it.

Chicago JOIN has taken the war on poverty into unorganized blocks, employing teams of student volunteers and JOIN members to canvass new areas of Chicago's Northside, trying to get a better understanding of local grievances, telling people about JOIN and bringing in new members. One paper written by JOIN for new student canvassers says: "Introduce yourself in a manner similar to this: 'Hello, I'm from JOIN, an organization in this neighborhood which is concerned about housing, school, and employment problems. We understand that the federal government is about to put a lot of money into this area, but it has not consulted the people who live here about how the money should be used. We were wondering if you could give us a few minutes to tell us what you think the chief needs of this area are.' " If a good discussion comes out of these questions, the canvasser is instructed to try to get the person "to agree to interview some people for himself" or he can suggest that the person "have some of the other people on his block get together with him sometime in the near future to discuss their problems and what can be done about them."

Using the war on poverty as the door-opener in canvassing does allow the organizer to discuss casually a whole range of economic and political problems related to poverty. He can stimulate thinking and writing about community problems and solutions and get people involved in organization through interview work. Of course, there are broad issues in addition to the poverty program which can open doors in a community and elicit good discussions. Generally, getting right down to the agency or slumlord or specific outside institutional structure on which the individual feels unfairly dependent is a better way to learn "what the people need" than asking someone what services he would like or how things should be done if ordinary people were running the show. But out of canvassing and informal talk about federal poverty plans, some people will want to demand that poverty money go to them and their neighbors rather than to the businessmen and patronage pockets downtown. Block groups may begin to formulate their own plans for helping the poor and push their community union to develop an area-wide proposal. In Baltimore, U-JOIN is preparing alternative measures for the city's $24 million anti-poverty plan. With a minimum of technical assistance (provided by Johns Hopkins economists), they will present a JOIN prospectus to a Governor's conference which reviews all city and county programs. The prospectus will be the result of weeks of small and large gatherings of working and unemployed people discussing and writing their ideas for a new Baltimore. According to a summary distributed by the League of Women Voters, the official plan U-JOIN opposes will pay 119 social workers ("Expediters") $12,000 a year to work a six-square mile area setting up street clubs ("to bring under control the anti-school behavior of delinquents identified as troublesome by residents and expediters in the area"), to help administer day-care centers, to coordinate legal service programs, and so on through the service gamut. U-JOIN has been bringing people to meetings with a leaflet appeal asking: Do we want our neighborhood invaded by more social workers and bureaucrats or do we want a war on poverty that will help the poor?

From small meetings of unemployed can come a meaningful basis for community organizing, as people are ready to fight to have poverty money go into the community union instead of the big agencies and will challenge the decisions of the official poverty forces, which ignore the program agreed on by the block groups in the neighborhood. Eventually demands have to be made on the city for a real war on poverty.

III—Challenging the Local Leadership of the War on Poverty

Rural Mississippians, Hazard miners, Cleveland welfare mothers, Newark housing tenants—all have shown how a few plain people can directly and dramatically expose the inadequacies and phoniness of plans designed by local politicians for poor people. While realizing a strategy of insurgent response may result in smears of an indigenous group or pressures on leadership to join the official force, a well-organized, politically sophisticated community union should eventually carry its counterattack right into the power structure behind the war on poverty, getting to the heart of the matter. Tactics like local mass tax strikes are means of demonstrating to local politicians the power of forgotten people and the needs they have. Such methods are more "militant" in the sense that they will force the poverty warriors to retreat with their program or defend it openly. There is no easy middle ground, as can be illustrated by several examples:

(a) Organize the community to flood token public service with large numbers of applicants.

The shortages of public services and programs to improve living conditions and job opportunities for the poor may be readily apparent in the city ghetto or the rural farm or a mining community, but rarely are comprehended by the affluent "outsider." It is commonly accepted that more poverty programs are not needed because existing ones are not used. The fact is that people who need them, for a variety of good reasons, stay out: They get "rough treatment" from the bureaucrats; they "never get accepted;" they don't know of their existence, etc. The politicians' myth that "we are doing all that we should" should be met head on—using one illustration, by jamming an existing service or training program with applicants, crippling the capacity of the poverty officers to extend the service intended. In organized areas, long lines could be extended around a recruitment office—lines which would convert to pickets and sit-ins as legitimate candidates for the program were denied access to the program being tested. Demands for improvement in the public service should include establishment of a community grievance committee to hear cases of improper procedures or mishandling of any applicant by a deputy or bureaucrat in the program's administration.

(b) Demand full control over a program operated in the local community.

The War on Poverty, like most federal programs, provides for "local participation" in decision-making, though the local power structure, unless it is powerfully confronted, manages to control things. Under Title II, many community "action" programs will locate offices in depressed neighborhoods to "coordinate" the different local programs or provide places for people to meet and "work on their problems." The professional staffs charged with running these offices will bring in community people as a nominal gesture to local citizen participation and as a way to create "better communication links" between the community and themselves.

To spotlight the fundamental issue of control by professionals rather than organized poor in the war on poverty, a community union could demand *total* supervisory authority over the professional staff working in the neighborhood. Mass pickets would demand the rights to hire and fire the professional staff and the right to set program priorities in the area. If demonstrations were held at the neighborhood office, an enormous turnout could be expected, giving visible evidence of the generally unrecognized commitment to the principle of democratic control in matters of relief and services to poor people.

(c) Establish a symbolic radical alternative program which competes with the city's plan.

An anti-poverty measure in many cities and towns will be the Job Corps provided in Title I. The local poverty officers will launch a recruitment campaign of some color and appeal for unemployed people to join countryside camps to get "work experience."

A community union could dramatize the absurdity of the local program by actually creating a *competing* operation for the city's unemployed—one which puts people to work at rehabilitating the neighborhoods. Street corner recruitment stands would be placed adjacent to the official placement center, drawing people out of the country and back into the city. The public challenge would be one that would go to the core of the poverty program's mission—determining whether it is to give training and experience to fill nonexistent jobs, or whether it is to create new employment.

How would a competing work program be paid for? For a short period, rent strikes could provide the funds for employing the jobless at fixing tenements. The expenses for improving the inferior public facilities of the city could be dramatically turned over to the mayor or the Poverty Board. The community would undertake its own fund raising drive to support much of the work. And, shortages of funds would be a justification for mass demonstrations, petitions, and public appeals for people across the city and country to support a movement to put the unemployed to work at meaningful tasks—creating decency out of the make-believe conditions of the Job Corps.

IV—Poverty Money for Organized Poor

Should a strategy of insurgent response include fund raising from the War on Poverty? Are funds available for groups which are publicly denouncing (or which intend to denounce) the fraudulence of the Johnson skirmish? It is one of the paradoxes (and tricks?) of the American way that there *is* a little.

However, since most proposals for federal money under the current legislation can be vetoed by a state governor, COFO in Mississippi is not likely to find support. (Money can, however, be sent around the governor via educational institutions). In Northern cities which have locked out the public from consideration of the anti-poverty blueprint, federal money to organized radical neighborhood groups should be written off. In states in which the Governor is taking an extremely active role in molding all rural and city plans into an overall state poverty strategy (such as Maryland) it will require extreme finesse to squeeze any but the most respectable representatives up to the trough. But if a city or county poverty program is being planned by many organizations (particularly small liberal ones) and the community action program is somewhat decentralized (as contrasted to the army approach), support for a community service program related to the organizing and political objectives of a community union may be obtained.

Newark appears to be this sort of exception and has parallels in other areas. The 63-man poverty board in Newark includes virtually all segments of the liberal establishment—trade union, civil rights, university, and non-partisan, charitable agencies. Election of the Poverty Board is by a self-appointed citizens' group in which any citizen can join after petitioning the secretary of the Board. The Newark Community Union (NCU) and the Newark SDS staff believe that money could be made available to the community union for a number of purposes. NCU is considering asking for a social-coffee center (an organizing office) and for salary to community people to work in the center (organizers).

Other independent "political" organizations based in poor areas may find support for education programs with adults, using specifically developed materials describing and analysing "problems" known to the neighborhood: Neighborhood legal firms may be created to defend local residents; regional or national conferences of community leaders may be formed for discussing the role of the poor in a grassroots war on poverty. VISTA volunteers (if they can be converted to a different type of community living and have good politics) may serve as office managers, or in some cases, organizers and can give their money to the community union. (Volunteers get $50 a month *in addition* to expenses for housing, travel, hospital and boarding costs.)

Like any establishment financial backing, federal or local poverty funds are to be seen as seed money to be replaced by more independent backing once the program is functioning. But refusing to ask for or take federal money should not be a *principle* of the movement. Indeed, we should *demand* it, realizing and planning for the consequences of a grant not being renewed.

A strategy of insurgent response to the War on Poverty is essentially a fight by poor people for control over the existing poverty money and for federal support to a real war on poverty. And that fight begins at the neighborhood level, where block groups write their own plans and send them downtown. Eventually poor people must get together and make demands on the whole national system. But the beginnings for a more shared abundance and democratic participation are found at the neighborhood level where ordinary people are talking to each other about how to change the ghetto and the outside country.

Rennie Davis, a graduate of Oberlin College, is director of the SDS Economic Research and Action Project, and a community organizer in a poor white neighborhood on Chicago's Northside. This article originally appeared in the Winter 1965 issue of Venture, *an SDS publication.*

AN INTERRACIAL MOVEMENT OF THE POOR?

by Carl Wittman and Thomas Hayden

Increasingly today we hear the call for a movement of the American poor. The call is exciting to anyone who cares about democratic improvements in our way of life, and who remembers with nostalgia and some bitterness the achievements and failures of the populist and labor movements of earlier times. But under the excitement is a sense of vast difficulty, and an historical knowledge of the tragic conflicts between groups of the same class situation which have prevented more constructive conflicts between truly opposed classes. Our comments here are meant to be incomplete and unpolished—a set of working notes for those in SDS and elsewhere who wonder about these problems as they work on them.

I. The Negro Freedom Movement

Any discussion of the prospects for an interracial class movement should begin with an assessment of what people in the Negro movement are doing and care to do.

In the South, especially the Black Belt South, the movement's most typical demand is for the elimination of explicit racial barriers to the opportunities which all other Americans have: the right to vote, travel, buy food, live where money permits, and work where one's skills are appropriate. The movement is conceived and led mostly by middle-class Negroes, specifically students, ministers, lawyers, housewives. But the increasing involvement of the urban unemployed and the sharecroppers is a sign that the movement, as constituted, is just as important to the Negro lower classes. The system which keeps a middle-class Negro from getting a good education or a job commensurate with his skills simultaneously scrapes the lower-class Negro between a reign of terror and starvation wages. There seems to be substantial Negro class unity about program within the Southern movement. Where there are differences they occur along status lines, with the more moderate and tradition-bound Negro leaders being classified as Uncle Toms.

Among the many effects of this movement, there are four which are quite important for our exploration.

The first is that it provides impetus for Negroes elsewhere, and precipitates action even where the terror conditions are not present. We in the North become especially conscious of the instrumental value of the Southern movement when we try to initiate a similar movement among a minority without this heritage, *e.g.*, Puerto Ricans. Although "freedom" in the South and the North has quite different meanings, the subjective identity which Negroes feel is perhaps the most valuable asset the Northern Negro movement has today.

The second is that the Southern movement, in a number and variety of ways, inspires greater commitment and greater activity from liberal institutions such as the churches and unions; it forces the government to legitimize, and bless, and therefore speed up civil rights activity; it awakens conscientious individuals to the possibility of doing something right and effective. In general it shakes things up everywhere—and provides a model of commitment and action which challenges those who are taking it easy or looking for a way to focus their anxiety.

The third is that the movement dramatically raises political and economic issues of a fundamental importance for the whole society. The default of Congress and the shortcomings of the private economy are just two of the issues which naturally become more pressing as the Negro struggle forces Americans to return to an examination of their way of life after many Cold War years of foreign preoccupations.

The fourth is that as the present Southern movement moves toward legal equality, which is beginning to happen in the urban areas and the upper rim of states, the way will be more open for the movement to consider new issues and make connections with the poor white population. This is not a mechanical one-two process, of course. Organizations like SNCC are already talking and programming on economic issues which are of deep concern to poor whites as well as most Southern Negroes. And it is certainly possible to begin experiments in organizing whites into political alliance, if not deep personal associations, with the Negro community today; *e.g.* many miners in Hazard, Kentucky, are changing their stereotyped conceptions of the Negro as they become interested in expanding their movement across all of Appalachia, where many of the unemployed miners are Negro. However, it does seem generally true that the establishment of desegregation is the first priority, and developing an interracial movement is much less feasible. (In this context the present civil rights bill might be very important in speeding the desegregation process.)

As desegregation proceeds, what are the possibilities for alienation between the Negroes and their real or possible white allies? The areas of possible alienation are twofold: between Negroes and *all* whites, and between Negroes and *poor* whites.

In the first instance, there is a kind of black nationalism that works uneasily within the integration movement itself. In many organizations there are disputes and splits over the color of leadership: whether whites understand Negroes or Negroes understand whites; whether whites, particularly white women, can be effective as organizers in the Negro community. These issues are among the most sensitive and difficult we face, and undoubtedly they will continue for an indefinite period of time. We suspect, however, that the tension in the movement will not be resolved on the side of an official black nationalist ideology, partly because it has not happened yet between Negroes and whites in general even in the worst conditions of racist tyranny. Even were it to develop in some organized form, we would guess that at some future time the possibility of Negro-white alliances would reappear because a program based primarily on race will not improve the terrible social conditions which provide the impetus for the movement. A permanent alienation should not develop unless two groups continually interfere with the deepest economic interests of each for a sustained period of time. . . . As long as the Southern Negro does not directly threaten the white's livelihood by actually taking his job or destroying the quality of the white child's education (and hence livelihood in this society), such estrangements are not permanent and can end whenever whites clearly see it is in their economic interest to unite with the Negro.

One clear example of this happened in Cambridge, Maryland: six months of intensive race warfare over the issue of a public accommodations referendum, with poor whites providing the core of segregationist action and opinion. Only a month later, however, the United Packinghouse Workers organized three locals in Cambridge, on a racially integrated basis, with militant Negro leadership carefully avoiding anything which would upset the 40 per cent white membership. After one of the locals was recognized, the victory party included dancing, drinking, and eating in racially mixed company, previously taboo in the town, and it occurred without incident. Without the movement, the Cambridge power structure could have defeated the union drive as it did in the past. The built-up alienation on the part of the poor whites was subordinated to a common interest which happened to be central to the lives of black and white factory workers.

Of course, we are aware that estrangement between the races can continue indefinitely, as it has in the South for a century. We are haunted not only by Southern history but by the problems dividing Muslims and Hindus in India, and Negroes and East Indians in British Guiana. But we remain convinced so far that permanent alienation can be avoided and overcome by a serious movement which fights for the interests of both groups. We know of almost no effort to organize in white communities in the South —and it would be foolish to be either optimistic or pessimistic until actual experiments are further underway. We need to know much more about the organizing problems faced by the Negro-white-Mexican coalition in Texas, and whether those problems are applicable to other areas of the South; we need to know much more about rank-and-file feelings within the white working class; we need to make contact with whatever radical individuals there are within the Southern union bureaucracy. These needs are briefly mentioned here to suggest some gaps in our present knowledge; the implications for our proposed or actual organizing campaigns remain to be discussed in a later section of these comments.

We realize that much of the preceding can be applied directly to the Northern civil rights situation, and that this is a symptom of the nationalization of the problem and the movement. Since the North is the place we generally work, however, there is need for a more detailed picture of trends.

Observed from the angle of current social alignments, the movement in the North seems pointed directly towards a difficult and violent period. As a movement it has developed very rapidly, with the mass base of support emanating from the metropolitan ghettos that run all across the northern rim of the country. There seem to be distinctive Northern conditions which tend to make the protest movement immediately volatile in relation to the white community. These are: first, the official but betrayed policies of non-discrimination; second, the change of the North into a "treadmill" instead of a "ladder," due to the automation of traditional low skill work; third, the greater isolation of the ghetto-dwelling Negro from the world of white people. These seem to be conditions conducive to militant tactics, distrust of promise, and a concern for radical economic improvement.

Various integrationist and separatist movements are now developing, most of them threatening the real or apparent interests of many whites, who now are so actively opposing the pace of integration that they can loosely be called "counter-revolutionary." Between these two contending forces, there is a crisis and a paralysis among the liberal organizations, and behind it all is the Federal Government encouraging mild concessions and preparing to maintain order. When looked at this way, it seems that a stalemate is likely to continue temporarily and then turn into a polarized and violent disorder ending in government intervention—without a change in the grim conditions of poverty and exploitation which are their irritants. We could speculate endlessly in this direction, but at a point it becomes fruitless because there is no way to predict reliably what will happen in the next few months.

There is another way to approach the problem which is more manageable because it avoids the problems of such sweeping prediction. This is through classifying various demands which are being made by the movement, and judging, first, the extent to which they might solve problems if they were enacted, and, second, the effect of these demands on existing or potential alliances with white groups.

The demands seem to fall into four categories:

1. *Demands to eliminate discrimination or de facto segregation.* These traditional and worthwhile demands would rectify a discriminatory situation, and the rectification would materially improve the Negro community. The prominent issues are open housing, fair hiring practices, and the end of gerrymandered school and voting districts. The major forces behind these demands in the Negro community are persons of middle-class aspirations, who may or may not be militant, for these barriers alone prevent their entrance into the mainstream of American life. Lower-class Negroes support these demands with conviction also, but more out of a belief that a basic change would occur if the demands were met. This seems to be supported by much evidence that the lower-class Negro prefers *improved* schools over *integrated* schools, and generally *improved* living conditions over *integrated* living conditions.

These demands have the full support of the liberal white community, for legal equality and equality of opportunity are part of the liberal ideology. No doubt the ire of the white unemployed, or working class, or voting property holder is sometimes heightened by many of these insistent Negro demands, but there is hardly any infringement of basic interests here.

2. *Demands which symbolically assert Negro dignity but neither achieve change nor alienate whites very much.* Examples of these are the anti-blackface demonstrations in Philadelphia, and demands for Cleveland school integration (integrated schools in poor white areas continue to segregate students by classroom).

These issues are pushed often by militant leaders who appeal to the racial bitterness of the Negro community for effective mobilization on further issues, or in some cases, unfortunately, for power without regard to the needs of the Negro community. These demands also receive lower-class Negro support because of the channel which they provide for the vigorous expression of a justifiable anger—but as with the first class of demands, these are not directed towards very much change in the economic conditions of segregated life.

However, the possibility of enraging or alienating liberal, middle- or lower-class whites with these demands is much greater than with the first set. The kind and depth of alienation is very important to consider here. It is not a case of *direct* economic deprivation being forced on the white, and in that sense it does not create what we tend to think of as permanent alienation. However, the impact on some whites is almost this severe, especially in the case of school integration. The experiences in Cleveland, where a lower-class Italian mob intimidated a CORE demonstration out of their neighborhood (over a question which clearly should be resolved on the side of the Negroes), and in New York where thousands of middle-, lower-middle-, and lower-class parents, without much visible coordination, gathered to protest the "pairing" of schools, demonstrate the immediate significance of this question. What is behind this "counter-revolutionary" response? All of the parents are in some sense racist, and this is one of the few occasions forcing a public declaration of their feelings—this is part of it. But the very fact that the racism was not so manifest before this might indicate that it is a feeling of secondary importance to the white person. What seems to bring it into prominence is the feeling that the proposed integration will destroy the "quality" of the school and prevent their youngsters from getting the education necessary to fit into the highly-skilled professions, those being the few left today which are at all secure. Is this a realistic fear? If it is, then this issue might create permanent alienation because, next to personal livelihood, the destruction of a son or daughter's future is perhaps the most serious threat which can be made to a parent. But on the other hand, if the fear of the white parent is not realistic, then the alienation probably can be overcome. We are inclined to think that the fears are very unrealistic. American education is responsive often to local parents' pressures, and "forced" integration probably will be coupled with the improvement of educational conditions for both black and white children. In addition, it is unlikely that there will be very extensive joint racial attendance at schools of the poorest ghetto groups and the white upper-middle classes because of their geographical and jurisdictional separation. As for the integration of lower- and lower-middle class groups, the threat of integration is likely to lead to either 1) the evacuation of the white groups from the area, if they are financially able, or 2) the actual integration of the whole neighborhood, with the resulting great potential for seeing common problems. In either case, there is not a serious long-term threat of severe alienation of the white community no matter how militantly the Negro movement presses the issue. Our tentative conclusion is that despite the initial antagonisms of the confrontation, there is relatively little danger of permanent alienation. But there is little direct social change either, since the fundamental need is for *more* and *better* education. The positive gains lie in the stir and pressure for change created in the various white communities, and the greater militancy and grass roots community focus of the Negro movement.

3. *Demands which are specifically racial, do not achieve very much, and potentially alienate large numbers of whites.* The clearest and most prominent example of this kind of demand is that of replacing white workers with black ones in a situation of chronic unemployment. Sometimes there is inarticulate anger behind this kind of demand, and sometimes there is a complicated theory of change. Usually the theory is that a violent clash over scarce employment opportunities liberates the Negro from self-doubt, makes alliances possible, and forces the middle and upper classes to act decisively to improve the economic and racial situation of the country.

Other issues of this kind are less clear-cut. The demand for a white student to lower his immediate educational chances by being bussed to a deprived Negro school might fall in this category instead of the second one, as we suggested before. So might the moving of a Negro into an economically insecure white neighborhood, although a violent white lower-class status reaction in these circumstances is not likely to be permanently alienating. Even the demand for fair employment sometimes might create alienating consequences, especially when it is seen as whites giving up jobs to fulfill Negro desires, or splitting the pie evenly. In small cities like Chester, Pennsylvania, where communications are relatively good between various groups, the idea that a job given to a Negro is a job taken from a white is quite obvious and unacceptable to all. In a larger city, however, this humanism is missing, perhaps because of the anonymity of the metropolis; in addition, the rude fact that there just are not enough jobs for everyone is much more difficult to see. Thus, the tendency to push harder and more vigorously for fair employment in the great industrial centers might be perceived as a by-product of racial encroachment more than as a failure of the national economy. Where unemployment is not so chronic as to convince everyone of its central importance in their problems, and yet severe enough to make one race threaten the other, tensions might be highest. At a certain point, the question of whether unemployment should be a "fair" situation for everyone could become less important than the question of how everyone can fight together for full employment. In many Northern cities we now face this delicate and potentially creative balance of feelings. (A part of this issue is what relation the Negro movement and the labor movement will have. Under increasing pressure from Negroes, the labor movement might decide to face squarely the problems of automation and stagnation, or they might see themselves as part of the privileged industrial elite fighting down the challengers.)

As we approach the end of legal discrimination in this country, we can expect the movement to debate—often with bitterness—the value in making this kind of demand for *racial* economic change as opposed to the demand for *class* economic change. The race-centered demand, which is the more alienating of the two, can find broad Negro support today although the new middle-class leadership will be pushing it the hardest. We should note the occasional unwillingness of the lower-class Negro, at least in Cambridge and Chester, to make demands that the white lose his job or that a white child lose his education, even when proposed by the militant leadership. These reflect some of the class differences *within* the Negro movement.

It is quite unreasonable, however, to expect that the Negro movement always will want to avoid alienating demands. Those who believe in the potential of an interracial movement, however, should be concerned with the dangers in this kind of demand and consider arguing against it, perhaps even at the risk of losing their voice in the Negro movement.

4. *Demands for political and economic changes of substantial benefit to the Negro and white poor.* Examples of these include improved housing, lower rents, better schools, full employment, extention of welfare and social security assistance. They are not "Negro issues" *per se;* rather, they are precisely those issues which should appeal to lower-class whites as well as to Negroes. They are difficult demands around which to organize, most probably for two reasons. The first is that they may lack a racial content and therefore might not be easy to shift towards in a movement with a heavy racial emphasis. But this can be overcome, for example, if these demands are linked with racial ones —if the issues of full employment and non-discrimination in hiring are linked. The second, and much more serious, reason is that no such demands can be realized on the community level. New York, for instance, is thoroughly unable to find even the resources needed to improve housing conditions in Harlem even if the city wants to; similarly, Chicago cannot conceivably use its available resources to fully retrain the Negro unemployed—and each of these problems is only a fraction of the entire condition of poverty that needs to be attacked in a nationally planned, financed, and integrated way. This in absolutely no way negates the importance of raising issues locally which can be solved only by national social change. But it suggests that in the absence of national social change, which is impossible to expect in the short-run, these demands in themselves may not result in the small vic-

tories which are required, presumably, if a movement is to keep its spirit. It suggests further that in the near future there might be a need for an organized national agency representative of the common interests of these local protest groups and able to mobilize and focus pressure that can be felt at national levels.

These difficulties are compounded by a leadership problem. The support for these demands comes most of all from lower-class Negroes and political radicals of all classes, races, and occupations. Much of the time the injection of these demands into the existing movement will be opposed by the middle-class leadership which prefers the first three kinds of demands. Such leaders are likely to have everything to gain and nothing to lose by the introduction of such issues.

Some mainstream organizations will shy away from this approach on the grounds that conservative support for civil rights will be lost if the issue is joined with proposals for broad new government economic policies. This is to be expected and, although differences need not be inflamed, they should be recognized as real since such new policies *are* needed. At any rate, nearly all the liberal institutions will go along in rhetoric with such demands, but few will follow up with a massive action program to make rhetoric reality. The Negro movement, where it believes in these demands, is usually more committed to a mass movement than are the sympathetic but lethargic white-led organizations. This failure of the liberal Left to come through with a total commitment to all the discomfort of a political crusade is another cause of the present lack of support for these demands in the Negro movement. Why should the Negroes, crushed as they are with a very specific form of exploitation, be called on to create a general social program and then wait for the whites to organize? Part of our whole crisis so far is that the white person has nothing specific to point towards when the Negro asks for *proof* that an interracial movement is possible. This is partly the reason for the importance of our present work in Chicago and Appalachia which involves white unemployed people. But it is important to remember that even if lower-class whites suddenly materialized as a mass movement looking for Negro allies in the struggle for dignity, there would be—and there are even when the question is raised today—immense difficulties rooted in the possible threat to certain Negro leaders. One SNCC member from Mississippi, in a recent Atlanta meeting, suggested that the "dream" of a Southern neo-populist movement would be a direct threat to the Negro organization to the extent that the organization is a means of finding and expressing a Negro identity.

Before taking up these questions of interracial relations, the prior question is: What do we know or believe about the possibilities of organizing with the other ethnic minorities and the white poor? Any discussion of a movement of the poor is incomplete and utopian without such an appraisal.

II. The Possible Allies of the Negro Movement

Economic deprivation is not an experience peculiar to the Negro in America. It is a class experience which cannot be overcome by a single race. Thus any potential allies of an economically oriented Negro movement will be the class affected by this phenomenon. The essential class unity of a group must not be overlooked: Any united movement must stress this, the only common ground which all members of the group share. Their common consciousness of poverty and economic superfluousness will ultimately have to bring them together.

However, at this stage, when only the Negroes are conscious of the possibility for real change, and when no more than rumblings are heard elsewhere, a general call to the depressed groups in society is not likely to have much success. The problem of deprivation is felt differently by countless groups, the major dividing characteristics being *ethnic identity*, *age*, *place*, and *occupational status.*

Ethnic Groups

Apart from the Negro, the other distinct ethnic groups are the Spanish-speaking Puerto Ricans and Mexicans, and the communities of southern and eastern Europeans in the large cities.

Puerto Ricans already show signs of willingness to ally directly with the Negro movement. They are found in large numbers in the industrial cities of the northeast, contiguous to or actually in the Negro downtown ghetto. The largest of these Puerto Rican communities, in New York City, joined the first city-wide school boycott in February 1964 (although not the second) and are participating extensively in the rent strike there.

A number of problems exist, however. If the Puerto Ricans are conceived as appendages to the Negro movement, then all the explicitly racial aspects of the Negro movement will tend to alienate the many Puerto Ricans. Any union of the groups is most certainly not possible through a racial appeal. The boycott in New York was organized around integration as well as equality of education, but since that time a greater Puerto Rican separateness has evolved and seems to suggest one difficulty of an immediate merger.

However, the contacts between the groups will naturally remain large, and will probably expand. The Puerto Rican and Negro leadership in the rent strike in New York City works in close alliance. The values of cooperation are great for both groups. Aside from the major argument of strength in unity, Puerto Ricans have a great deal to gain from the experience of the Negro movement; and Negroes can see real, rather than rhetorical, possibilities for an alliance on economic issues which can be quite impelling. A good example of this sense of mutual benefit in operation occurred in the first meeting of Negroes and Puerto Ricans in Chester. After a session in which many Puerto Ricans were upset about the possible dangers and consequences of action, a Negro woman approached a student who was trying to lead the discussion, and told her not to worry: "These people have never had anyone try to help them before; you have to be patient."

But even without the complications of Negro-Puerto Rican relationships, certain other factors mitigate against successful organization of this group, especially in the smaller cities: If things are not going well for the Puerto Ricans, they move back to Puerto Rico, or to another city. Six thousand Puerto Ricans lived in the

Chester ghetto four years ago, at the time of the first major immigration. Today there are less than 1,000. Even if this is not the case everywhere, the psychological presence of the island homeland and the possibility of return may make an all-out movement for change less appealing than for an American Negro who doubts that moving out is a real alternative for large numbers. Another problem is that although color and class consciousness exist among Puerto Ricans, there is not yet a widespread consciousness of the need for struggle as there now is in virtually all sections of the Negro community.

However, we might speculate that the deepening of economic slump, the inadequacy and betrayal of alleged pro-Puerto Rican organizations such as the International Ladies Garment Workers Union, and the inviting example of the Negro revolution, are the conditions leading to a further upsurge of Puerto Rican activity, and at least a working alliance, if not always a close and happy one, with the Negro organizations.

For the summer, groups in every city in the East should take note of the Puerto Rican community. The economic status of these groups is usually abominable, and housing, welfare, jobs, and schools are all potential burning issues. The impetus to change stemming from the New York successes and from any local offers of assistance could be enough to develop movements elsewhere. And since highly developed internal community organization already exists in many places, the problem of finding and stimulating leadership to take the initiative is probably minimal. Especially along the New York-New Jersey-Philadelphia-Baltimore-Washington coastline, the possibility of greater Puerto Rican action should be explored.

Mexicans provide a comparable minority in size. Those in the cities of the Midwest, especially Chicago, are in a position analogous to that of the Puerto Ricans in the East. . . . A second group has resided for longer periods of time in the Southwest from Texas to California. Important work has been done to forge an alliance between these Mexican-Americans and other groups. Easily the most promising example is the Texas Democratic Coalition, which is a voter registration and political organization unifying

Mexican, Negro, labor, and liberal forces across the state. However, the stable residence patterns of Mexican majorities, as in Crystal City where last year the "white power structure" was utterly deposed, the lack of political representation in Texas for such a large minority, and the cruel forms of direct exploitation in west Texas, might make the coalition idea less applicable to the Mexican problem in the North. Where the idea might be extended, however, is farther to the West—for instance, to San Diego and Los Angeles, where the crisis of Negro and Mexican poverty can converge along with increasing lay-offs and job insecurity in the aerospace industries which are organized by the International Association of Machinists and the United Auto Workers. It should be high-priority for SDS to find the people and resources to begin organizing in this southern California area. We already have excellent informal offers of assistance from political and union leaders there, and should consider taking this up as a major organizing campaign.

. . .

All these ethnic groups share with the Negroes a key position in American society: They are segregated, separated, and exploited. For as long as they have been in the "land of opportunity," this has been the case. The other generations of migrants, organized labor, and the midwestern farmers were all dealt into the more protected lower-echelons of the establishment in the twenties, thirties and forties. The crisis today rests largely on the fact that the orthodox manner of dealing people in, even if all white Americans ceased their racism, is disappearing as automation cuts into the mass production centers of the economy. The very segregation of the colored ethnic groups, however, has led to problems concerning the prospect for alliances. Differences, often divisive ones, exist between the Negroes, Puerto Ricans, Mexicans, and Indians. But it seems possible to bridge many of the differences which impede a political alliance, especially as the peril of slump and the promise of a movement become more sharply counterposed. But whether ethnic-centered demands will be accompanied by demands for general economic change does not depend solely on the existence of a long-term slump or the spontaneous development of a new consciousness. It depends also on organizing experiments which we have not begun.

Of groups in the urban North which might be directly antagonistic to the Negro movement, we must mention the eastern and southern Europeans, who are in the anxious lower sector of the establishment. A number recently immigrated here, especially after the 1945-48 transformation of eastern Europe, but the vast majority stem from the immigration waves of the late nineteenth and early twentieth centuries. They were the manual labor of the early industrial revolution in America, and were part of the industrial union movement. As a consequence, today they are mostly manual laborers in highly-paid industrial sectors. They form a large part of the group of Americans who are lower-class in status but middle-class in income.

Often they remain in the center of the industrial cities, however, and now are often contiguous to the expanding Negro ghettoes. They should not be seen primarily as a constituent of the American poor, but rather as a group which finds itself defending its position. They are threatened by automation, which is striking hard at the jobs the old ethnic minorities possess. But they are threatened also by the Negro movement in a number of ways. Their children are more likely than the Negro children to win the few jobs which will be remaining in the production sector of the economy—the artisan, craft, service, and new technical fields. This is due, of course, to their being white and having some money. But the point is that the Negro demand for decent jobs threatens many of these groups directly. In addition, the "encroachment" of the Negro on the border of their territory is threatening. They struggled for a long time to arrive where they are, and the increasing proximity of the Negro threatens their new-bourgeois position. Still further, although their schools are not much better in quality than Negro schools, education remains their key to the highly-paid jobs, and is seen with great protectiveness. The attacks on Negro pickets by Italians in Cleveland during the January school crisis is probably a classic example of this phenomenon.

These groups remain tightly-knit cultural centers, and have not been integrated completely into American society. They have been the centers of machine politics and the underworld. They have a well-developed system of mutual assistance and defense, and the violence of their response to the attack on their community's integrity may simply be a function of their need for this security. The breakdown of the neighborhood is especially a threat to them.

The conclusion we draw is that this group will play a reactionary role in the impending economic crisis. Unless they are hard hit by automation and can be organized around their employment status, it is difficult to see how outright conflict can be averted. The possibility of organizing them as ethnic groups around ethnic issues (such as the establishment of cultural centers) seems of no relevance to a coalition of forces demanding economic improvement.

The size and growth pattern of these ethnic populations is not known and should be researched. They exist in great number in West Cleveland, and the study project includes Portuguese and Greek communities. In Chester, where the worst ghetto is contiguous to a Polish section, tentative attempts to probe the reaction of this group have been inconclusive. In Chicago, census tracts show that some of the largest concentrations of white poverty are in these ethnic ghettos. A series of surveys and experiments is likely to produce much more accurate information on the response of these groups to a program of general economic improvement, and we shall find new approaches to them also. Otherwise, they loom as a serious immediate threat to our movement.

Age Groups

Age is another major factor in a discussion of potential members of our coalition, because America is organized to discomfort both its young and its old.

Some groups were either left out of, or arrived too late to partake in, the great establishment formed at the height of America's economic strength, and today they are undercut further by automation. This is precisely the case with the youth of America:

They "arrived" in the labor force too late to fit in.

Among the hardest hit in the whole society is the young Negro. The insurgence of a demand for equality combined with his increased economic superfluousness in the South leads to rapid migration North. This rate reached 50 per cent for Mississippi Negroes in the 15-24 age group in the 1950-60 decade. Thus the youth's chances of getting work in the depressed center-cities of the North is even less than if he were older.

But, disregarding the race factor, the rate of unemployment for all high school dropouts and those who do not continue their education beyond high school is more than double the national figure. They are entering a labor force without skills necessary for a high paying job, but lack of education is not the major problem. Although it is true that any one youth can increase his chances for getting a job by acquiring a needed skill, the total number of unemployed will not decrease significantly if the level of education is raised.

The choice for the non-college youth is difficult: He must either break into the limited market for skilled labor, take a low-paying, insecure job in the service field, or fit into some niche that is open to him. The need for skilled labor remains, of course; traditional artisans (chefs, jewelers) are not threatened by automation, and the normal openings remain, through family contacts; the crafts (carpentry, plumbing, printing) absorb a small group. Those who are lucky can acquire the skills necessary for our new automated society (the electronics specialists, machine operators).

For the most part, however, especially in groups with any initial disadvantage (race, lower income, residence in depressed areas) the chances are that they will not get a secure, high-paying job. The four-dollars-an-hour industrial jobs which their fathers have are disappearing rapidly, industry by industry. Even in the most successful union settlements in automation-threatened industries, the best the union can get is a guarantee not to fire anyone; the ILWU contract on the West Coast last year is an example of a progressive union which realized that on a local or even industry-wide basis, this was the best they could do. Other unions, such as the United Mine Workers, have agreed to permit automation to proceed more rapidly, worrying only about those who maintain their jobs. In either case, the opportunities for youths entering the labor market are cut off completely.

Unless there is some niche (a job with a family firm, the opportunity to start a new business), chances are the youth will end up in a low-paying service job. Sales clerks, office-boys, managers of small retail stores and public accommodations are all unorganized, and wages rarely are more than the minimum required by law. Aside from the fact that $1.25 an hour is not enough to support a family in urban life, the crisis becomes more acute because of the standard of living which these youths are used to enjoying. Factory workers can afford to raise a medium-sized family in a middle-class area, but their sons will not be able to.

Thus a large group of what Labor Secretary Wirtz calls "outlaws," the unemployed, or highly insecure youths facing a closing and formidable labor market, is growing constantly. These are perhaps the most invisible of the invisible poor, however—especially those who do not have some other identifiable characteristic (race, residence in a depressed area, etc.). It may be that the government is taking steps to avert a crisis before the group becomes politically vocal, or because of the correlation between crime and unemployed youth. The government program plans for the development of skills and mere labor-intensive work (CCC-type camps). To the extent that there is frictional unemployment, the skills program may reduce unemployment, although the ability of the government to carry on such programs successfully is at present seriously in doubt, judging from the slight success of the Manpower Redevelopment Program. The camps will reduce youth unemployment slightly, but it is not a permanent solution to the problem and may in fact heighten young people's consciousness of their common problems, the social and economic origin of such problems (as opposed to seeing it as individual failure), and the magnitude of the problems.

The outlook for the organization of high school students into the movement is very promising. In the Negro community, especially in the South, high school groups exist practically wherever the movement exists. These organizations focus mostly on civil rights direct action or on the acquisition of educational skills, and it is not clear whether the youth can deal with their complex economic problems without an adult movement working with them. Chicago SNCC includes a city-wide system of high school groups, mostly in the Negro schools, who work around the issues of curriculum reform and school boycotts. In Chester and Swarthmore, the Student Political Action Committee developed contacts with white as well as Negro high school students, but the white students are mostly from middle-class homes and so far see themselves as college-bound rather than economically insecure. Somewhat similar patterns are visible in the work of the Detroit Education Project with Negro youth in the Barbour neighborhood, and with high school students in suburban areas.

Outside the Negro movement, there is a great deal of concern with the youth by educators, law enforcement officials, and social workers. Each interprets the problems of this group in his own light: The educators see the solution in a wider curriculum to help the student fit the new contours of the labor market; the law enforcement official will solve their problems by strict discipline and keeping them in school; and social workers see them as a product of poverty and broken homes, to be helped through careful understanding. But there has been no attempt to help this group see its own major problem—its uselessness in an automated society.

One of the priorities in research is to develop methods in working with these youth. They are particularly prone to right-wing and racist appeals, but perhaps must be organized around their own economic insecurities, and only observe later that their own demands coincide with those of Negroes. But broaching the race issues is not the only barrier which must be faced and overcome. The primary problem is finding them. Where this group overlaps with some other poverty category, *e.g.* race or depressed region, they are among the most vocal. But elsewhere it is likely that their frustrations will not be vocalized. In those cases where their parents are industrial workers making good union wages (and many of them will be from this group, for they most frequently cannot find employment where their parents do), there is no reason why they will not subsist off their families until they reach an age when they think employment is easy to find. This does not mean that they are not potentially active, but only that, left alone, they will rarely give spontaneous verbalization to their real problems. It means that we must find concentrations of these youth, and after probing into their attitudes toward economics, employment, and race we must find a program which will appeal to them if possible, and fit into our concern for full employment. It seems likely that without a pressing sense of obligation (of the kind that a father who is laid off feels) and a group consciousness, they will not respond immediately to a call for direct action on economic issues. Alternative approaches which seem feasible are to begin organization on a smaller unit around those issues they deem important (social activities, police) or to tie them into another movement, presumably of white unemployed who have already entered the labor movement. It may be feasible at this point in Chicago to begin to organize groups of high school students, dropouts, and recent graduates without work, attempting either to involve them with the broader full employment movement, or in their own issues.

. . .

Organization by Area

Although the problems of the economy are nationwide, the poverty which results is not spread evenly to every nook and cranny of the country.

The depressed areas include:

1. Appalachia, including the southern tier of New York state, all of Pennsylvania, West Virginia, eastern Kentucky, and Tennessee, western Maryland, Virginia and North Carolina, and northern Alabama. This area suffers from the automation of the coal industry, the depressed railroads, and the general economic malaise. Northern Minnesota and Michigan's Upper Peninsula share this area's depressed mining conditions.

2. The industrial metropolises, including practically every major city in the north: Washington, D.C., Baltimore, Philadelphia, Boston, Pittsburgh, Newark, etc.; the string of small cities

from Wilmington, Delaware, to Newark, New Jersey; the north-central areas of Buffalo, Cleveland, Akron, Cincinnati, Dayton, Detroit, and Chicago, and much of the West Coast.

3. The depressed agrarian areas: the Black Belt, stretching from eastern Louisiana across much of Mississippi and Alabama, through central Georgia, most of South Carolina, and south-central Virginia; the eastern shore of Maryland; southern Delaware, southern New Jersey, and northern New England.

4. Isolated cities and regions which are hit by cancellation of federal contracts, changes in world prices, and other unexpected crises; presently Long Island and upstate New York are representative.

The territorial basis of organization should be carefully considered. Not only are economic conditions varying on the regional, state, and municipal level, but political organization may be appropriate on these levels and on the ward and neighborhood levels as well. It is clear that solutions to the problems of these areas are only at the national level, however, and it continually must be kept in mind that such organization is strictly a means to exert pressure nationally and to gain strength for the movement, and not an end in itself.

Economically, the movement has relied most completely on the city or municipality level in the North. It is the Chester movement, the New York rent strike, and the Chicago school boycott; to the extent that a greater consciousness has been achieved, it has been in terms of federations of these municipal movements. This is natural, for in the industrial Northeast and North Central states, the city is the place of great poverty, and cities are not contiguous, and thus they lend themselves to separate movements.

Within the city, organization has proceeded on a district and neighborhood level, and where the density is great, in the block and tenement level. It is on these levels that exciting work is being done, not only in more intensive participation in reform movements, but in the development of leadership and discussion which may be the basis for radical thought and participatory democracy. Among the uneducated, the poverty-stricken, and the segregated, there is a lack of leadership and administrative ability, and even of an ability to focus on issues and verbalize general dissatisfaction. It is also here, however, that there is an absence of vested interests in continued exploitation, and possibly the seed for a different society. After months of cooperation, the residents of the second ward of Cambridge, Maryland, not only discuss basic flaws in the system and verbalize what their economic and social rights are, they also have developed institutions and patterns of behavior which are foreign to middle-class America. They refuse to talk seriously about taking jobs away from white workers as a solution to their unemployment. Many are not taking the now-available surplus food: They say someone who needs it more may not get it if they take it. In Chester, too, women on a march refused to block the school, arguing that stopping a white child's education was not their goal.

The major problem with organization on this level is that while it contains the most opportunity for new values, it is not the locus of decision-making. Only a block clean-up, anti-rat campaign, and at most a rent strike can be organized here with any material changes possible. In Newark, and increasingly in Chester, federations of block organizations are the basis for a city-wide movement, and these may be models for others to follow.

Outside the industrial areas, a regional approach seems more viable. The Black Belt has been the target of voter registration, and the shared problems of Appalachia make it optimum for regional organization.

In translating local insurgency around economic issues into political terms, the same question of location is relevant. On the precinct ward level, the most one can do is publicize issues, and perhaps shake up the machine by destroying traditional patronage channels and even winning a city council election in one or more constituencies. Even on a city-wide level, only limited solutions to problems exist. Majorities within city limits of groups with which we are concerned hardly ever exist; where they do they have no actual power (Washington, D.C.), or are split racially (Cleveland). Direct political action can probably only force others to make concessions in their benefit, and not actually displace the rulers. On the other hand, the destruction of reactionary machines may well lead to urban renewal and some material benefit (although the tax base of those places where poverty exists is usually lower than in richer communities). In addition, the popular frustration created in seeing the inability of the municipality to act to solve basic problems brings on a greater consciousness of scope and depth of those problems. The election to state and federal legislatures of representatives who are liberal, and at least will not block reform, is a worthy bi-product of the movement, especially when it does not destroy the race and class identity of the people.

On the state level, there is a great possibility of effecting reforms through direct and political action. Again, however, those states which contain the largest incidence of poverty are least able to afford such programs as quality education, adequate welfare, and area redevelopment. Little except publicity and some reform can come on this level. However, there are other advantages to state-wide organization. Where there is more than one group affected adversely in the state by economic conditions (as is the case in Pennsylvania, an industrially-depressed Southeast, ghost coal towns in the Northeast, Appalachian rural poverty in the center, and unused steel capacity in Pittsburgh) there is great potential for these groups seeing their common problems and beginning to make sound alliances. In Texas this apparently is already happening with Mexicans, Negroes, labor and liberals.

Ultimately, however, the national level is where political pressures must be directed. This pressure undoubtedly will take many forms: Mass demonstrations, independent and reform Democratic candidates, and other activity might well be coordinated by a nationally-representative assembly of the movement. This is a very intricate problem, especially since the Negro movement is at this stage already, while its national liberal-labor allies live in impotent desperation below the establishment. How and whether to work out a national political organization is a problem which will require much sensitive exploration in the days ahead.

Organization by Occupation and Employment Status

The concept of organization by occupation and employment status is basic to this discussion, and is the last major criterion.

Our premise is that a movement can be developed among persons whose economic role in the society is marginal or insecure. What groups, then, fall into this category by this criterion?

First, the *unemployed* present an important potential force. Due to the high levels of unemployment among Negroes, the civil rights movement is growing more militant in its demands and program. It is not at this point a chronic problem for whites, as mentioned earlier—a situation which leads to many of the tensions within the disadvantaged class. However, there are many instances of white unemployment; areas where highly skilled men are being laid off because of military shifts is just one example. And unemployment very definitely is a chronic *threat*, if not yet a reality, to whites.

The Chicago JOIN project is attempting to organize in a situation which includes these factors, especially the higher amount of Negro than white unemployment, the present relative "normalcy" of white unemployment levels, the growing apprehension among whites about their employment, and some patterns of anti-Negro feeling. An attempt is made to appeal to persons in their common status of unemployment, with organization proceeding simultaneously in different neighborhoods among whites and Negroes. Not surprisingly, Negroes are deeply concerned to do something about the problem. More surprisingly, the whites, though fewer in number, express a real interest in becoming involved in JOIN, and most see racism as a diversionary issue. The advantages of initiating a project with the explicit intention of building interracial unity around the jobs issue are quite obvious: The movement is immediately political; the service-centered aspects of the project do not become more consuming than issues and program, etc.

But one barely-started project does not constitute evidence that the white unemployed want to, or can be, organized politically. There is good reason to question whether objective conditions (the social psychology of the unemployed, and the pace of unemployment itself) permit effective organization. Some unemployed whites may be more embarrassed than Negroes by their unemployed status, and see their problems as personal or obscure rather than social and clear. Many are not working because the only jobs they can get are not lucrative enough to compete with welfare or the other means of obtaining income. Some are too disillusioned by past disappointments. Others are just momentarily unemployed, the rapid turnover and transient nature of this group being one of its characteristics. These feelings are all supported by the fact that the problem is not always chronic and because few institutions express a real concern about it. In addition, many of the unemployed will be hard to find, since they are not registered and receiving unemployment compensation checks.

However, these qualifications by no means apply everywhere, and two growing forces could reduce much of their significance. The first is the expanding rate of unemployment which could become a chronic problem for whites unless drastically new ameliorative policies are enacted. The second is the growing visibility of the unemployment problem and the consequent incentive to see it as an issue on which action legitimately can be taken. Together these trends are likely to create a far greater consciousness and movement by the unemployed themselves. The better unions as well are likely to become involved in the political organization of their unemployed, or the unemployed generally. In this case, organizing work might become easier for us, although new problems of remaining fraternal but independent in relation to the unions would arise. An especially good opportunity for this effort exists on the West Coast, in San Diego as already mentioned, and in Seattle where 10 per cent unemployment exists in an unstable defense-based economy.

An even larger group defined by their job status is the mass of *employed but economically-insecure* persons—heralded in traditional ideology as the true agency of social change, but today a perplexing and divided group.

These often are reactionary people, many trying to consolidate the achievements made during the generations since their families immigrated here. Many in the craft unions, which are organized to defend a single skill in a tightening market situation, are very likely to be racist and conservative. A good example is the building trades unions who, in New York, fought bitterly to preserve their racism and nepotism against the Negro jobs movement. It is likely that such persuasion will have to come in the streets as well as at the negotiating tables.

The industrial unions seem more likely to sense the need for progressive economic change, but today they might be tied too deeply to the Democratic Party and private enterprise to be a mass political force campaigning for a transformation to planning and abundance. So long as this is the case, the possibility for alliances between labor's rank-and-file and Negroes or the whole underdog class is jeopardized. Often the unions are fighting for the jobs of those who are working already, and the best they can hope to achieve on an industry-wide scale in the face of automation is an agreement that the machines will proceed no faster than the pace of natural turnover through retirement or quitting. Thus the union local, or any other local institution, cannot do very much by itself; it is modeled to work on a local level around local issues, and the problems it is confronting here are national ones that stretch beyond even their industry. Therefore, even though the rank-and-file is capable of more militancy than the union leadership much of the time (as the rising numbers of contract rejections, wildcat strikes, and various attitude surveys indicate), this potential militancy may be blocked indefinitely, rather than drawn out and channeled into political action.

We will be in a sensitive situation in this area, because our immediate identification is with the Negro movement and the problems of the unorganized poor—and these are not the primary and immediate constituents of the American labor movement. We should take up several opportunities for organizing work with the employed union men, however. One need is to attempt building political coalitions in places such as those on the West Coast—but coalitions spurred by the intensity of the Negro movement, not coalitions which compromise the Negro movement for the sake of its less militant allies. Another need is to engage directly in support of strikes where locals request assistance and where we can be of aid, make close contact with the rank-and-filers, and learn the techniques of strike organization. A third need is to participate in union educational programming; it seems possible, for instance, to help develop curricula on social problems to be used in many of the summer and year-round labor institutes and forums. A last need is to be involved directly in the labor movement with others of our persuasion, making an informal "legitimate" radical force pushing for policy and leadership changes and supporting and pressing the most militant wing of the CIO leadership.

Another potential participant in our coalition is the migrant worker, often described as the worst off and the most exploited of society's poor. Students and some unionists have attempted either labor organization or educational improvement among these poor, never with a great deal of success. Some of the problem seems to be the failure of the AFL-CIO to commit itself seriously enough in the southern California drive, but the problem of organizing in this area runs deeper than the matter of commitment. It may be the case that if the migrant worker were to "win" on the issue of unionization or wage-hikes, the growers would introduce the automatic machinery which they have been holding back while labor exploitation was so cheap. In that case, which we think is probable, the future for the migrant is coming to resemble that of the rural tenant or field hand being replaced by machines. Although there is no sign of a slowing of migration, ultimately the migrants may recognize the lack of opportunity in the cities and will remain where they are, unemployed, or join the welfare rolls in the North as the next best alternative. If they stay south, organizing becomes a separate problem; if they come north, they dissolve into the groups we are discussing.

In summary, there are various open possibilities for organizing among the 50 million or more "non-Negroes" who now are in a state of poverty or economic insecurity. What we know does not point towards anti-Negro or fascist attitudes throughout these groups of the poor, contrary to what some premature defeatists declare. We find a diverse series of situations, but most of them are characterized by:

1. The impact of growing economic insecurity.
2. A widespread feeling of alienation and a discouragement with existing economic policies.

Now with an official "war on poverty," there is a chance

that the poor will feel a greater common consciousness of the legitimacy of their problems and the inadequacy of government programs. In addition, it is striking to observe that almost no attempts are being made to organize the poor for social change—and no verdict can be reached until a long-term attempt is made.

Interracial Problems of an Interracial Movement

After this sketchy appraisal of organizational possibilities among various groups of the American poor, the question of an interracial movement must be taken up more directly.

We hope for a movement of all the poor, at a time when the Negro community is creating the only major movement in American society. The problems inherent in this situation are several and sensitive. We realize they will not be settled on paper, but only in actual work. Nevertheless it is critically necessary to state at least what the problems seem to be about.

The first is that in very few instances are *any* white persons demonstrating a commitment to Negro causes, and in almost no instance is there actual evidence that *poor* whites can be mobilized. This makes it seem unfair to ask that the Negro movement take up economic issues as well as the directly racial issues which burden it today.

The second is that if whites *were* mobilized somehow, they would not represent an unambiguous sign of hope to the Negro movement. This is because many Negroes believe, with excellent historical justification, that the whites would dominate the movement and eventually receive the social rewards. This attitude is sharpened by the growing "black" ideologies of the new militant middle-class Negro leadership. These ideologies variously require Negro control of the Negro organizations, Negro staffs in the field, and a program of specific hostility to the whites of all classes. The usual psychological justification for such a program is the need to expunge alleged pent-up hatred of the Negro masses for the white man, either as a way to keep people moving or as a way to force action out of white society. Many integrationist ideologies, held by Negroes and whites, agree on the need for control and much of the time on the need for Negro staffs, while opposing the anti-white features of the program wherever it might permanently alienate whites and Negroes who live in the same class circumstances.

The third problem is that the issues are not always conscious matters of debate, but they arise in the form of emotional tensions between people and organizations within the movement.

What are the arguments *for* an interracial movement?

1. The alternative is more likely to be fascism than freedom. We are not convinced that violent conflict between Negroes and lower-class whites will force the American establishment to even make significant concessions, much less dissolve itself. The establishment might merely ignore the trouble and leave it to the local police, or it might use troops to enforce order. In either case, poor Negroes and poor whites will continue to struggle against each other instead of against the power structure that properly deserves their malice.

2. Since the Negroes are today the most *experienced* force for change, it is doubtful that they will fall to the rear of a movement of the poor. In generations gone by, the Irish, Italians, Jews, and other ethnic minorities rose to the partial security of the establishment through a labor movement and political machines which subordinated Negroes. That was an unforgivable action. But the process is not inevitable; it depends on the balance of forces at any one time. Today it seems inconceivable that Negroes would put up with less than a central role in directing the movement. Quite the contrary; would they not have *leading* roles in an interracial movement if their own action fosters it?

3. The economic problems of the Negro are class problems. They cannot be solved by the elimination of discrimination. The creation of decent housing, education, and employment requires massive change. No such massive change could improve the poor white without improving the life of the poor Negro. Some argue that the economic "solution" for the Negroes lies in compensatory treatment, or a "Marshall Plan for Negroes." This is quite true, and should be done, but it cannot compensate for joblessness except with a job—and there will not be enough

jobs until there is a political movement that successfully demands them or, alternatively, a guaranteed income, from the government. Private business is not creating them and will not create them.

4. The psychological argument that the Negro must expunge hate is questionable on several grounds. It presumes that hate can be liberated while other feelings, such as kindness or openness, are suppressed, whereas it is doubtful that any such mechanical process exists. But even were the psyche to operate in this way, the strategy of liberating hate begs two questions: First, is it morally justifiable to want to liberate hate alone? And, second, after the liberation of hate, how will the living conditions of lower-class Negroes improve?

These questions convince us of the need for a loose alliance of some kind, however difficult. In this context, we should approach the problem of the new Negro leaders and black ideologies more directly. We believe that the Negro community should be, and is, the main repository of guidance over the Negro movement. We believe that a racially-integrated staff legitimately should use the criterion of race in tactical and strategic decisions about organizing. We believe that much of the racial tension within the movement is rooted in our initial refusal to decide upon and maintain a *staff* policy of racial equality. Finally, we believe that the black ideology alone is incapable of leading to improvements in the everyday living conditions of Negro people. It can be one vital way of stirring people into participation, but it cannot eliminate poverty. The elimination of poverty, we think, requires the mobilization of all the power of the 75 to 100 million Americans who suffer it or suffer over it.

This is the same case we would take to the whites, for example, in the office of the Chicago project. Although the Chicago situation is quite hopeful so far, we realize it is illusory to expect the instant removal of prejudice among many whites. The whites must be organized on economic issues which are more important than their racial ideology. Perhaps today this is more possible than in the past because it is hard to imagine the poor white improving his economic condition without confronting a Negro movement already involved in many of the same issues. In this situation we think whites would decide to identify with the Negro struggle were it generally parallel to their own. Of course, the whites could opt for prejudice and further poverty—then we all lose. Whether this choice is made, perhaps, depends in large part on the organizational role we play.

This discussion no doubt will continue, and will be painful to us all. It should not become more important to argue than to organize, however, for only in organizing will the proof be found. So it is organizing we intend to do. Too many people are hungry and kept down, and we are mad. The question that remains is *how.*

Notes Toward a Definition of Our Role

We are left now with the need to ask what the foregoing implies for our political work. By "our" in this context we partly mean SDS and ERAP—this is a working paper on immediate problems we face—and we partly mean any other persons or organizations sharing the concern with racial justice and an end to poverty. Some of what we say, therefore, will be specific to SDS-ERAP, but most of it is intended to apply to the general community active around these issues.

The immediate questions center on our role in the Negro movement, the emerging economic-class movement, the relation this work has to the campus, relations with professionals and the important liberal-left political organizations, the national organizational structure of our movement, and our political program. What follows, it should be stressed, is a set of working notes, not a "blueprint" about which we are confident.

First, Negroes among us should and will continue to work in the Negro community, supporting wholeheartedly all the demands of the movement, stressing a program that includes economic issues, but attempting to avoid programs that lead to the permanent alienation of potential class allies. There also is potentially an important role for Negro organizers among the white poor where we are trying to develop interracial movements and organizations. For instance, Chicago JOIN will involve at some point interracial organizing teams in both the Negro and white neighborhoods and unemployment compensation centers. The effectiveness of this approach is not certain. But it would be impressive and certainly right for a Negro to argue *to whites* that blacks and whites should adopt the direct action tactics of the Negro movement for the sake of class gains. Some whites certainly should continue working where possible in the Negro movement, loyal to its program, but remaining committed to economic and class problems. The rationale for such work lies primarily in keeping in touch with that movement, and not in trying to change its direction. The contributions which whites, as whites, can make are: (1) trying to show the Negro community that there are whites, especially those without any vested private interest, who are concerned as human beings; (2) helping to make connections between those in the Negro movement who are interested in economic issues and any other segments of American society with similar concerns.

However, many whites should turn their organizing attention to the whites in the "Other America." This is by no means as immediately promising as work in the Negro movement; nor is the problem as "legitimate" in the eyes of the middle and upper classes; nor does it hold out the excitement and relationships that the Negro movement does today. But it is the first priority, the task no one else is going to undertake, and one of the best contributions to the Negro movement itself.

The student base of our movement must remain solid and must increase greatly in scope and quality. Our primary concern is not with the immediate value of students to the Negro and economic movements, although students today are among the main catalysts of change. We are concerned also with improving our quality of work and making opportunities for radical life vocations. Whether students stay in college, or leave to work in the movement, they need constant immersion in the content of at least the social sciences and humanities. Much of this can be accomplished in study groups or conferences connected intimately with the problems of the movement. In addition, students can develop various technical and administrative skills which are invaluable in working with the movement. Finally, the campus chapter or group working in the Other America is a valuable workshop in relating academic endeavors to real human problems, building up an understanding of collective, cooperative leadership, and gaining invaluable experience in politics and organizing. Thus there is an educational need we must constantly meet, and there are ways to meet them within the active fibers of the movement itself. The result of deliberately improving the student base can be the creation, over the next several years, of the independent presence of a new radicalism.

Besides this key group of organizers, we must mention the on-campus groups, the middle-class professional and cultural workmen, and the liberal organizations, as they fit into the organizing work. What should be the relation of the economic movement to these forces? SDS still needs to keep aiming at a broad social movement, with room for moral and aesthetic concerns, work on educational reform, and other activity which argues with the prevailing normative structure of society. However, what we are concerned with here are the specific ways in which these groups fit into the economic movement. An entire paper should be done on this subject; but, again, we mean only to broach it here.

The intellectual groups, first of all, can turn their intellectual resources to the many areas of research which any self-educating and program-centered movement needs. Second, they are effective transmitting and recruiting agents in the constant search for new personnel. Third, in their part time they can be a crucial volunteer force in the movement and in the community—doing everything from busy work to helping create the lines of a winning political coalition.

The relationship with the liberal-left community is a problematic one which becomes more pressing now that domestic conflict and activity are becoming widespread. If the unions and religious groups are lumped together into a "liberal establishment," two very important but very inadequate generalizations can be made: (1) that these institutions are not primarily or above all interested in ending poverty and racism, because of the short-run threats to leadership and to organizational stability; (2) however, these are the most interested and committed of all our institutions, and we must find a close but critical relationship to them.

These generalizations disguise the fact that certain unions, certain churches, certain regional organizations, certain chapters, etc., are outstanding in their character and program—and it is through the careful selection and identification of these groups that we will find vital sources of new power and support. It would do no good to catalog these groups here; we have not explored relations sufficiently with them to have a clear working grasp of who within the liberal-left frame today can move with us into a radical coalition. Making these bonds is one of the most important horizontal-organizing responsibilities before us.

In particular, we will find rewarding contacts with individuals or small groups within the institutions who wish to push for a greater allocation of institutional resources towards the basic work we want to do. These individuals therefore are a source of left stimulation within their institutions and a source of essential support for us. Concretely, the Chicago project was supported directly at first by a tiny handful of trade unionists; now it is viewed much more sympathetically and it is the object of a healthy discussion within many of the liberal-left organizations of Chicago. Through contact with individuals in these large organizations, we gain not only support and the "cover" of legitimacy, but their transmitted wisdom, skills, and experience.

We believe, of course, that nothing less than a wholly new organized political presence in the society is needed to break the problems of poverty and racism, but it must be a force which today explores for many of its allies within the liberal institutions. Only through such development will the institutions themselves ultimately go through the healthy conflicts that lead towards greater radicalism.

As we sketch, however briefly, this configuration of united or mutually supportive groups which potentially make up our movement, it becomes clear that SDS and similar groups must consider future organizational forms with great care. It is likely, in the case of SDS, that our traditional campus-related work will suffer increasingly from (1) the weight of the "old guard," (2) the emphasis on national and local political movements at the expense of certain student-centered programs. These dangers can be averted, however, if we are able to discover new organizational forms which permit the natural beginnings of a people-centered, instead of student-centered movement. Each in its own way, many organizations can take practical steps towards these natural beginnings.

For instance in SDS: ERAP and the Peace Research and Education Project could easily become separate but overlapping forms open to students as well as "adults" while still keeping a working connection to an SDS student-centered program. This will permit a greater integration of many persons and groups hitherto "outside" our community because of its student identity.

The SDS national staff, working closely with the ERAP and PREP staffs, would need to continue campus education and action programming, not only on the peace and economic issues, but as well on educational and cultural ones. Structurally, this means SDS would become the student movement tied to ERAP and PREP but also a movement within the student community itself, politicking with the National Student Association, and the major religious and student civil rights groups as well as building the orthodox chapter units on campuses. Enlarged research and field staffs would be required, of course, for the whole complex of organizations. If from this there eventually flows a more integrated organization, a Movement for a Democratic Society, for example, that will be determined by social and psychological developments that are difficult to predict.

These developments quite naturally will involve cooperative relationships and perhaps even mergers with various civil rights, peace, labor, student, and other groups, which deeply share our goals. No doubt there will be difficulties in relationships with other organizations, too, due to political, racial, and other tensions. At present it seems very important that we strengthen our own existing resources (without becoming rigid), rather than engaging in any discussion of new horizontal relations with other groups—unless that discussion is about clearly-feasible goals based on trust.

We must also be prepared to radically change, or even dissolve, our organization if conditions someday favor a broad new movement. As insurgent movements develop on their own around the country, we anticipate the hopeful possibility that realignments will occur leading toward a new national movement. In time there might need to be a representative national framework for all this variety of local insurgency. But that will not be determined by an organizational scheme so much as by unpressured discussion and conscious attempts to find compatible local-insurgent groups which truly need the leverage that national organizations can bring. Our role today is not to "call" for that movement nor to suggest its appropriate organizational forms, but to keep the hope open in our thinking, dialogue, and, most of all, our work.

We deliberately understress ideology in these comments, largely because SDS has already made viable beginnings in this area but has not begun to deal exhaustively with questions of organizing strategy. However, there are certain "ideological problems" that demand inclusion here.

The first is that in trying to build a broad, open, and democratic movement it will be quite difficult to maintain a radical ideology. We want to stress, in a thorough way, the need for democratic participation in a society with a publicly-controlled and planned economy, which guarantees political freedom, economic and physical security, abundant education, and incentives for wide cultural variety. The initial, but not the only, problem here is that we need a way to keep discussing the problems of goals while we are immersed in day-to-day activity. There is not a natural relationship between tactics and ends—it must be cultivated in at least the few we have mentioned at an earlier point. And with the tremendous influx of staff we expect, it will be difficult to keep that general sense of openness and fraternity needed around the organization as a basis of freely-shared discussion.

We will need also a more detailed and materialistic content to our ideological thinking. It is not enough, of course, to cry out for abundance; we must be able to think fluently about what it would mean in the homes and neighborhoods and cities where people live.

But the harder problem is that we persistently will be troubled at the community level by the variety of "irrelevant" or "dangerous" issues we appear to "smuggle" into our work. There will be immense pressures, and undoubtedly vicious smear attempts (indeed, they already are beginning), which will create a demand within SDS to modify the program. There is much common sense in this view. It will make a hard life easier within the labor movement, in the community organizations where we work, etc. But if the issues really are interrelated, as we say, then in some sense we have no choice but to confront them as such. The answer would not seem to be in "postponing" the announcement of our deepest value concerns and commitments, since that merely postpones a confrontation and compounds it by making ourselves obviously hypocritical in the eyes of people with whom we are supposedly honest. The possible amelioration of this difficulty, which will be with us indefinitely, perhaps lies in the future of the poverty and racial crises, and within the matter of with whom we work and how. With an examination of these related phenomena we will bring this long commentary to a close.

There is now, of course, another war on poverty besides our own. It is not a war that will be won, however, because it is not intended to redistribute power and wealth. The Johnson "war" will not create the aggregate demand, nor establish the public planning that is required for a solid onslaught on misery. For example, the new Johnson "camps" may reduce unemployment, but mostly among those who are not counted on the unemployed rolls anyway since they never joined the labor market. Similarly with manpower retraining: The problem is not fundamentally one of readjusting the skills of the work force, although that is needed, so a "solution" along these lines is not likely either. What the "war" will do, or what we should attempt to make it do, is make the problems of poverty visible, dramatic, and legitimate to work on; stimulate the poor to further develop a consciousness of their social, rather than individual, plight; and even create the basis for class disgust with the men in Washington.

With civil rights, the crisis also involves a new piece of legislation which is not going to solve the problem, but which will create the basis for clarifying its deeper nature. Even with our doubts, we believe that over the long run the Negro movement, or the major part of it, will agree that our freedom is chained not only by racism but by economic problems general to men of all color. We very much favor the present civil rights bill to the extent that it secures some greater dignity and because of the chance it presents for wiping out the racist stalemate that delays a confrontation over the poverty that accompanies our plenty.

These issues tend to be converging. But we do not bank on tendencies, or presume that we are an elite waiting for "the masses" to see the Way. *We are people and we work with people.* Only if conscious *cooperative practice* is our main style will our ideology take on the right details; only then will it be tested and retested, changed, and finally shared with others. There is no guarantee of succeeding no matter what we do. But clearly it is not an ideology that will give us a legitimate and radical place; rather, it is the role we play in the community, as aides in developing a voice and a power among the poor. The manner of this work will be basic to any change in the direction of a new society. The meaningful participation in politics, the moral reconstruction that comes from cooperation in positive work, and the forms which evolve in this struggle may be the main social basis for a democratic America.

"An Interracial Movement of the Poor" was written as a contribution to the original organization of SDS's Economic Research and Action Project, in the winter of 1963. Tom Hayden was a graduate student at the University of Michigan, and now is a member of the staff of the Newark Community Union Project,

the ERAP project in Newark, N. J. Carl Wittman is a recent graduate of Swarthmore College, and past president of the Swarthmore Political Action Committee, a liberal student group that has had close contact with SDS.

3. The Campus Revolt

The function of the university is not simply to teach bread-winning, or to furnish teachers for the public schools or to be a centre of polite society; it is, above all, to be the organ of that fine adjustment between real life and the growing knowledge of life, an adjustment which forms the secret of civilization.

W. E. B. DUBOIS
The Souls of Black Folk

FROM THE *PORT HURON STATEMENT*

Students for a Democratic Society has been continually interested in university reform, and may be credited with sparking anti-administration sentiment on many campuses since the appearance of the Port Huron Statement *in 1962. The following excerpt from the* Statement *is something of a manifesto against the social and political conservatism of academia.*

"Students don't even give a damn about apathy," one has said. Apathy toward apathy begets a privately constructed universe, a place of systematic study schedules, two nights each week for beer, a girl or two, and early marriage—a framework infused with personality, warmth, and under control, no matter how unsatisfying otherwise.

Under these conditions university life loses all relevance to some. Four hundred thousand of our classmates leave college each year.

But apathy is not simply an attitude; it is a product of social institutions, and of the structure and organization of higher education itself. The extracurricular life is ordered according to *in loco parentis* theory, which ratifies the administration as the moral guardian of the young. The accompanying "let's pretend" theory of student extracurricular affairs validates student government as a training center for those who want to spend their lives in political pretense, and discourages initiative from more articulate, honest, and sensitive students. The bounds and style of controversy are delimited before controversy begins. The university "prepares" the student for "citizenship" through perpetual rehearsals and, usually, through emasculation of what creative spirit there is in the individual.

The academic life contains reinforcing counterparts to the way in which extracurricular life is organized. The academic world is founded in a teacher-student relation analogous to the parent-child relation which characterizes *in loco parentis*. Further, academia includes a radical separation of student from the material of study. That which is studied, the social reality, is "objectified" to sterility, dividing the student from life—just as he is restrained in active involvement by the deans controlling student government. The specialization of function and knowledge, admittedly necessary to our complex technological and social structure, has produced an exaggerated compartmentalization of study and understanding. This has contributed to: an overly parochial view, by faculty, of the role of its research and scholarship; a discontinuous and truncated understanding, by students, of the surrounding social order; a loss of personal attachment, by nearly all, to the worth of study as a humanistic enterprise.

There is, finally, the cumbersome academic bureaucracy extending throughout the academic as well as extracurricular structures, contributing to the sense of outer complexity and inner powerlessness that transforms so many students from honest searching to ratification of convention and, worse, to a numbness to present and future catastrophes. The size and financing systems of the university enhance the permanent trusteeship of the administrative bureaucracy, their power leading to a shift to the value standards of business and administrative mentality within the university. Huge foundations and other private financial interests shape the under-financed colleges and universities, making them not only more commercial but less disposed to diagnose society critically, less open to dissent. Many social and physical scientists, neglecting the liberating heritage of higher learning, develop "human relations" or "morale-producing" techniques for the corporate economy, while others exercise their intellectual skills to accelerate the arms race.

The university is located in a permanent position of social influence. Its educational function makes it indispensable and automatically makes it a crucial institution in the formation of social attitudes. In an unbelievably complicated world, it is the central institution for organizing, evaluating, and transmitting knowledge. . . . Social relevance, the accessibility to knowledge, and internal openness—these together make the university a potential base and agency in the movement of social change.

1. Any new left in America must be, in large measure, a left with real intellectual skills, committed to deliberativeness, honesty, and reflection as working tools. The university permits the political life to be an adjunct to the academic one, and action to be informed by reason.

2. A new left must be distributed in significant social roles throughout the country. The universities are distributed in such a manner.

3. A new left must consist of younger people who matured in the post-war world, and must be directed to the recruitment of younger people. The university is an obvious beginning point.

4. A new left must include liberals and socialists, the former for their relevance, the latter for their sense of thoroughgoing reforms in the system. The university is a more sensible place than a political party for these two traditions to begin to discuss their differences and look for political synthesis.

5. A new left must start controversy across the land, if national policies and national apathy are to be reversed. The ideal

university is a community of controversy, within itself and in its effects on communities beyond.

6. A new left must transform modern complexity into issues that can be understood and felt close-up by every human being. It must give form to the feelings of helplessness and indifference, so that people may see the political, social, and economic sources of their private troubles and organize to change society. In a time of supposed prosperity, moral complacency, and political manipulation, a new left cannot rely on only aching stomachs to be the engine force of social reform. The case for change, for alternatives that will involve uncomfortable personal efforts, must be argued as never before. The university is a relevant place for all of these activities.

But we need not indulge in illusions: The university system cannot complete a movement of ordinary people making demands for a better life. From its schools and colleges across the nation, a militant left might awaken its allies, and by beginning the process towards peace, civil rights, and labor struggles, reinsert theory and idealism where too often reign confusion and political barter. The power of students and faculty united is not only potential; it has shown its actuality in the South, and in the reform movements of the North.

To turn these possibilities into realities will involve national efforts at university reform by an alliance of students and faculty. They must wrest control of the educational process from the administrative bureaucracy. They must make fraternal and functional contact with allies in labor, civil rights, and other liberal forces outside the campus. They must import major public issues into the curriculum. . . .They must make debate and controversy, not dull pedantic cant, the common style for educational life. They must consciously build a base for their assault upon the loci of power.

As students for a democratic society, we are committed to stimulating this kind of social movement, this kind of vision and program in campus and community across the country. If we appear to seek the unattainable as it has been said, then let it be known that we do so to avoid the unimaginable.

THE COLLEGE COMMODITY

by Roger Siegel

An unusually potent weapon in the arsenal of collegiate traditionalism is what might be termed the "marketable goods" or "commodity" theory of higher education. It is at the base of the argument which at its simplest takes the form, "If you don't like Oberlin, leave. You chose to come here, don't forget." Or less crudely, "If you're unhappy here or dissatisfied with the kind of educational and spiritual institution that Oberlin is, you can always transfer to a college or university more in harmony with your own particular way of life, or more suited to your particular needs and interests." Like soap, one can shop for the institution that works best. If dissatisfied with one brand, one can always turn to its eager competitors . . .

The more sophisticated version of the argument is essentially "that Oberlin offers, and has every right to offer, a certain, particular form of education, including its general environment for learning. It is the Oberlin ethos of education, not the school's physical plant, that was the moving spirit of its founders and its educators, and this ethos must be the continuing concern of those entrusted with Oberlin's preservation and growth." The logic of the liberal rational creed: Truth is not prescribable. The right of a man or body of men to preach, to inculcate, to attempt to extend their beliefs as they see fit must remain unchallenged in a free society. In the same tradition, the right of transfer remains an option. If transferring is admitted impossible in a particular case, the reasoning might be that one can at least come to terms with the institution, to give it a fair chance over an extended period of time, to confront its philosophy of things with an open mind, and to wait and see how one will feel later on. The student always has the opportunity in the future to put his own views into effect, to build his own college as Oberlin was built, or, through the proper channels, to become a reforming alumnus. But Oberlin offers a certain kind of education in a certain environment; Oberlin is an avowedly x, y, and z college. Other schools are available that offer something else again. Certainly we are not happy if a student feels unfulfilled here, but his problem, outside of the counselling and guidance we can offer him, is external and not internal to Oberlin.

To one who would emphasize the humanist aspects of this same liberal-rational creed, such a "market" approach to education is likely to appear intuitively disturbing. Colleges are not soap. The concerns of education, the human spirit, the human condition, are not soap. One's own grievances about a school only secondarily arise from any "economic" considerations or other relatively abstract considerations. In my own case they have arisen more directly from personal feelings of pain, injustice, or bitterness when I have felt myself or another the victim of institutional failings or constraints, when the dissident have been pursued as deviant, depraved, or merely "disturbed," the protesting or bored explained away as "irresponsible." They have been due to what I have felt to be a failure or refusal to take "human" truths into account, or to a tendency to distort them, in the name of a ready principle or convenient "necessity." Too often the human condition has succumbed to the ethos, or its most militant champions; the "lazy" and "irresponsible" have born the brunt of institutional irresponsibility and laziness. It is disturbing that in an institution dedicated to the free pursuit of truth, argument can rest with reaffirmations of the *fact* of the ethos, but offer nothing in its defense.

But it is true that a recognition of the real problems involved rarely solves genuine differences, even if it may make a settlement more reasonable and more just. And it does no good to question the integrity of the argument's proponents, or accuse them of wanting to depersonalize the university. They turn to the market argument precisely for salvation *from* the market—to prevent the corruption of the liberal ethos by its detractors in the outside world. And though it is by no means the only or even perhaps the best approach to the problem, it does us very well indeed to consider the "economics" of education. Rather than deny that we are dealing with a market commodity, we might recognize instead that we are dealing with quite a different kind of commodity in quite a different kind of market.

It is precisely that colleges are not soap. I might well be held extravagant if I could not find a brand among the bewildering variety available on the market a soap that suits my tastes and needs, even my peculiarities. (Leaving aside the important, but here unnecessary complication of cost.) Even then, I and my fellow dissidents, constituting an unfulfilled consumer market, could appeal to the profit motive of manufacturers. However, there is something less than a bewildering variety or even a generous sprinkling of small, high-level coed liberal arts colleges, all with top-rate conservatories and art museums, a substantial library, and an unusually strong economics department; institutionalizing different philosophies of student academic and moral freedom, differing in policies on course requirements, testing-out opportunities, and opportunities for independent work, research, and "creative expression." There exists, as far as I know, only one college with the former, and unless the latter are to be considered trivial, Oberlin's uniqueness stands as an important example that our higher education is a rare and scarce resource. There is hardly an abundance of variously situated colleges and universities competing for the allegiances of variously situated students, or for that matter, of faculty, administrators, and funds. In this instance, abundance is a deception, not merely because of differences in cost, location, size, and standards, but primarily because the college serves considerably more and more complex functions for the individual than does, for instance, soap. More factors are important and mere numerical similarities are less significant. Despite the broader range available to the student if he decides on the lower ranks of state universities or small coed colleges (which seem in any case more to imitate than to compete with each other), this student finds himself with a very limited number of choices within his acceptable range, and the best of all available worlds which he can choose may be hardly the best of all possible worlds, either in terms of his all too inadequate early insights or his later wisdom.

The same is of course true for the faculty member. Faced with the same limited facilities, he is going to base his decisions on any number of considerations, including salary, opportunity for advancement and research, the quality and emphasis of his department, the quality of the student body, living quarters, cultural and educational facilities available for his children, neighborhood, and proximity to cultural centers. He rarely chooses (or is chosen) on the basis of the school's ethos, which he probably believes in or adheres to only in a very general sense. Even if he desires to make a primarily "ethosical" choice, he can rarely afford to. On the other hand, competent faculty members are scarce, and the school is forced to rely on a diversified faculty, with different moral upbringings, educational backgrounds, and educational philosophies. Depending on the particular balance of supply and demand, either the teacher or the schools may have the favored choice at the moment. But lacking the advantages of a self-perpetuating sect which may characterize the completely parochial school, both are forced to "compromise."

This doesn't mean, of course, that the school doesn't desire and even encourage diversity in both its student body and its faculty, as Oberlin certainly does to a degree. It may be quite happy to reap the fruits of its relative educational monopoly and draw into its campus all kinds of students—trained, taught, and fashioned with the resources of the entire intellectual world. It may even incorporate diversity into its ethos. If it does lure diverse people and ideas to its campus, however, it must consider the psychological, sociological, and academic consequences of putting all its animals into four-foot cages, of encouraging diverse elements while admitting only a narrow framework for their expression. Even the Army has had to reform somewhat in the light of sociological and psychological realities. The colleges are faced with certain moral considerations as well.

The implications of recognizing the college as a commodity discredit the "commodity theory." The student has contracted into the complete and inviolate ethos of the school, however seen and interpreted, with withdrawal his sole option. The view is invalid if only because he was not given his pick of intricate ethoses.

It is an invalid view if only because the greatness, or even the continued existence of the school, are dependent on the resources and products not of a school of thought but of the world of thought and the limited opportunities for their employment. And only in a very limited and general sense is the ethos a factor in their allocation. Oberlin cannot claim itself to be an "avowedly *x*, *y*, and *z* college" that also "avowedly happens to have a monopoly of X, Y, and Z scarce resources." Like it or not the educational advantages that a college has to offer are largely dependent on its relative monopoly of valuable scarce resources.

Isn't my argument, though, vulnerable in its very guts? What if the ethos has been crucial to the growth and success of the school? Why can't the ethos be argued and defended in terms of its products? Why can't it be shown, in addition, that certain safeguards and limitations are necessary to the more important benefits that Oberlin offers?

I would grant this point with glee. It can, it should, it must be shown. The switch is delicate, subtle, but crucial—it is the tradition itself, not the *a priori* right of the tradition, on which the argument hinges. The tradition is placed on its merits. It is made arguable, subject to dissection, division, and dissent.

I may be overemphasizing the importance of this shift in position. It hardly settles matters, it hardly resolves conflicts—an open ear isn't an open mind, open minds aren't always of the same mind. But besides being fertile ground for aphorisms, this shift in position does provide useful results. First, it distinguishes the interpretors of the ethos. It clarifies the obvious—that the ethos is not monolithic and neither is its legion of adherents. The garden is put on show: One man's rose is found to be another man's thorn; what are clear benefits to some are seen as dangers or necessary evils by others; different elements of the tradition will be argued as the crucial ones. Secondly, it forces a painstaking reappraisal of causal links. One can argue that "clear necessities" are unfounded or erroneous or attack the "It might work at —— but it could never work at Oberlin because . . ." formulation. The fine in the ethos can be shaved of vacant assertions and pompous norms. Historical fact can be separated from causal necessity: For example, referring to the claim that the magnificence of Allen Art Museum has depended upon the dedication of men whose profound insights into the educational and spiritual values of art were connected with the educational and spiritual values of art that Oberlin has preserved, one would be able to argue philosophically to the separation of educational and artistic insights from ethical and religious beliefs, personally to the distinction between dedication and concurrence, empirically to the development of other fine art museums outside the Oberlin Gestalt, historically to the intellectual contributions of many diverse beliefs and commitments, economically to the financial and material contributions of many who were motivated by any number of reasons (including the relative scarcity of college art museums) to bestow their beneficence on Oberlin. One has open to him the fashioning of new links, the drawing of new chains. Yes, yes, yes, yes, yell all you want, but if they just won't listen?

It is true that this article has been concerned not so much with a philosophy or methodology of activism as with a justification of activism against what I have argued is an illegitimate weapon that seeks to smother activism in the name of its own liberal creed. Yet I think it leads to more than just the conclusion that the tradition must be argued on its own merits. A recognition of the vague and often ephemeral relationship between the school's ethos and its success implies that the activist need not be limited to presenting his humble pleas only to see them rejected at the next meeting of men's board or the board of trustees. He has a right to more effective voice than that. He is not begging for recognition by the cult, or merely that he be allowed to plead before it. He is demanding a right to effect what is a part of his own birthright, his right to his nation's facilities for education. Reformists or activists have the right to avail themselves of every legitimate political means to convince and to force change, and by legitimate I mean within the "ethos" of a democratic society.

My own views, briefly, are that a good strategic and moral assessment of available means must recognize political and social realities; what stands in the way are not merely the idealisms of dedicated men, but also departmental jealousies and rivalries, red tape, academic stasis, external pressures from other interested parties, alumni ignorance, and the private and personal conflicts of private and personal men. It is important that such efforts for change be "political" efforts, based on what blandly might be termed "power realities" and not, as has often characterized Oberlin politics, irrational expressions of what may have been quite legitimate personal grievances. An excellent example of good political strategy was the 1957 Oberlin student movement to abolish compulsory chapel attendance, which culminated in 500 X's signed on attendance slips during a particular assembly. This strategy, which was preceded by all the usual attempts at less "forceful" political solutions and which came face to face with precisely the problem of the immovable ethos, made use of the political power of the parents, who would have vigorously opposed any mass suspension for violation of what appeared an undemocratic and immovable regulation, and forced successful "negotiations." Another example has been the efforts of the *Oberlin Review** to spotlight alternative policies in effect at other colleges and universities, and to analyze their problems and effects. The "Four-Class Dorm" series was an unusually comprehensive and insightful treatment.

I will probably be accused of advocating anarchical procedures, whatever those might be. A fascinating analogy would be the facilities and scarce resources represented by cities, and how one would treat the following argument: "If you don't like Chicago, you don't have to live here. You can always move to San Francisco"—particularly if cities weren't subject to elections and democratic government. I'm not arguing that cities are the same as colleges, although there are important similarities, nor am I quite advocating that the board of trustees be extended to include the student body. However, I think that some differences in politics are necessitated by some differences in the form of government: for example, the intervention of foreign powers.

The argument has been used by some people in power in some instances, especially as a last resort when the logic of the

* [Editors' Note: The student newspaper at Oberlin College, usually fairly liberal.]

case has turned against them. My purpose was not to stress the frequency of the "commodity" argument's use, but to show it invalid. If its actual use has been exaggerated, all the better.

Roger Siegel graduated from Oberlin College in 1963. "The College Commodity" originally appeared in Focus, *an Oberlin student publication, Vol. III, 1963.*

THEODICY OF 1984: THE PHILOSOPHY OF CLARK KERR

by Bruce Payne, David Walls, and Jerry Berman

Today there are two words that describe and characterize the common bond among the majority of American intellectuals; those words are *confusion* and *concern.* As truly political men, we are concerned about our common life, with respect to both its meaning and its purpose. We desire to act and yet we cannot seem to answer the question "For what?" Purposes do not appear as "self-evident" in the age of impersonal government and mass organizations. The meaning of the American political consensus seems to blur. For instance, we rightly insist on protecting liberty, and yet the meaning of liberty seems interchangeable with the meaning of alienation and loneliness. Americans have always pursued "prosperity," but today they find that prosperity is not necessarily interchangeable with happiness. In the end we often find ourselves unable to act or to read meaning into life. With Paul Goodman, we find more and more that we are "growing up absurd."

Few men in American life are more concerned with the present and future of American society than Clark Kerr, President of the University of California and past Chairman of the Institute of Industrial Relations at the Berkeley campus. Not only has he given much time to research the present trends of the American community, but he has set down his ideas and findings in several pamphlets, articles, and his most recent book, *Industrialism and*

Industrial Man. (Besides these important contributions, Clark Kerr has served the public as a labor management arbitrator.)

Whereas most of us are confused and concerned about the prospects for America, Clark Kerr claims to know this future in many of its more important aspects. More importantly he believes this future is "necessary" and "logical," and, more profoundly, an improvement over the present state of American life. Since it is a better future for Americans, we are encouraged at least explicitly to act in accordance with the prophetic vision and help make it a reality. Not the vision of the philosopher or moralist, but the vision of the social scientist—making predictions and calculations on the basis of known facts—is the presumed meaning of Clark Kerr's future society.

History, says Kerr, reveals "a pattern to all the apparent chaos" about us. It is the "process of industrialization." Once a country begins to industrialize, its history can follow only the logic of industrialism, which is "designed to be the ever-lasting thread of the future." In Kerr's opinion there is no turning back and there is no alternative to industrialism once a country has chosen to industrialize.

We become suspicious of this interpretation of history when we discover that the end of industrialization is "pluralistic industrialism" for all countries. The nature of this "good industrial society" happens to be the *American* answer to the questions of industrialization and the basis of the decisions by the American industrial elite. Pluralistic industrialism turns out to be the result of American culture, ideology, and organization.

In America the cause and legitimacy of industrialization can be ascribed only to "liberty." Time and again Kerr defines liberty as "the absence of restraint" and the right to "act as you please," which are our common notions of liberty. America in the Declaration of Independence happened to desire "happiness." Happiness, declares Kerr, is prosperity. Prosperity is the promised land for which we make sacrifices. From this seed industrialism begins and continues to be the essence of American history. From this viewpoint Americans did not contract for an equal opportunity to live and develop their potentials, but rather their agreement was based on a desire to gain "satisfactions" from "wealth." Upon this desire, rational or irrational, there has been built the industrial complex we know today. For Kerr there is no use being concerned for what we have given up in exchange for this age of large, impersonal organizations and mass society. There is no escaping the logic of industrialization.

Although the general trend toward industrial society is clear and seemingly irresistible, Kerr argues, the exact characteristics of the new order are not inevitable. To predict, one must first choose. What is chosen and what is required by the "logic of industrialism" is often unclear, but it is certainly clear that Kerr prescribes the kind of society that he predicts.

This new society is to be a society of the "managers and the managed." "Everywhere there develops a complex web of rules binding the worker into the industrial process, to his job, to his community, to patterns of behavior."

These rules cover every aspect of economic life. They are to be devised by the managers, who are the leaders of the "New society, the vanguard of the future." Interestingly enough, the managers are also to perform the "role of protest," though it is to be a "more restricted and passive role."

Some of the specific features of this society might be pointed out. Religion, custom, and tradition, Kerr and his associates argue, will eventually be destroyed by industrialism. Some traditional institutions will be preserved, but most of them will not. Agriculture for instance, is not a way of life to be preserved, but will become rather an industry with a single purpose of the production of food in the most efficient possible manner. This stands in striking contrast to the words emblazoned over the doors of the Agricultural Hall on the Berkeley campus. Only a few hundred yards from Kerr's office in the modern University Hall, these words state the historic aim of the School of Agriculture:

TO RESCUE FOR HUMAN SOCIETY
THE NATIVE VALUES OF RURAL LIFE

The family, too, is to change in character. The destruction of the institution of the extended family seems already to have taken place in advanced industrial societies like our own. "There is no place for the extended family in the industrial society; it is on balance an impediment to requisite mobility." The function of the nuclear family is constricted. It is to be "largely a source of labor supply, a unit of decision-making for household expenditures, and a unit of cultural activity."

This sort of family is necessary to provide the society with the mobility required by constantly changing occupations and places of work. Certain jobs become obsolete in industrial society, and retraining will be necessary.

The point of this argument is that Kerr intends to argue quite seriously that the "web of rules" is the only force holding society together. These rules of the game determine the division of labor and the power relationships in the society, and for Kerr, these are the primary factors in the society.

What this society means to individuals is broadly defined in the four-man study. Regarding the worker, they [the authors] state that "in his working life he will be subject to great conformity imposed not only by the enterprise manager but also by the state and by his own occupational association. For most people any true scope for the independent spirit on the job will be missing."

There is to be little danger of strife between the managers and the managed, for most of the members of society will have both types of roles. Moreover, *there will be little cause for strife.* The economic wants of the people will be more and more satisfied, though never fully, since aspirations will rise proportionally.

More importantly, there will be little conflict because all the basic questions have been answered. A consensus will have been developed around the goals of production efficiency and individual self-interest that will allow conflict only at lower levels. Society has achieved consensus and it is perhaps less necessary for Big Brother to exercise political control. Nor in the Brave New World need genetic and chemical means be employed to avoid revolt. There will not be any revolt anyway, except little bureaucratic revolts that can be handled piecemeal.

Under this system, ideology and politics (and Kerr seems characteristically to make little distinction) become "bureaucratic gamesmanship." Politics is still seen as conflict, but that conflict will be over narrower issues. "It will be less between the broad programs of capital and labor and of agriculture and industry; and more over budgets, rates of compensation, work norms, job assignments."

Nineteenth century Utopians would have found little which is original in Kerr's new society. It is fundamentally identical with the managerialism of St. Simon, the militarized capitalism of Bellamy, and even, perhaps surprisingly, with the old Marxian dream of a society where "the government of persons is replaced by the administration of things"—because under its beneficent aegis persons have been reduced to things. . . .

Students will be particularly interested in the position of education in the new society. Even after accepting industrialism's goal of prosperity, one might well feel there is a certain inconsistency in having a leading theoretician of industrial organization as the President of one of the nation's leading universities. It is disconcerting to realize that these two roles are not seen as contradictory in the least by Kerr. As the "handmaiden of industrialism," education has itself become a leading industry. Kerr considers education to be a functional imperative to an order based on technology. As there is a "relatively smaller place for the humanities and the arts," the system of higher education becomes keyed to the production of specialized careers—professionals, technicians, and managers.

The principal functions of education are to train the bulk of the population to "receive instructions, follow instructions, keep records," and to train the managers, engineers, and civil servants to operate this system. The increasing importance of the funds obtained for research activities adds to the need for patterning the university more along the lines of the industrial organization. Each participant has his carefully delineated role within the "great web of rules," the authority allotted out to each person is carefully subordinated to the principle of efficient productions and control.

Kerr is well aware that intellectuals and students can often be most disruptive to the carefully laid plans the managerial bureaucracy has for the new society. Since Kerr assumes the goals of society are already embodied in the things that be, students and intellectuals "are by nature irresponsible. . .not fully answerable for consequences. They are as a result never fully trusted by anybody, including themselves." Especially by Clark Kerr, we are tempted to add. At the same time the conflict within societies takes place increasingly in the realm of ideas. Thus the student can be a "tool as well as a source of danger," in these intellectual skirmishes. Even so Kerr also remarks that "in some cases students may be taught things they must 'unlearn' if they are to make good production workers."

Kerr's history as President of the University of California suggests how he proposes to control this apparently natural tendency of some students to refuse to see education as merely another technical procedure designed to fit them to a specialized niche in the process of production. In October, 1959, the "Kerr directives" were first promulgated under the guise of being a liberalization of University policy toward political activity. A quick series of "clarifications" removed certain of the more objectionable provisions—such as restrictions on the power of the academic senate and such obviously unconstitutional provisions as qualifications on the freedom of students to lobby in the legislature on matters concerning the University. While the directive did certainly liberalize certain rules on political speakers and the distribution of literature, the attempt to codify the regulations on the student government amounted to a severe reduction in the actual scope of its traditional authority. The old restrictions had originated in the political stress of the thirties and the later period of McCarthyism. Under a principle of "salutary neglect" they had been enforced only intermittently.

By the fall of 1961 the major points of the clarified directives seemed to establish two general policies: 1) an "open forum" for discussion of public issues, and 2) "limited purpose" student government. The open forum was tested at the UCLA campus by an invitation to Dorothy Healy, former chairman of the Communist Party of Southern California, to speak on the campus. At this time an old graduate of the Berkeley campus promised the University a million dollar trust fund on the condition that no members of the Communist Party be allowed to use University facilities. President Kerr immediately stated that it had been the policy of the Board of Regents since 1944 to prohibit Communists from speaking on the campus on the grounds of "incompatability with the educational ends of the University." This line of reasoning becomes more comprehensible if one assumes the end of the university education to be the production of individuals with the particular skills required by the existing industrial order more than the preparation for citizenship and training in distinguishing truth from error.

The "limited purpose" nature of the student government revolves around the "on campus–off campus" distinction and the question of the right of student government to represent the interests of the students whenever this may be opposed to the interest of the administration. The National Student Association has held that these distinctions indicate a grave misunderstanding of the student community. To limit student government to "on campus" issues, narrowly defined, is to deny that students have any common interests whatsoever outside the price of cheeseburgers in the cafeteria and the type of background music to be played in the student union. This reasoning parallels Kerr's concern for protecting the individual from the associations to which he belongs—be they labor unions, professional societies, or student bodies.

At the bottom of Kerr's theoretical concern for restricting the scope of student government is his concept of the "absolutism of the group," the strangely vague process through which the individual is tyrannized by these intermediary organizations between himself and the state. There seems to be a definite, if curious, relation between Kerr and defenders of the "Beat Generation" who maintain that man can gain some portion of freedom and attain a certain measure of human virtue only in isolation, never through acting in concert with other men.

The most recent addition to the Kerr directive was announced to the students this past year. Student political groups (YD's, YR's,

YAF, SLATE, etc.) are forbidden to use the campus for their business meetings on the grounds that the University's charter states that the University must be kept free of "political and sectarian influence." The Kerr administration does not recognize the argument that it is precisely when they yield to the pressure of small but vocal elements in the state—as by exiling campus politics—that they place themselves subject to political influence. But it is not to be expected that the University would recognize any obligation to encourage student participation in politics. Kerr believes it is sufficient to allow these groups to sponsor speakers on campus. In a manner very consistent with the rest of his system of "liberal pluralism" Kerr refuses to admit the necessity of connecting thought with political action.

The new society of industrial pluralism, while requiring a great degree of conformity in the work individuals do, is designed to increase their degree of individual freedom. "The great new freedom, it is argued, may come in the leisure of individuals. Higher standards of living, more leisure, more education, make this not only possible but almost inevitable. This will be the happy hunting ground for the independent spirit. Along with the bureaucratic conservatism of economic and political life may well go a New Bohemianism in the other aspects of life."

This is not an unusual sort of argument, particularly in America. One assumption behind it is that men are motivated primarily by self-interest, and that freedom is the ability to do as one likes. It is an argument in the Madisonian tradition, and a number of fairly standard criticisms may be applied to it. With many others, we would challenge this idea of irresponsible freedom. The freedom to do what one feels he ought to do, the freedom to do one's duty, are concepts which argue against the one-sided view that man is no more than a self-interested beast. And certainly freedom for economic self-interest can hardly hold much meaning for individuals in an economy of abundance.

Further comments at the end of *Industrialism and Industrial Man* remind us that the arguments made by Kerr and his associates go far beyond the arguments of the eighteenth century liberals. "The new slavery and the new freedom go hand in hand.

Utopia never arrives, but men may well settle for the benefits of a greater scope for freedom in their personal lives at the cost of considerable conformity in their working lives. If pluralistic industrialism can be said to have a split personality, then the individual in this society will lead a split life too; he will be a pluralistic individual with more than one pattern of behavior and one dominant allegiance."

The new system, then, involves not only a division of the society, but the division of the individual. The separation of the parts of an individual's life prevents any one part from having overriding importance. Kerr has argued in the past that groups are dangerous because they tend to interfere with individual freedom. The aim, therefore, is to prevent any one group or institution from having any great part of the loyalty of an individual. It may be worth noting that loyalty is not a word that one finds often in the works of President Kerr. When it does appear, in fact, it is usually found to be "loyalty to the plant," or something similar.

Kerr rejects, notably, any idea of civic or political loyalty. His citizen is a "private citizen" and not a public one. For civic or political loyalty demands that the individual integrate his diverse roles into a whole personality, just as it demands that he accept responsibility for the whole political society. This fact lies behind Aristotle's dictum that man is a "political animal," one who discovers himself and his being only through political society. Loyalties, in Kerr's argument, are specialized, fragmented into "roles"; they reflect Kerr's complacency regarding the individual of split or multiple personalities. A man is, Josiah Royce argued, what he is loyal to, and he urged nineteenth century Americans to "be lóyal to loyalty," and to the idea of the whole man. Kerr rejects politics and civic loyalty because he rejects man as such. He accepts a "system" in which men are only parts, and schizophrenic parts at that.

Challenging this system, we would argue that it carries with it a great potential for destroying itself, and with terrible results for the citizens who make it up. We are convinced that at least for most people, this system would not create the "happy hunting ground of the independent spirit." It would rather lead to a heightened sense of alienation, both from the society itself and from other individuals. It is that very lack of a sense of control over one's own environment that has produced such feelings in America. It seems, moreover, that the closer we move toward the industrial society, the more we find ourselves faced with boredom and apathy and alienation.

A little reflection reminds us that these feelings are dangerous. Bored and alienated people do surprising and destructive things to escape their sense of boredom. They are seldom moved, but when they are, the bitterness produced by years of unsatisfied needs may vent itself in reckless fury.

Whether such destruction results or not, however, makes little difference if the feelings of the individuals in the system are as we have argued. Kerr's system throws the individual back completely on himself, with no serious support or loyalty from any group or idea except the "web of rules." Intermediate loyalties between those to family and to nation are destroyed or rationalized in the terms of self-interest. Kerr argues that his "system" makes "Big Brother" unnecessary. It is too efficient to need him—a kind of rationalized 1984. Yet when the groups between the individual and the state become so specialized and remote as to lose all meaning, when the individual loses all sense of a "public," Big Brother is not far off. For the isolated individual is unable to act with his fellows to control the system. Convinced of his own isolation, he can acquire the sense that the "system" is concerned for him and for his welfare at all only by a fevered personal identification with an "ego-ideal," with the Messianic chieftain who is at once "one" with the citizen and elevated far above him. "Big Brother" arises when man can no longer find brothers of his own.

It should not be thought that the basic themes in the predictions and prescriptions for the new society are the creations of President Kerr and his associates. The basic choices have been made and are being made by the populace, even in Kerr's eyes. We dislike President Kerr's picture of education and the new society intensely, but we are forced to admit that this picture is true to the standard of American fears of loyalty and prejudice against politics. The American people have believed in self-interest, and many of them sense that this ethic has cheated them. As yet, however, they have been unable, in all but a few instances, to substitute a new one.

Yet there is at least one ideal that still survives in our society, although it has been a part of our civilization for more than 800 years. That ideal is a university, a community of scholars bound together by the search for knowledge and truth, and feeling a responsibility to their society. That ideal declares that teaching and learning are more important than economic self-interest, and where that ideal has been a reality, some men have been able to face the future with self-confidence and hope.

We believe the defense of that vision and the attempt to make it a reality are profoundly important. For in fact, the vision is losing to Kerr's adherents, and not only losing in California. The defeat of the vision of the University is, of course, only part of the general social process of which Kerr is both analyst and advocate. But students have a special duty to combat that process on their own part of the battlefield: the university campus. "History" may be moving in the way Kerr believes it to be. *Brave New World* or *1984* may be the destiny of men in some ultimate sense. We do not believe that this must be the case. But in any event there is all the difference in the world between resisting any such trend and advocating it, between hoping to postpone 1984 to 2025 and hoping to establish it, as Kerr seems to, in 1975.

Bruce Payne, David Walls, and Jerry Berman, when this article was written, were students at the University of California (Berkeley) and members of SLATE, Berkeley's liberal political party. "Theodicy of 1984" originally appeared in The Activist, *Vol. 2, 1962.*

THE STUDENT RIOTS AT BERKELEY: DISSENT IN THE MULTIVERSITY

by Joseph Paff, Bill Cavala, and Jerry Berman

"The intellectuals (including the university students) are a particularly volatile element . . . capable of extreme reactions . . . more extreme than any group in society. They are by nature irresponsible, in the sense that they have no continuing commitment to any single institution or philosophical outlook and they are not fully answerable for consequences. They are, as a result, never fully trusted by anybody, including themselves."

CLARK KERR in *Industrialism and Industrial Man*

The University of California at Berkeley has earned a reputation as a "hot-bed of radicals" because of a small group of students who have demonstrated the audacity to be excited by such issues as free speech, academic freedom, political participation, and awareness. They have rarely been able to dent the apathetic detachment of their fellow students, but they have succeeded in finding successors for themselves and maintaining a continuous and vocal expression of dissent. Amid the quiet ebb and flow of dutiful students preparing to take up positions in the society of affluence and technical progress, they can be "seen" and "heard" by the starkness of the distinction which divides them from their fellows.

This activity arouses criticism from the respectable and the right-wing among the public, and provokes fear and hostility among administrators. Gradually, then, a net of rules has been built up restricting campus political activity to a bit of ground in front of the University, where the bearded and the vested vie with more acceptable organizations like the YD's or the NAACP in soliciting funds and membership.

This September, the University barred political activity in the last bastion as "illegal" and contrary to existing regulations. The prohibition provoked what can only be called a student rebellion. An estimated 5,000 students have participated in demonstrations; faculty, press, public, and politician have all expressed themselves in varying degrees of vehemence; the riot squad of the city of Oakland was called in by the University. Nor has the crisis ended. The Free Speech Movement (FSM) has managed to sustain interest and activity among its almost faceless mass of adherents.

Yet this rebellion has not been "building" to a climax through social or historical forces. The student society, impermanent and transient, does not build movements. The perfect example of the society of the alienated and the uprooted, it produces rebellions, dictated by the force of circumstance rather than the force of history. From a single student defying University regulations by setting up his organization's card table, a movement involving thousands of students demanding their rights springs up. More astonishingly, such a movement has been sustained against fantastic odds and threats of violence. Curiosity, if not concern for civil liberties or the American university, make it a movement worthy of attention.

The sequence of beginning events is simple: The defiant student set up the table; a police car appeared to take the student away. To the politically active student, in each instance, the car symbolized the action of unjust authority and the threat to his political rights. To the rest of the students, the car was a source of excitement, curiosity, and a degree of sympathy. The political students organized a sit-in around the car to prevent the student from being taken away; the apoliticals joined in.

Revolt against a police car seemed legitimate to many of the apoliticals. The fraternity student who works off much energy in the purposeless collection of street signs or red lanterns found it much more marvelous to capture a police car. He might not sit down; he would, however, very likely stand around. This is a form of rebellion the American community has always condoned: the "honest prank" of the "boys will be what the community wants them to be: tight fun" even if it injures people, wrecks property, or disgraces the community. Students, to some extent, will be what the community wants them to be: Tight political controls and loose social controls produce the expression of resentments in useless and purposeless aggression. Fraternity students came to one demonstration to drink, jeer, and throw eggs; the object of hostility was of little importance, whether it was the police or the FSM.

There were others among the outer ring who sympathized with the demand for free speech. Normally, they feared to act because of anxiety regarding clearances or jobs, or were unable to act for lack of a vehicle of expression. Some who felt politics to be "unreal" still felt it unjust to whisk a student off in a police car for so trivial an offense; indeed, it was unjust because politics was unreal.

For all these reasons, the students of a large, anonymous university lost, for a moment, their feeling of being strangers to one another. Different in their motives, they lost their fear of difference in a common feeling of rebellion, and in a sense of equality in banding together.

All this is easy to explain. It is difficult, by contrast, to capture the tone of subsequent events which transformed a formless rebellion into a dedicated movement. Those who knew the history of student conflicts with the administration expected students to be defeated by feelings of impotence and to relapse into attitudes of apathy. This time, however, there was something different. The sheer size of the crowd which had assembled provided a new excitement almost akin to exhaltation.

One of the students, Mario Savio, leapt to the roof of the police car and began to address the students. Savio's action captured the imagination of the crowd; he began by talking to them, and ended by talking *for* them because he gave form and voice to the symbols of their rebellion. The police car, the crowd itself, the administration building in the background—all the symbols of resented authority and group strength found their way into his address. "We," he shouted, "are being denied our rights by 'them' "—pointing to the deans assembled on the balcony of the administration building. "We will stand around this police car until they negotiate with us." Savio's ability to symbolize and articulate the crowd's sentiments gave form and foundation to an otherwise easily dispersed enthusiasm. Elected to represent the group in negotiating with the administration, he was able to unite student groups and student government leaders of varying persuasions under his leadership in an almost prodigious united front.

The issue was as American as free speech. Yet if it is remembered that it is "free speech" in the particular sense of being "against the denials of the university," the reason for the continuance of group sentiment and cohesiveness becomes even more apparent. The dangers to free speech are so many and diffuse in American society that a fight for free speech must have its visible enemies. Once the enemy is a university administration, the meaning of the fight also takes on deeper salience for the student. Free speech becomes the fight of the individual for his own recognition as a *person*—a recognition of his significance and dignity. A rebellion over free speech is a protest against bureaucracy and its impersonal processing of the student, against the petty and trivial red tape, the two-dollar fine to drop a course late, the penalty for a misplaced IBM card, the misspelled name on a form card, the many windows and forms one must confront to make a change, express a grievance, solve a problem. Maybe this is all "necessary" because of the size of a "multiversity," but no one has to value its anonymity, its dispersion of passion, its enervating pinpricks. A student rebellion, gathered in front of a building or in hallways, form windows, arrows pointing the right direction for a line to form, has to evoke sentiment and resentment which, when allowed to coalesce, is very difficult to disperse. Reason must also deal with the reasonableness of the fragmented person who wants to be a whole man.

This movement became something more than the action of "irresponsible" children. Students discovered that a basic commitment could overcome fears of impotence, exposure, and ridicule. Having come to "play," they stayed to defend their dignity: They demanded a different role than the accepted image of the student as a fumbling adolescent. Some fraternities—as the egg-throwing incident demonstrated—retained their childish attitude; over 650 other students from the same fraternities signed a petition to apologize for the egg-throwers and to commit themselves to the basic goals of the movement. For the moment, the student had become an adult concerned about his university, its meaning, and freedom.

As a movement, the students have to be taken seriously. Their dedication and coherence were demonstrated that Friday night when the students surrounding the police car held their position in the face of 500-1,000 police drawn from Berkeley and Oakland. Conflict was averted, but for a time it seemed imminent. There was talk of tear gas; a student leader advised students to loosen their ties and "go limp" and "take the number of the policeman" if they were hit. The scene had a certain macabre quality: The President of the University, who had called in the police to break up the so-called "riot," appeared at the disaster area to get a "feeling" about it.

Many police, tense and expectant, complained of a "loss of morale" when finally denied an opportunity to demonstrate their efficiency. Faculty and administrators drew analogies to the labor disputes of the thirties and forties; some saw the work of "outside agitators" as responsible. (One faculty member was in tears, predicting violence and curiously asserting that it was "all my fault.") The San Francisco newspapers had predicted a riot—calling out a crowd of bystanders expecting bloodshed. Terror and the expectation of violence were on every hand; the verge of chaos had been reached.

All of this, parenthetically, took place on the eve of Parents' Day and a football game. It was insane and it was terrifying, throwing into stark contrast the old university and the new, the trivial and the important. It illustrated the tension of the university cast in the modern world, unsure of its identity, a sprawling jumble of buildings and people desperately confused about its own meaning.

To the "public"—that unknown and amorphous body to which every interpreter of the situation is forced to appeal—student life is a strange and bizarre condition that is little understood. Higher education on a mass scale is a new development and few people have anything other than a high school experience to draw upon for comprehension. It is this experience, and the image of the

University presented in the mass media, that structure the public's perception and understanding.

The "picture" of students and the University presented in the press is conveyed in a medley of overlapping and conflicting clichés —frequently presented simultaneously. Since high school experience provides no relevant analogies for understanding student *political* activity, it is the clichés that shape the "public" picture.

One such cliché ignores the political aspects of what occurs and places demonstrations in the same category as football game "rallies" or "panty-raids." Such activities can be smilingly and condescendingly shrugged off with a paternalistic admonition, or perhaps lead to a "they ought to get tough with those damn kids."

A second myth sees the demonstrations as a result of "subversion" by those who would channel the energies of youth into dangerous political paths. There are many who would argue that this subversion occurs in the classrooms; others point to "outside agitators," or such "non-students" (a recent addition to the list of "subverters") as returning SNCC workers from the South. Under no circumstances could it be imagined that there is any spontaneous root to political action. That a young man would shout drunken obscenities at a "Big Game Rally" is natural, but that he would demonstrate for his political rights, he had first to be brainwashed by propagandists.

Third, a few journalists see student protest as an expression of legitimate grievances. It appears only in the stories of those reporters who take enough interest in what is going on to go beyond university handouts and thirty minutes of camera snapping at a noon rally and actually talk to those concerned.

All of these "interpretations" were superimposed on the protest demonstrations of the past six weeks—frequently all in the same day's paper. A wonderful palimpsest was created in the *Oakland Tribune* when one picture presented pretty girls sitting in warm sun, a second showed a student addressing the crowd, and a third was a subtle close-up of the Essentials of Marxism—with a helpful caption, "a textbook of Marxism was among the crowd."

The first cliché vanished first; the Indian Summer theorists with their meterological explanations were discredited when the activities survived a few cold wet days. The other theories remain to this date—and both hold sway not just with the press, but with the faculty and administration as well.

That the "old style" administrator should be unable to see the possibility of political action that is not the result of "outsiders" or "subversive" students is not astonishing. The rah-rah spirit of pre-multiversity days lives on in many an aging dean, and Berkeley's world-famous panty raid is less than 10 years old. The *in loco parentis* mentality is still present; thus Vice-Chancellor Sheriffs can smile at the outer ring of beer-drinking fraternity boys and talk of their "piss and vinegar" in defense of the University (forgetting so soon panty raids and the massive senseless riots of 1957) whilst maintaining a position of utter intransigence toward the political demonstrators in the center.

The actions of President Kerr, nationally famous educator and labor mediator, champion of the "new style," "liberal" successor to the conservative Robert Gordon Sproul, are much more difficult to comprehend. With the selection of Kerr, liberals and intellectuals breathed a sigh of relief—the closed "old boy" world seemed shattered and the hope of decentralization promised a more open system both intellectually and politically.

How then do we explain the sudden restrictions on student activity and, more seriously, the near insanity of his reaction to the subsequent student protests? To consider the former question first, we come face to face with the multiversity in all its "multiness"; *who* made the decision? Despite the theory of decentralization, the fact is that Kerr has pursued a policy of concentration of power, reflected in consistent appointment of weak men to every major subordinate position. The price of such a policy—a pervasive incompetence at lower levels—can in fact lead to a decrease in control when the weak-sister appointees fail to recognize the consequences of seemingly minor decisions.

Aside from the specific decision and its bungled execution, there is little debate that the general intention was to quiet down student political activities in response to "public pressure" of some sort or other. The San Francisco *Chronicle* stated that the decision was a response to the "pressure" from "West Coast Goldwater" supporters—presumably smarting under the picketing of the Republican convention last summer. The more widely held theory, and the one generally admitted to by administrators, is that the *Oakland Tribune*, edited by William Knowland, objected to students meeting on the campus to organize picketing of the *Tribune* for its alleged racially biased hiring policies. The plausibility of this theory gains further credibility from the fact that two bond issues for University construction were on the ballot in the election to be held one month later. (Both were subsequently backed by the *Tribune* and both were passed; the bond issue of two years earlier had been defeated the first time. . . .)

The actual execution of the decision suggests that the "multiversity" has not yet developed a coherent or workable substitute for the stern but personal paternalism of the "old style." The days when Sproul could address thousands of students by name are nostalgically remembered; confronted with three thousand rebellious students he surely would have addressed them. Had Kerr been in the crowd not one in twenty students would have recognized him. The perception of the students and their demands is dominated by the old style mentality; the mechanism for treating the thirty thousand "children" is an impersonal and poorly manned structure. In short, the multiversity as *alma mater*, a bureaucracy *in loco parentis*, is a monstrosity.

But is it then just a question of growing pains? Can we explain the present situation as a result of old men from the "old regime" manning the automated machinery of the old order? Our fears are far from allayed when we turn our attention to the "new men" —for their conduct reveals a loss of authority and with it a readiness to rely on force. Kerr's visit to the campus during the tense Friday confrontation was like that of a general touring the trenches. The prospect of his unleashing between 500 and 1000 policemen on the students caused even his most ardent supporters to pause. In the days that followed, none of his actions suggest that the Friday behavior was the result of a momentary weakness. In a series of statements to the press Kerr referred to the "Communist tactics" of the demonstrators; he observed that 40 per cent of the student leaders were "non-students;" and with mathematical (and ideological) precision he pointed out that 49 per cent of the students "followed the Mao-Castro line." [sic]

The intensity of this outburst can be understood if we recognize that for Kerr the "issue" is essentially one of "betrayal." He views the University's freedom as a difficult political matter due to her immense involvement in the "outer world." Fittingly, he was addressing the American Council on Education on the subject "Autonomy and Interdependence" the day the demonstrations began. From his perspective, the main threats—and they are, for him, vast—come from the political world and from the community at large. All "restrictions" on free speech and political activity are presented as politically necessary to protect what hasn't been given away. Given this view of himself—as holding back a great tide of reaction or Know-Nothingism—any hand from behind that is not a pat on the back is seen as a knife in the ribs.

His reaction to the demonstration—surprising to many—is very much in character. In 1962, when the "Kerr Directives" (a set of regulations concerning student political activity) were under attack, Kerr responded with an open letter to the chairman of the student group attacking him, poutingly stating that if the students didn't like what he had given them, he would reintroduce the regulations which his conservative predecessor had used during the McCarthy years.

This time it was the same story again—an utter refusal to accept any criticism from the university community as legitimate. Given a self-image of the "liberal defender" of intellectualism and academic freedom confronting a dangerous world of extremism, it is easy to see why Kerr can see only Communists to his left. This same position is expressed by many of the so-called "liberal" faculty as well; thus sociologists Phillip Selznick and Seymour Lipset called the demonstration "collectivist" and "totalitarian" and introduced motions to the Academic Senate condemning "violence" and praising peace and order. From Lipset's vantage point of the "realized left," there is simply no legitimate space on that flank; to clarify the issue, he insightfully likened the students to "Ku Klux Klanners."

There were other members of the faculty who placed their Red-baiting tactics in a context of "strategy" and realism. Since the public was going to interpret the demonstrations as youthful rebellion skillfully manipulated by subversive agents, it was a political masterstroke to direct their fury away from the campus by stating that many of the participants were non-students and that their leaders were professional agitators and Maoist-Castro-ites. (Frequently SNCC summer project workers were placed in the same camp.) The fact that the political protest to Kerr's actions is also discredited, and the students made to appear "dupes," is not important. What *is* important is to deflect the expected onslaught away from the ivory towers and their sand foundations.

The faculty seems to share Kerr's appraisal of the fragility of the University in the face of "public pressure." Between the totalitarian left and the reactionary right there is presumably a narrow space in which the University lives. Few seem to raise the possibility that this view may be compounded of the faculty's guilty feelings regarding its leftism in the thirties and the anxieties surviving from the age of McCarthy in the fifties. The space in which freedom is possible is a narrow one, and it is the task of the administration to maintain it.

For those willing to stay within that space and accept its rules, the rewards are high. Kerr is an unparalleled fund raiser, and his successes have provided a richly furnished sanctuary.

It was logical that the faculty should adopt the pose of professional social science, denouncing the tactics ("activities") of the students as maladapted to their ends ("preferences"). The issue is a family affair, in the faculty view, and needs no more than family methods. Lipset argues that the direct action tactics used in the South are totally inapplicable to Berkeley, for *here* there is access to the centers of power and decision. Lipset, the doyen of political sociologists, assuredly does have access, but the same does not apply to those who challenge Kerr's interpretations of reality, nor to those students who would negotiate from a position other than that of humble mendicant. "Access," impressive though it may be as a term, is a decidedly relative affair.

The faculty's position, like that of President Kerr, reflects an "insider bias" that fails completely to understand the problem. The issue, to the faculty, remains essentially a misunderstanding, caused by a "lack of communication" and to be resolved by "clear and precise" statements of the problem. This thesis is vague enough to fit the facts, but neither the faculty nor Kerr have realized that the problem lies largely in the fact that students are "outsiders," to whom being listened to is as important a part of "communication" as is hearing accurately.

There is no conclusion to this story: The movement continues as the article goes to press. The events rush on in confusion and chaos. Yet the events themselves are no more than symbolic of what is really at stake: the identity of the modern university, the relations of faculty, administrator, and student. Once, a university implied the community of scholars, in which faculty stood *in loco magistri*, not as a genre separated from "students." Events at Berkeley and elsewhere demonstrate—were any demonstration needed—the central importance of the administration in the modern university, an administration which claims to speak as the voice and conscience of the faculty and the parent of the student.

It is also evident that the student does not want a bureaucracy for a parent, and, when given an opportunity, he will express a desire to be free from parental governance altogether. He wants political freedom, or, to be more exact, wants the chance for dignity and responsibility. As Tocqueville knew, "responsible" use of freedom can be learned only by men who are given responsibility.

It may be necessary to fight a battle before freedom is secure. Some assert that the great private universities fought that battle long ago; it may now be in the process of being fought at Berkeley. Yet the fight is made more difficult because President Kerr does not join the combat squarely. The language of liberalism provides a cloak for restriction. The Kafkaesque network of rules and passages is covered by the term "multiversity" and by the imagery of decentralized pluralism. If Kerr is an enemy, he is hardly an honest one. Yet, if he is a friend of the free university, his equivocation and his retreats in the face of critics hardly create confidence in his ability as a defender of the university's liberty.

Nor can there be trust in the faculty. Its members realize the expanding sphere of administrative power; they feel the amorphous quality of the university, its lack of purpose and definition, and the senseless expansion of facilities for expansion's sake. Yet they have been unable to join together for their prerogative to be free. Isolated cases aside, their record in the defense of civil liberties is abysmal. Until they overcome their past impotence, their destiny is simple. They will live in an organization, while dreaming ineffectually of a community.

The issue is momentous: whether the university will mirror the worst in America, its sprawling character, its aimlessness, and its anonymity, or whether it will stand as the symbol of its best ideals and its hopes for quality. It would be shameful for the rest of America, and tragic in the event, if the students—wise and responsible at one moment, fumbling and emotional in the next—were to be the solitary voice worthy of respect.

Jerry Berman, a graduate of the University of California (Berkeley), is an editor of the California Law Review. *Joseph Paff and Bill Cavala are students in the political science department of the University of California. "The Student Riots at Berkeley" originally appeared in* The Activist, *January 1965.*

AN END TO HISTORY

by Mario Savio

Mario Savio is a former student at the University of California at Berkeley. A junior majoring in philosophy, Mr. Savio dropped out of school to devote full time to leading the Free Speech Movement. This article was edited from a tape made by Mr. Savio while he was engaged in a sit-in in Sproul Hall on the University campus. Police arrested 800 students at the sit-in, and the leaders were given jail sentences. "An End to History" originally appeared in Humanity, *December 1964.*

Last summer I went to Mississippi to join the struggle there for civil rights. This fall I am engaged in another phase of the same struggle, this time in Berkeley. The two battlefields may seem quite different to some observers, but this is not the case. The same rights are at stake in both places—the right to participate as citizens in democratic society and to struggle against the same enemy. In Mississippi an autocratic and powerful minority rules, through organized violence, to suppress the vast, virtually powerless, majority. In California, the privileged minority manipulates the University bureaucracy to suppress the students' political expression. That "respectable" bureaucracy masks the financial plutocrats: that impersonal bureaucracy is the efficient enemy in a "Brave New World."

In our free speech fight at the University of California, we have come up against what may emerge as the greatest problem of our nation—depersonalized, unresponsive bureaucracy. We have encountered the organized status quo in Mississippi, but it is the same in Berkeley. Here in Berkeley we find it impossible usually to meet with anyone but secretaries. Beyond that, we find functionaries who cannot make policy but can only hide behind the rules. We have discovered total lack of response on the part of the true policy makers. To grasp a situation which is truly Kafkesque, it is necessary to understand the bureaucratic mentality. And we have learned quite a bit about it this fall, more outside the classroom than in.

As bureaucrat, an administrator believes that nothing new happens. He occupies an a-historical point of view. In September, to get the attention of this bureaucracy which had issued arbitrary edicts supressing student political expression and refused to discuss its action, we held a sit-in on the campus. We sat around a police car and kept it immobilized for over thirty-two hours. At last, the administrative bureaucracy agreed to negotiate. But instead, on the following Monday, we discovered that a committee had been appointed, in accordance with usual regulations, to resolve the dispute. Our attempt to convince any of the administrators that an event had occurred, that something new had happened, failed. They saw this simply as something to be handled by normal University procedures.

The same is true of all bureaucracies. They begin as tools—means to certain legitimate goals—and they end up feeding their own existence. The conception that bureaucrats have is that history has in fact come to an end. No events can occur, now that the Second World War is over, which can change American society substantially. We proceed by standard procedures as we are.

The most crucial problems facing the United States today are the problem of automation and the problem of racial injustice. Most people who will be put out of jobs by machines will not accept an end to events, this historical plateau, as the point beyond which no change occurs. Negroes will not accept an end to history here. All of us must refuse to accept history's final judgment that in America there is no place in society for people whose skins are dark. On campus students are not about to accept it as fact that the University has ceased evolving and is in its final state of perfection, that students and faculty are respectively raw material and employees, or that the University is to be autocratically run by unresponsive bureaucrats.

Here is the real contradiction: The bureaucrats hold history as ended. As a result significant parts of the population both on campus and off are dispossessed, and these dispossessed are not about to accept this a-historical point of view. It is out of this that the conflict has occurred with the University bureaucracy and will continue to occur until that bureaucracy becomes responsive or until it is clear that the University can not function.

The things we are asking for in our civil rights protests have a deceptively quaint ring. We are asking for the due process of law. We are asking for our actions to be judged by committees of our peers. We are asking that regulations ought to be considered as arrived at legitimately only from the consensus of the governed. These phrases are all pretty old, but they are not being taken seriously in America today, nor are they being taken seriously on the Berkeley campus.

I have just come from a meeting with the Dean of Students.

She notified us that she was aware of certain violations of University regulations by certain organizations. University Friends of SNCC, which I represent, was one of these. We tried to draw from her some statement on these great principles—consent of the governed, jury of one's peers, due process. The best she could do was to evade or to present the administration party line. It is very hard to make any contact with the human being who is behind these organizations.

The university is the place where people begin seriously to question the conditions of their existence and raise the issue of whether they can be committed to the society they have been born into. After a long period of apathy during the fifties, students have begun not only to question, but, having arrived at answers, to act on those answers. This is part of a growing understanding among many people in America that history has not ended, that a better society is possible, and that it is worth dying for.

This free speech fight points up a fascinating aspect of contemporary campus life. Students are permitted to talk all they want so long as their speech has no consequences.

One conception of the university, suggested by a classical Christian formulation, is that it be in the world but not of the world. The conception of Clark Kerr by contrast is that the university is part and parcel of this particular stage in the history of American society; it stands to serve the needs of American industry; it is a factory that turns out a certain product needed by industry or government. Because speech does often have consequences which might alter this perversion of higher education, the university must put itself in a position of censorship. It can permit two kinds of speech: speech which encourages continuation of the status quo, and speech which advocates changes in it so radical as to be irrelevant in the foreseeable future. Someone may advocate radical change in all aspects of American society, and this I am sure he can do with impunity. But if someone advocates sit-ins to bring about changes in discriminatory hiring practices, this can not be permitted because it goes against the status quo of which the university is a part. And that is how the fight began here.

The administration of the Berkeley campus has admitted that

external, extra-legal groups have pressured the University not to permit students on campus to organize picket lines, not to permit on campus any speech with consequences. And the bureaucracy went along. Speech with consequences, speech in the area of civil rights, speech which some might regard as illegal, must stop.

Many students here at the University, many people in society, are wandering aimlessly about. Strangers in their own lives, there is no place for them. They are people who have not learned to compromise, who for example have come to the University to learn to question, to grow, to learn—all the standard things that sound like clichés because no one takes them seriously. And they find at one point or another that for them to become part of society, to become lawyers, ministers, business men, or people in government, very often they must compromise those principles which were most dear to them. They must suppress the most creative impulses that they have; this is a prior condition for being part of the system. The university is well structured, well tooled, to turn out people with all the sharp edges worn off—the well-rounded person. The university is well equipped to produce that sort of person, and this means that the best among the people who enter must for four years wander aimlessly much of the time questioning why they are on campus at all, doubting whether there is any point in what they are doing, and looking toward a very bleak existence afterward in a game in which all of the rules have been made up—rules which one can not really amend.

It is a bleak scene, but it is all a lot of us have to look forward to. Society provides no challenge. American society in the standard conception it has of itself is simply no longer exciting. The most exciting things going on in America today are movements to change America. America is becoming ever more the utopia of sterilized, automated contentment. The "futures" and "careers" for which American students now prepare are for the most part intellectual and moral wastelands. This chrome-plated consumers' paradise would have us grow up to be well-behaved children. But an important minority of men and women coming to the front today have shown that they will die rather than be standardized, replaceable, and irrelevant.

GOD IN THE COLLEGES: THE DEHUMANIZATION OF THE UNIVERSITY

by Michael Novak

The following article is a discussion on two levels. The first level discusses the growth of a peculiar brand of "non-militant" agnosticism among college students. The second level, the one we are most concerned with here, points to this development as only one symptom of a larger phenomenon: the total destruction of all commitment. ". . . the American consensus has forced a 'commitment to nothing' upon our universities." Students, Mr. Novak argues, are no longer concerned with veritas, *the search for the truth. They are, rather, obsessed with propriety. Though Mr. Novak is not associated with "the new young left," his thesis has a clear relevance to the campus revolt.*

The professor looked into the faces of the freshmen in Philosophy 1. "How many of you," he asked, "believe in the existence of God?"

He walked up and down a little. The class was intellectually alive and usually argued. No hands went up.

"Good. I'll give you Anselm's proof for the existence of God." In a few minutes of lecturing, the professor presented Anselm's proof. "Now," he paused. "How many of you see anything wrong in this proof?"

No hands went up.

"Well, then, some of you now believe in God. How many?"

Still no hands went up. When the professor told about it later, he shrugged. "What can you do when thinking doesn't seem to make any difference?"

The experience of this professor is not a solitary one. The fact that the life of personal conviction is separated from the life of academic intelligence is frequently remarked in university life. The phenomenon is not even confined to this country, for it is well known in England. In *Lucky Jim*, Kingsley Amis makes fun of the non-commitment and the sham which he finds in middle-class education; Wilfrid Sheed's American-English novel, *A Middle Class Education*, extends the observations well beyond the classroom. In our day it is precisely this that education in England and America has become: middle-class. John K. Galbraith's *The Affluent Society* brought the emergence of the new and numerous educated class to our attention; it is there for anyone to see.

The present essay pretends to no special statistical wisdom; its material has been gathered from a long-time interest in religion and the university, from reading, from conversations at Harvard and other colleges. Undoubtedly, the essay has fuller relevance for the liberal arts college; I have hardly broached the problem of religion in the scientific and technological schools. Also, in the smaller colleges and the huge state colleges, the focus may be somewhat different.

How does God fare in a middle-class education? What happens to religion in a middle-class education?

First of all, we must remember that since medieval times the West has been becoming a middle-class civilization. The rise of the bourgeoisie has been concomitant with the rise of technology. And underneath the social and economic changes that made Europe capitalist and then industrialist, there was a change in world view. Even though the bourgeois classes might cling to the conventions and forms of an older tradition and an older faith, the impersonality of business and the objectivity of scientific method were molding their weekday spirits and their habitual attitudes. The very bourgeoisie that nourished the technological and scientific revolution nourished within itself an intellectual avant-garde that strove to point out to it how very empty its forms had become. The avant-garde was usually increasingly irreligious: from Voltaire and Hume, Comte and Zola, to Shaw and Russell, it has come to take its battle *vis-à-vis* religion as won. For its point has been that our culture is now at base irreligious, that the bourgeois businessman who pretends differently is either hypocritical or blind. Catholicism was long content with the status quo, and Protestantism for a long time praised the thrifty and the rugged and the strong. Thus the war on poverty which Marxism declared and which the democracies have taken up is (though it need not have been) a secular war, and the ideals which international civilization now pursues are secular ideals: the abolition of poverty and disease, of ignorance and indignity, of colonialism and tyranny. Giving itself to science and technology, our culture makes religion not central but optional, and the avant-garde has been trying to point out—and to form—change.

Secondly, it is necessary to see that while Europe was torn nearly to its death by the ideological and physical contortions of recent revolutions and wars, America and England have tried earnestly to go on as before, as if nothing has happened. The war washed away the intellectual foundations of Europe's past, and intellectuals like Camus, Sartre, Marcel, Barth, and Guardini have fought desperately for intellectual starting points—whether they deny or affirm the possibility of religious faith. But in America and England, philosophy and art showed little such desperation; men tried to pick up where they had left off, a little more tired, a little more angry, worried about the bomb, but not fundamentally changed. Moreover, education in England and America has become financially cushioned as never before. The government, corporations, and unions all give grants for specialized research or simply for the maintenance of students and professors. A distinctly comfortable and entrenched kind of existence is growing up. The small, modestly optimistic world view which Europe shared before the wars is still almost possible. The radicalism of the American 1930's has been fragmented by prosperity and by disillusion with ideology.

Although the colleges pride themselves on the awakening of young minds, on the asking of the Big Questions of life (who and what is man, whence has he come, where is he going, what is love, what is passion, what is reason, is there a God), it is soon clear to college students that the Big Questions don't count—in academic standing, or in later life, or in research grants.

In the first place, the standing assumption is that ultimate questions are in principle unanswerable, and hence not worth asking seriously. This assumption may not discourage freshmen, but over a four-year period it is pretty well driven home. In the second place, nobody is much interested in students' answers to such questions, or deems them worth putting in competition with anybody else's. Even among the professors it is assumed that ultimate questions are nonintellectual, personal, and, if matters of supreme importance and self-commitment, nevertheless not matters for passionate academic dispute. The university, on principle, concentrates on statistics, historical facts, historical intellectual positions, logic modeled on the discourse of the physical sciences, and ample documentation. Even the literature courses, under the impact of the New Criticism, have the students noting the occurrences of words, running down allusions, and abstracting from the conditions of history. The Anglo-American university has committed itself to all that is "objective," countable, precise, publicly verifiable. Though this commitment suits the middle-class temper capitally, it stifles religion almost to death.

A Tiny Taste of Rebellion

Not only religion is stifled. More fundamentally, it is possible —it is even common—for a student to go to class after class of sociology, economics, psychology, literature, philosophy, and the rest, and hardly become aware that he is dealing with issues of life and death, of love and solitude, of inner growth and pain. He may never fully grasp the fact that education is not so much information and technique as self-confrontation and change in his own conscious life. He may sit through lectures and write examinations—and the professors may let him do merely that—collecting verbal "answers," without really thinking through and deciding about any new aspect of his own life in any course. The dilemma of education has always been to combine merely mental skills with personal experiencing and growth. The educational currents in American colleges tend to oscillate from one pole to the other; and at present the attention in college to the formal and the public easily leaves the inner life of the student untouched.

It is true that in a place like Harvard, or among more serious students everywhere, the young collegian may experience beneficial crises of growth. He gets a taste of rebellion against his origins; he may become, for a while, "avant-garde." The folks at home find him restive, critical, hostile, in his approach to a world he had hitherto peacefully shared. He has learned to despise the organization man and the many patterns of conformity in mass culture; he has learned a certain contempt for suburbia and its values. Yet he likes the comforts of home. Worst of all, in college he has not really had to rebel (except perhaps against not having Latin on his diploma). The college gave him rebellious, critical books, but also gave him a cool grove to read them in. No commitment, no crusading is asked of him. The college merely wants him to "have the facts," to show mental control of the concepts. Yet he, so everyone tells him, is not at all like the collegians of the thirties, or even of the forties. He is cautious, quiet, studious. And no wonder. So is the institution in which he is studying. The higher-powered institutions are committed to testable information and techniques; the patterns of conformity in lower-powered institutions do not far transcend the interests of the society that fosters them.

"*Say Nothing*"

Middle-class Christianity—the bourgeois Christianity which Nietzsche, Kierkegaard, Péguy, Bloy, and others so hated—was always prudent, small-visioned, secure. It dared little, with its gaudy-colored plaster statues, or its devices to protect the little world of the entrepreneur. In the person of many university professors, middle-class secular humanism is not much more daring. It thinks of itself as humble in its agnosticism, and eschews the "mystic flights" of metaphysicians, theologians, and dreamers; it is cautious and remote in dealing with heightened and passionate experiences that are the stuff of much great literature and philosophy. It limits itself to this world and its concerns, concerns which fortunately turn out to be largely subject to precise formulation, and hence have a limited but comforting certainty. (It has a particularly comfortable ambiance if it works within the physical sciences, or mathematics, or the statistics of sociology and economics.) If we cannot control the great uncertain questions in the universe, nevertheless we can make a universe of little certainties we can control.

The agnosticism—atheism would be too strong a word—of the classroom is not militant. It is only, in principle, unconcerned. It is bourgeois Christianity all over again, to so great an extent that, in college, in spite of differences in belief, the behavior of agnostic and of religious man is pretty much the same.

The agnosticism of the classroom does not have to be militant. Once upon a time it was fighting for its life; now it is an accepted part of the college scene, in fact the predominating part. The old battles between positive science and religion which delighted, or angered, our grandfathers—about chance and design, monkeys and Adam—seldom resound now in academic halls. The distinction between empirical and theological activity seems pretty well recognized; each side preserves a certain calm and only occasionally do tempers flare. Perhaps psychologists more than others are given to writing off religion as illusion; anthropologists, in turn, are habituated to data on revelations and recurrent religious themes, and are correspondingly casual about the traditions of Judaism and Christianity. One school of analysis in philosophy, of which Russell and Ayer among others are examples, believes that nothing that cannot be reduced to sense experience can have meaning, and most religious questions of course lie outside this restricted zone. Some partisans of another movement, linguistic analysis, following the later Wittgenstein, do not require the discourse of faith and theology to conform to other kinds of discourse, but study it in its own right; but religion does not lie in words.

Professional disciplines aside, a bland tolerance seems to be everybody's ideal. Say nothing that will offend. Say nothing that involves personal commitment. Stay close to the public facts. "You've got to teach these youngsters to forget the shoulds and musts they came here with," one new teaching fellow was recently admonished by his program director. "The students have to learn to be objective." And of course such a critique is excellent, since some shoulds and musts are what a man dies for. But there seems to be correspondingly little concern about which ones he will acquire and keep.

Professor Raphael Demos of Harvard was once quoted as saying, with perhaps his touch of irony, "*Veritas* means we are committed to nothing." It may be that the American consensus has forced a "commitment to nothing" upon our universities; we are a pluralist people, and it seems very difficult to discover a way to teach about those differences on ultimate questions that make us so. The colleges make a "commitment to noncommitment," have a "faith in non-faith." They demand perpetual re-examination and have nowhere to rest.

Thus the new middle-class tolerance of the colleges neither destroys nor transforms the religion of the incoming freshmen. Of one hundred students who marked themselves "atheistic or agnostic" on the poll of the Harvard *Crimson* in 1965, only ten felt "obliged . . . to enlighten others to abandon their faith." The new tolerance merely established, officially and in principle, that personal conviction be separated from teaching and learning. If a student wishes to commit himself to answers to ultimate questions (by commitment to some personal synthesis, or to traditional religion or ethics, or anything), he may do so—is even encouraged to do so—but not publicly, nor officially, not in his daily work. He will do well to keep his answers to himself. In term papers and on tests they will not be welcome; there he is obliged to prove rather that he knows facts and correlations, and can run, seeking, as well as anyone else. No one in *official* university life seems to care about his convictions.

There is good reason for the university's position. One of its tasks is to turn out professional men. Think of the difficulty there would be in correcting exams and term papers if each student were engaged in a highly personal way in working out a position important to himself. What if the student found that something of importance to him was of minor importance to the course—or outside its confines? The dilemma of professionalism versus full human experience is a pressing one and cannot be solved by making light of it.

Trials by Weak Fire

How relevant is this dilemma to the actual church affiliations of college students? A Catholic report published in *America* (April 8, 1961) quotes Bishop Robert E. Lucey as saying: "The dangers to faith and morals are at least as great in a downtown office as on a secular campus." The national survey of *Time* magazine (1952) is cited to the same effect. "No appreciable number of defections," say Newman Club chaplains at the University of Illinois and the University of Iowa; those which do occur "result rather from weak religious background prior to college than from campus living and experiences." The Harvard *Crimson* poll I referred to earlier records a high rate of defections (40 per cent among Protestants, 25 per cent among Catholics, 12 per cent among Jews) among the 310 students who answered. But in almost every case the defection had its roots in precollege days, especially in high school experience.

Although it is not clear what constitutes religious "strength," it is clear that if the student's faith goes through a personal trial-by-fire, that is his affair. There are few courses in critical theology, few in modern Biblical theory, few in the theory and practice of organized religion, to help him explicitly and formally to mature his theological intelligence. In the view of some religious men, this is a good thing; religion, after all, is not something that can be formally taught. It is a living commitment to be enkindled from person to person, a life to be lived rather than lessons to be learned. Besides, formal theological studies imply a living content of religious experience; but it is precisely this living content which in our day most men no longer possess. If religion is to enter the university, it must enter first at the most elementary level: in experience, in awareness, in slow and gradual exploration. The traditional words are not relevant to the present religious development of most men. Our times are sub-, not only post-, religious. The institutionalized forms of religion did not originate in modern life, and modern science and technology have grown up outside them; the two worlds of religion and modernity are strangers to each other. Were there to be merely formal courses in theology at the university, genuine religious life would fare hardly better than at present. As the New Criticism is to art, so is critical theology to religious awareness. Theology, like the New Criticism, has a role to play, but it is neither necessary nor sufficient for religious life.

If we admit that theologians would also contribute to the professionalism and formalism already thriving in the modern university, who might do better? The answer, I suggest, must be that the greatest contribution to the religious life of the university could come from teachers and scholars—formally religious or not—who could lead the student to the profound human experiences lying below the surface of the academic curriculum.

These experiences are often "prereligious"; they are barely starting points for full religious life. But they are the only foundations on which anything living can be built. I mean man's experience of his fragility, of his transitoriness, of his tininess, his consciousness of his uniqueness on the earth, of his endless and restless questioning; his personal choices whose motives and consequences he cannot fully know; his vast ability to be proud and to fail, to be isolated and to love, to be—and yet not to be—the master of his own destiny.

These experiences, and others like them, underlie the statistics of economics and of sociology, the laws and hypotheses of psychology, philosophy, and other disciplines; they are at the source of great poems and novels and histories now often taught as if they were technical puzzles.

Large and unsettling personal questions arise from these experiences. And it is by their answers, explicit or implicit, that men finally differ from one another: how they react to achievement, to pride, to love, to suffering, to feelings of life and energy, to death. Implicit in the actions of every man is his own particular bias and approach to economics, to social and political affairs, to all matters with which he deals. What are the biases and beliefs that make a student unique and color all his judgments even in his professional concerns? Instead of concentrating on this question, and hence helping the student toward self-discovery, the university takes the easier path: it tries to maintain an area of "objectivity" and "fact." But the truly crucial element in human knowing (I repeat: even in professional knowing) lies in the recesses of our personal judgment. Our critical sciences, unlike our creative arts, have favored the "objective" over the "subjective." Our universities favor the one pole over the necessary two: notional-verbal competence over the self-knowledge and self-commitment that also affect professional careers, and make up personal life.

Untested Pretense

If university teachers could right the balance, would religion begin to thrive? Those who have made faith central to their lives —who believe in the reality and relevance of God, and the interaction (in dark faith) of God and men—hold that it would. And if theology, as such, came to the campuses and became there embattled and truly controversial, this would be welcome; for the very fact that fundamental questions were posed would transform the experience of university life.

No one can know what the full consequences of such a transformation might be, but surely it would mean that university people would be far more closely engaged with the world outside than they are today. Religious men in colleges could follow the example of the clergymen who took part in the Freedom Rides, went to jail, went on a hunger strike in the name of justice and brotherly concern. Religion has played a large role in the commitment of the young Negroes to struggle for their rights. It must suggest other ways of acting when situations in our society call for justice and compassion and protest. Religious men must be "active." They are obliged to consider the forms a just society should take, and ways to achieve them. Again, in the silence, self-control, and patience required by the tactics of passive resistance, they find an excellent school in the "passive" strength of religion. The intellectual resources from which such a transformation might grow are now latent on our campuses. And they are quite carefully neglected.

Meanwhile, the student on the secular campus works out his

religion for himself. Often his previous religious background will have been uncritical, informal, and unsophisticated; he may be the first member of his family pursuing a university education. His grasp of religious concepts like faith, hope, love may well be far less precise and intellectually defensible than it ought to be; his university career will offer him very little formal help in clarifying and criticizing them. It is possible that college life may be for him, then, a period of searing but private examination. For a time at least he may stop going to church or synagogue, and believe himself atheist or agnostic. But the chances are—in most schools and among most students—that no such honest and fruitful personal critiques will occur, at least none of any lasting depth. Where they do seem to occur, experienced religious men are pleased. "It's a more thoughtful kind of religion," seems to be the consensus of chaplains near Harvard. "It's better than merely going to church out of habit. They may be missing church services and undergoing changes now; but they'll be back when they return to their local communities and all the better for it."

But will they be? The fact seems to be that even among the more searching students, religion follows the pattern of their other personal convictions. The pattern of conformity they are taught in college, by which they systematically separate their inner convictions from the "objective" work of the classroom, will simply be continued in their business affairs, legal practice, or work of whatever kind in later life. A civilization pervaded by the laws and spirit of technology—on which profit and life itself are based—is a civilization prone to expediency and nonmoral, nonpersonal considerations. The vice of academicians is to become intellectual technologists; this vice prevails. The consequent bourgeois life of the American university becomes with hardly a hitch the middle-class life of the organization man and the suburbanite. The pretense of nonconformity and intellectual liberty on campus is seldom tested by real and fundamental disagreement; for such disagreement is usually "subjective" and not amenable to the kind of debate the university tacitly approves. "Liberals" and "conservatives" in politics, for example, seldom touch the basic issues separating them; they both try to argue in terms of "facts"; but why they are committed, each in his separate way, to different ideals, and what precisely these ideals are and whence they are derived—this kind of discussion does not suit the pragmatic and "objective" temper of present intellectual life. It is too intangible, dialectical, personal, however lethal, in its effect upon action.

"*God Is Not Dead*"

One might have hoped that the religiously committed private schools in America might have made by now some major contribution to American intellectual life. In part, they have been too concerned with putting up buildings, with more or less ghetto-like defensiveness, and with hesitating between secular standards and their own long-ago tradition. In part, general American intellectual life rules out of professional discussion the very commitment which the religious schools primarily exist to foster. In any case, the potential strength of the religious school now goes almost for nought.

One might have hoped that religious men within the secular colleges might by their understanding and their leadership have restored to American universities a chance for a living and critical experience of religion. It is true that the Danforth Foundation, the National Council for Religion in Higher Education, and other groups are trying to favor the presence in our universities of talented religious men. But the strident tones of Fathers Feeney and Halton, and of William F. Buckley, Jr.'s essays and talks have sometimes soured the air. And for decades there have been too few men, at once intellectual and religious and wise on the campuses. Vast empty spaces seem to surround the Niebuhrs and the Tillichs. The churches are filled with worshippers but intelligence has fled from the ranks of religion. Who or what can bring it back?

What, then, is the place of God in our colleges? The basic human experiences that remind man that he is not a machine, and not merely a temporary cog in a technological civilization, are not fostered within the university. God is as irrelevant in the universities as in business organizations; but so are love, death, personal destiny. Religion can thrive only in a personal universe; religious faith, hope, and love are personal responses to a personal God. But how can the immense question of a personal God even be posed and made relevant when fundamental questions about the meaning and limits of personal experience are evaded?

"God is dead . . . What are these churches if they are not the tombs and sepulchers of God?" Nietzsche asked. But much of Western humanism is dead too. Men do not wander under the silent stars, listen to the wind, learn to know themselves, question, "Where am I going? Why am I here?" They leave aside the mysteries of contingency and transitoriness, for the certainties of research, production, consumption. So that it is nearly possible to say: "Man is dead . . . What are these buildings, these tunnels, these roads, if they are not the tombs and sepulchers of man?"

God, if there is a God, is not dead. He will come back to the colleges, when man comes back.

Michael Novak graduated from Stonehill College in Massachusetts, and holds a degree from the Gregorian University in Rome. He was a doctoral candidate and a Teaching Fellow in Philosophy at Harvard when this article first appeared, in Harpers, *October 1961. He now teaches religion at Stanford University.*

SEX AND THE NEW MORALITY: CONFUSION AND HUMANITY

by Thomas Conrad

It is fashionable for the older generations to view the sex lives of the younger generation as different quantitatively but not in essence from their own. This fond assumption has to do with the anxieties of the older generations rather than any careful and realistic view of the present generation; the assumption is generated by a massive fear of social change and instability. The change and instability are present, but it is only some parts of our generation and a handful of the most imaginative older people who can see the new morality as something leading to greater humanity and the affirmation of individual worth against a fearful collectivity.

Most discussions of the sexual behavior of our generation, when they rise above prurient sensationalism, make the mistake of isolating sexual patterns from the rest of the life of youth. Such separation has not been true for some time, and part of what we will want to explain is how the separation has been destroyed.

Some observers suggest that the "cultural shock" of entering college largely erases previous learning in the realm of sexual behavior, putting the new student in an anomalous situation and thus leading to a sudden increase in sexual activity. This thesis seems just as false as a pure Freudian one, in which any secondary socialization (such as that obtained in peer groups after puberty) is immaterial in comparison to learning in infancy. What the Freudian view suggests is that the effect of changed community standards (the community being the peer group, our generation) is that more people will be behaving sexually in ways that promote anxiety than were behaving in such ways when the community standards supported (and in the more distant past, coerced) abstinences which tended to follow from fears of sex. This observation is a kind of circular reasoning, because the learning of fear in connection with sexual desire and activity was one strategy of a social system fearing on a more basic level its own instability. Fear of sexual activity is not something inherent in any organized social system; it is not a basic concomitant of social organization, but rather an accidental and largely irrational extension of a more basic fear of social instability, as should be clear from the ravings of certain types who point to the moral decay of Rome and draw parallels to the America of today.

It is continually suggested by professional moralists that American culture, and particularly the advertising of the mass media, is being bombarded with sexual symbolism which will lead to moral decay. The trouble with this view is that sex needs no advertising; those who have not been psychologically ravaged by their parents are well aware that sex is pleasant and desirable and the objections of our generation to the "bombardment" are on other grounds.

Those of our generation who think about the sexual effects of advertising at all tend to be revolted not by the sex, but by the fact that sex is being used for some irrelevant purpose. Buy this product, suggest the ads, and you will get laid more often; the tacit assumption being that gimmicks and external appearances are the only determinant of the "successfulness of one's sex life." The reply to this is that a quite large percentage of this generation would rather have a less-than-technically-perfect night in bed with someone for whom they have deep affection than a frolic in the hay with someone attracted by sparkling white teeth, sexy cigarettes, and absence of B.O.

The case does not rest there, however. Attractiveness, in the sense of external appearance which excites sexual desire, is in fact an important factor in the initiation of relationships; the perceived danger of the advertising is that it tends to destroy the differences in taste which act to assure that most people will be physically attractive to at least a sufficient number of others. The current ideal, as represented in *Playboy* for example, is a female having breasts much larger than average for the late teens and early twenties; most cannot match this "ideal." The somewhat uneasy and defensive attitude of many males in our generation is to the effect that "more than handful is wasted." Many similar examples of the reaction to mass-media stereotypes can be cited.

The defense reactions of both sexes in our generation to impossible and basically impersonal standards of physical attractiveness are a clue to more basic conflicts. Physical attractiveness is obviously not a suitable criterion because once the fear of sex is at least partly conquered in the individual and the community, each person is desiring many more people at a given time than would be prudent or physically possible to pursue. No one argues against this observation in the case of the men, but many would deny it in the case of the women. The case with the women of our generation is different, but for reasons which have little directly to do with desire per se: the women are still socialized to believe that female sexual desire is at least slightly abnormal and reprehensible, and thus a factor which should not be so conscious; and practical factors make it still somewhat easier for men than for women to act upon desire for more than one person. In short, the fact of sexual attraction does not by itself "validate" sexual action; some other basis must be found for choice.

If sexual action in our generation were a question of accidental couplings, as the hedonists of *Playboy* suggest and the professional moralists charge, there would be no emotional turmoil of the sort which is thoroughly evident. Extreme positions are always the easiest to take in human relations. In the present problem, we have the traditional moralists and the pure hedonists. The traditionalists are clearly fools and fanatics; their view of the world is quite unrealistic, and that view is inhumane. But the pure hedonists are likewise at least fools: it is palpably true that the effects of sex can be bad, and that random coupling on the basis of simple passion is likely, sooner or later, to cause someone damage. The reply which pure hedonists make to this last observation is that if everyone had a liberal view of sex, and pregnancy were controlled by foolproof means, there would be no reason to limit sexual action and no damage would be possible. It may be true that unlimited sexual activity could be made painless in the distant future. But that is almost a metaphysical question. It is not the question which this generation faces. The practical questions come down to ones of the form, Should I sleep with my girl while she has a hangup about sex ruining the relationship, a hangup which I can't do anything about? Or: She's sleeping with him, but she really wants me, only he's blowing his mind right now and she knows he needs her—should we sleep together secretly? It's worth noting that tangles of sex and love which in previous generations were the problem of tiny minorities of "deviants" are now problems being faced every day by significant proportions of a whole generation.

A key question which arises at this point is, Why is there such a propensity to get into sexual-emotional tangles of almost Byzantine complexity? It is true that much of what happens can be explained as cycles between withdrawal and complex tangles, but where does the apparently greater tolerance for complex hangups in comparison with previous generations come from? One obvious factor is the greater sexual freedom; "sex is fun," and when it is available as a concomitant of involvements, there are reasons to maintain the involvements. Another factor arises from the fact, as it was put by one woman, that sex is often as much a reassurance as a strictly physical passion. More generally, protection against the attacks of the older generations requires a type of "community" which by constant interaction and mutual emotional involvement in nonsexual ways encourages sexual attachments. Thus we have the incestuous group, where almost all the logically possible sexual attractions are actually present at least in latent form, and where much of the Freudian theory of family groups is played out. Another concomitant is the degree and amount of communication about each other's sexual as well as other emotions; the "community of knowledge" is one of the aspects which most shocks and infuriates the older generations, who see it as a flaunting of indecent behavior.

The degree of honest communication in our generation, even on delicate emotional problems, represents one aspect in the revolution of which sexual behavior is one part. The parental generation's communication on sexual matters was very largely split; the men talked to each other and boasted, and the women (those with courage) pooled their knowledge. In our generation, people quickly learn in college if not before that free conversation about sex between the sexes is approved behavior, and that those who refuse such discussion are considered (not without accuracy) to have a hangup about sex. What the freedom of communication between the sexes represents, however, is part of the still-ongoing revolution in which sexual roles as traditionally defined are being critically reexamined. It is getting harder for men in our generation to use women as punchboards without guilt. It is getting harder for women in our generation to play the useless plaything or whining suppliant to men. Much of the trouble comes from the fact that this revolution in the mutual perceptions of the sexes and thus of the human kind is not as complete as our generation would like it and as we try to behave. The women of our generation were mostly reared by parents who had gone beyond extreme reactions and counter-reactions on feminism to a kind of weary acceptance of women as long as they were not too uppity, much the same reaction as that of certain liberals toward moderates and extremists in civil rights. The result is that many women in our generation feel vaguely or even acutely uncomfortable as equal "sisters" of the men; they must be taught by the older women and the men that "sisterhood" is good, and remnants of the earlier training-by-indirection often remain. The shift in roles is somewhat easier for the men, both because there has always been an underlying male guilt over the subjugation of women and because the traditional male role of toughness and aggression has always required most men to play a part ill-suited to them. Traditionalists have, of course, attacked the development of "Unisex" (our thanks to *Time* magazine for the word) as another breakdown of moral fiber. The feminists have also attacked it as a sellout of the new-traditional female role. Whatever other effects the revolution in sexual roles and mutual expectations may have, it has the effect of no longer requiring people to spend so much time and energy warping their personalities into standard forms and feeling guilty or worthless if they fail. And in passing it is useful to note that it is no accident that the same generation which started seeing men and women as people rather than the opposite sex has also made some effort to impress upon their elders the fact that Negroes are the same species as whites.

But let us return to the question of sexual choices. If they are not made on the basis of mutual desire alone, what are the bases? The quasi-traditional basis of sex-with-love is the formal theory for most of our generation: but there are problems. Once sex outside marriage is accepted, no other clear guidelines are available. The initial reaction is usually an attempt to find some general theory to place in opposition to the general theory of the traditionalists. The result, arguments about "what is love," is natural: if love is a necessary and sufficient condition for sex, the burden of decision is merely displaced into attempting a definition of "love." Sometimes the results of these explorations are laughable (as lampooned in the movie, "Lord Love a Duck": "Is it love or sex, and six sure-fire ways to tell the difference") but mostly the results are a minor tragedy. Countless relationships in our generation move into mutual analysis and finally into being talked to death because a general theory is being sought: often the mutual analysis is a cover for natural anxieties, a cover which is particularly undesirable in that it raises all the anxieties without, in most cases, being an efficient way to resolve them.

After the first two or three affairs, the stupidity and emotional unattractiveness of general theories has become evident, and the individual moves toward what is often called the new morality, or the morality of specific consequences. The basis of the new morality is its attention to predictions of consequences in specific cases rather than more general, dogmatic, and inaccurate predictions suggested by or implicit in traditional moralities. But once one has made the consequences of his alternative actions clearer, a rather traditional problem appears: so what? In theory, no one is to be hurt, and no one is to be used as an object. But most choices imply that several people will be hurt and/or used. The moral choice is not simplified by being based on a more accurate and sophisticated theory of consequences. On the contrary, it is made more complex. The new morality does not have any answer in an absolute sense. It is only in the process of attempting to apply the morality of specific consequences, in the process of seeing more and more clearly the fact of human interdependence, that the new morality has its value. The lesson is one in the ethics of ambiguity and in the concern for the welfare of others; specific decisions are not guaranteed to be sensible and compassionate, but the long-term effect is a humane sensitivity the older generations might well cultivate, if it is not too late.

Thomas Conrad, a graduate of Oberlin College, is a graduate student in political science at Columbia University. Mr. Conrad is the author of the forthcoming The Analysis of Central War. *This article was first published in* The Activist, *November 1966.*

STUDENT SOCIAL ACTION: FROM LIBERATION TO COMMUNITY

By Thomas Hayden

For several weeks students [at Southern University in Baton Rouge] have been demonstrating against segregation practices in the community, and recently a number of them were expelled for their part in the activities. I happened to read a copy of the letter of expulsion sent from President Feltin Clark to student leader D'Army Bailey, dated January 18 of this year (1962). President Clark based the expulsion on Rule 16 in the Southern University Student Handbook. The rule reads:

Lack of University Adjustment. The University reserves the right to sever a student's connection with the University for general inability to adjust himself to the pattern of the institution.

For expelling these students whose fervor for freedom was unadjustable to the university pattern, President Clark has been sharply criticized. Indeed, the attack on Negro college presidents generally has increased since the beginning of the student direct action movement in 1960. The Negro college president, symbolized in Dr. Clark, being a recipient of state funds and therefore an agent of the racial status quo, is loudly maligned by all integrationists as a tyrant, a moral weakling, and an aggressor against the hopes of a struggling generation. One imprisoned student demonstrator, for example, has declared that the Southern University officials are working hand-in-hand with segregationists.

Curiously, the attack on Dr. Clark is concentrated upon the issue of racial integration alone, and not on the issue of education that is also involved in Rule 16. Dr. Clark's actions are symptomatic of an educational philosophy and practice quite as undemocratic, though less brutal and spectacular, as the philosophy and practice of racial superiority. What has "general inability to adjust to the pattern of the institution" to do with acquiring a higher education in a democratic system? I wonder why our stylish social reformers, many of whom are college presidents and professors, are not as critical of the paternalistic educational habits as they are of the "Uncle Tom" racial practices of President Clark.

No part of the American university system is demonstrated more lucidly by the Southern incident than the doctrine of *in loco parentis*, the doctrine that is the key to understanding the organization of our extracurricular life. What exactly is this Latin phrase? According to the volume *College Law*, published by the American Council on Education:

> The power which the officers of a college may lawfully exert to restrict and control the actions of its students is based upon the fact that, in law, the college stands in the same position to its students as that of a parent—*in loco parentis* (in lieu of parents)—and it can therefore direct and control their conduct to the same extent that a parent can.

In fact, this means the university—that is, the incorporated institution run by the regents or trustees—circumscribes the form and content of student social life and academic pursuit. It is the moral guardian of the young.

The historical origins of *in loco parentis* are ambiguous, as far as my perhaps inadequate research can determine. Perhaps the doctrine evolved partly from the early English universities, where faculty ownership was customary. This form of control, as Dean Kathryn Hopwood of Hunter College suggests, is "quite at variance with the genesis of the European universities, such as the ones at Bologna or Paris, where the students employed visiting scholars to teach them."

In America, of course, ownership is removed from the hands of students and faculty and the university is either a state agency or a private corporation. If these happenings have tended to divest students of autonomy, certain other distinctly American developments led to the institutionalization of *in loco parentis*. One of these, perhaps, was the delegation of educational control to the states, an act which induced a close relationship between home and school. The fact that many early American colleges were dominated by religious orthodoxies and dedicated to specific religious ends is probably relevant, too, in considering the ascendancy of *in loco parentis*. Whatever configuration of historical events gave rise to the doctrine, we know that it has been around for a long time, and that it is deeply rooted in the American educational system. We know, for instance, that in one of the early colleges, a master beat a student with a cane and the courts were asked to decide whether canings could go on outside the school buildings as well as within; the court said that the authority of the executor—I mean, the administrator—extended beyond the limits of the classroom—a theory that is still relevant to the university and social action.

To really experience the nature of the controversy requires a yet deeper examination of the meaning and application of the doctrine itself.

First of all, *in loco parentis* is not a closed issue legally, much as many deans would like us to believe it is. One contemporary observer of higher education, Professor Gordon Klopf, acknowledges that while most legal precedent establishes the right of universities to serve *in loco parentis* "the real testing of this issue would vary from case to case and court to court." For instance, there is some evidence that state-financed universities are not necessarily responsible for the libelous material printed by their student editors. Or again, a recent Supreme Court decision involving Alabama State sit-in leaders indicated that due process is a right students can demand; and if due process, what other constitutional rights can they seek? There are plausible grounds, furthermore, for claiming that first amendment restrictions, such as speaker bans, are not constitutional. These trends and events, I believe, help to perforate the solid legal justification of *in loco parentis*. But, more important: when and where a law is thought unjust and improper, the responsible citizens and institutions affected by the law should challenge it. That is the relevance of constitutionalism and liberal democracy. The fact that *in loco parentis* has substantial legal base is not so much an index of [its propriety as it is an index of] university and community approval of the doctrine. When a dean dismisses anti-*in loco parentis* crusades by legalisms, he is evading the moral and educational issues. As Neal Johnson points out, he is confusing the legally founded "right" of the university to act *in loco parentis* with the legally unfounded "responsibility" to do so. He is thus avoiding the fact that moral and educational decisions must be made prior to invocation of *in loco parentis.*

So much for detours into the history and legal basis of paternalism. I want now to present my criticisms of the doctrine in a somewhat organized way.

First it is paradoxically discriminatory that our vaunted "educational elite," the people that society places its best hopes upon, are subjected to greater social restrictions than most persons of comparable age, save imprisoned convicts. To go to college involves a tacit surrender of the first amendment freedoms of speech, press, and assembly and often the freedom of privacy. It means arbitrary hours for women students and compulsory functions for both sexes; it means dressing in a certain way for a certain meal that is served only at certain times; it means the "double jeopardy" of receiving punishments from the university for crimes committed in and adjudicated by the city; it means tolerating personal dossiers and students who spy for the dean of men or congressional investigating committees; it means the supervision and regulation of privacy; it means living under threat of punishment for "conduct unbecoming a student," of "inability to adjust to the university pattern." Margaret Mead has commented forcefully on the distinction between the work force and student force in the same age range:

> A handful of tugboat employees or flight engineers, because of their admitted rights in a complex system in which they are working members, can hold up a city or a country until their demands are met, but in some states students are not even allowed to vote.

And, unlike parents of students not in college, parents of studying children must both support them and, correlatively, retain control of their conduct or delegate comparable control to some quasi-parental educational institution. In either case the student is treated like a dependent child.

Needless to say, student extracurricular activity in most universities is articulated by the administration in terms of either the "preparation" theory or the "privilege" theory. The first of these goes like this: college is a "preparatory" period when the student, through incubation, is equipped with the skills he will need in life later on. "Preparation" means involving the student in a make-believe laboratory world of student activities where he can safely practice being a citizen. This process is affirmed by one dean of students in these terms:

> I propose a system whereby we use our decision-making processes as teaching tools, allowing students the opportunity to observe, criticize, and question, but not actually to exert direct control. The element of "let's pretend" has some value as a way of teaching.

Are we to take this as a serious educational philosophy? If we do, let us also remember that it is a feasible way to remove substance from politics, leaving the emptiness of gesture. Let us note, too, that it neatly sterilizes the content of debate and controversy, while leaving the form intact. Let us note, finally, that it is a convenient means of preserving the university status quo, maintaining harmony with legislators, rich alumni, and worried parents. And, nicely enough, all in the name of building democracy!

But does the student really learn from making decisions that can have no certain consequences, that are posed and controlled and subject to veto by the dean of students? I think not. For any decision to constitute a useful learning experience, the individual must sense in a real way the responsibility for its consequences. And some decisions must affect the local status quo if decision making is to be distinguished from the boredom of perpetual rehearsal.

I found one of the most devastating examples of the pretend theory of learning in an article in the University of Wisconsin *Daily Cardinal* of November 17, 1961. The author, in analyzing the student government constitution, finds that "Student Senate shall. . .legislate on any matter aiding in the planning, supervision, and co-ordination of student activities *in accordance with University regulations.*" The Senate "can thus vote only to uphold University rules. It is constitutionally mandated to maintain the status quo."

This does not mean that students are shackled completely at the University of Wisconsin. It simply means that they violate the constitution every time they do something creative; this violation gives the administration a "constitutional" excuse for veto action every time an "unconstitutional" act is not to their liking. Incredibly, the government of laws coincides with the government of men. I wonder how many students in America share the mood of the student journalist's last brief paragraph:

"Rather makes the whole thing a farce."

Linked to this theory that college is a preparation for democratic life is the administrative creed that attendance at a university is "a privilege, not a right." This follows the narrow line of argument that the student chooses to attend such-and-such a university, pays his tuition, enters a contractual relation, and must leave at the university's insistence. The student is essentially an outsider, someone who takes what he gets, or else. But if this be one's conception of the fundamental relation of the student to his academic community, then the academic community will hardly obtain certain of its social and educational ends. Socially, the ends will be thwarted by the segregation and occasional intimidation of the student population from the educational community which should be whole and integrated. Educationally, the ends are thwarted by analogizing the university to a corporation or any form of business enterprise which produces "college graduates." The ideal, and the only ultimately practical university (I hope to argue today) is composed of a host of scholars, each of them students and each of them teachers to some degree, finding unity in the common task of leading the examined life. To designate some as members by "privilege" and some as members by "right" means that the former group has only a submissive role in the general search for knowledge and values. They can search, but not too boldly; they can inquire, but not into everything; they can participate, but not in the actual governance of the community. They can be forbidden certain associations. Their academic life habits can be regulated without explanation. They can be suspended, or expelled, for at any moment they might find themselves "unable to adjust to the pattern of the university."

Having briefly examined the institutional role of the college student, I want to look more closely at the student generation emerging. Several influential studies in recent years suggest rather alarming facts about the nature of student culture. In his book, *Changing Values in College*, Philip Jacob found that 3 per cent of the students interviewed "gave top priority to being active in national affairs or being useful." Seventeen per cent expected that participating as a citizen in the affairs of the community would be one of the activities giving the "most satisfaction in life." Asked what was the university's most important function, the goal of "getting along with other people" received five times as much support as the goal of "citizenship participation." A second study, done by Dr. Edward Eddy at the University of New Hampshire, concluded that most students perceive college life as a "parenthesis" enclosing something neither related nor relevant to the rest of life, except as it assured a better job. Another more recent study is contained in a 1,000-page collection of essays by social scientists, edited by Nevitt Sanford and titled *The American College*. One of the author's major concerns is the university's failure to challenge and truly educate a huge bloc of students who are fair achievers but without strong goals or commitments to anything. One of the most astonishing surveys was reported by Dr. Herman H. Remmers just a few years ago. "They play it so safe," he said, "that they've lost their feelings for the basic tenets of American democracy." He found that three of every four students believe "that what the nation needs is a strong fearless leader in whom we can have faith," 50 per cent were willing to compromise freedom of the press; 83 per cent thought it all right for the police to use third-degree tactics.

What are we witnessing here? Surely it is the decomposition of democracy in this country. People are becoming more remote from the possibility of a civic life that maximizes personal influence over public affairs. There is a deep alienation of the student from the decision-making institutions of society. C. Wright Mills suggests a widening separation between "social structure" and personal "milieu." As our major institutions expand, and science and technology generate an increased need for division of labor, expertise and specialization, and the life of nations becomes more interconnected, fewer and fewer individuals are able to perceive truly beyond their immediate and limited circles, their milieus. An even smaller number have even the semblance of an integrated understanding of social realities and social change. Take the University of Michigan: Who here has any conception of the structure of even this university, the location of authority—formal and informal, the role of the faculty in policy making, the impact of federal research funds on the education of the individual, the relations with legislators and alumni and foundations?

Less and less do we transform private troubles into public issues. For instance, the man who is sick with the commercials he sees on television tends to disconnect the set instead of complaining about the capitalist system that created pseudo-needs in people—a prerequisite of mass society—so as to continue profit in times of overproduction. Similarly, the freshman in the quadrangle does not connect the fact that he can see his girl friend in the apartment but not in the quad with the fact that the State of Michigan is politically gerrymandered so as to entrench nineteenth-century Americans like Senator Elmer Porter in the Senate and House of Representatives. The student who is upset by the idiosyncracies of the Negro cleaning lady in his corridor does not connect his upset with the fact that more than one-third of all Negro women in America are forced to be domestics or the fact that salary rates for Negroes have been, on the average, one-half of the rates for white men for the past twenty years.

As the perimeter of personal vision becomes closer, several terrible things happen. A sense of powerlessness evolves, powerlessness with regard to changing the state of affairs evoked by the ideology of "complexity," a powerlessness that is often hidden beneath joviality and complacency. To the student, things seem to happen because of a mixture of graft and manipulation by an unseen "them," the modern equivalent of "fate." To the extent that these powerless participate in public affairs, they participate with impotency, adapting themselves to the myriad of rules, initiated and imposed from without, that constitute the university game (after all, who wants to be a martyr over dress regulations?). They seek to conform their actions to what the Top People like, they just try and get by, feeling pretty content most of the time, enjoying the university's benevolent laxity about drinking regulations, building up their exam files, "playing it cool."

A recent Gallup study of youth concluded, among other things, that youth will "settle for low success [and] won't risk high failure." There is no willingness to take risks, no setting of dangerous goals, no real conception of personal identity except one made in the image of others, no real urge for personal fulfillment except to be *almost* as successful as the very successful people. Much attention is paid to the social status (meeting people, getting a wife or a husband, making good solid business contacts); increasingly much more attention is paid to academic status (get grades, get honors, get into medical school). Still neglected generally, however, is the intellectual status, the personal cultivation of excellence of the mind. Nevitt Sanford writes: "To develop a skill in selling one's personality may appear far more important than to develop any personality worth selling." That the universities should encourage social acceptance is only natural; they are, of course, only acting *in loco* middle-class *parentis.*

The university and society are not just impersonal to the student. Where members of an institution are linked by the *functional* bond of being students, not by the *fraternal* bond of being people, there develops a terrible isolation of man from man only dimly disguised in the intensity of twist parties or the frightening riots that broke out at Lauderdale because the city lights wouldn't turn on the beach at night. Albert Camus' novel, *The Stranger,* creates a paradigm of the man lacking relatedness to anything at all. In one part of the novel the Stranger's mother has died and he himself goes swimming and to the movies with his girlfriend. That evening she asks him to marry her, to which he nonchalantly consents. Next she asks if he loves her, and with the same detachment he replies that he doesn't think so. In this perhaps extreme case, don't we see the contours of a generation consciously drifting *but not even prepared to commit itself to drifting?* A teacher in Austin, Texas, made this point plain to me when he joked: "Students don't even give a damn about apathy." Can we call this attitude human? Doesn't it involve a perception of life that is unreal, as articulated by one coed who said: "For the most of us, war is a great big fairy tale told by our parents. We don't believe that it can happen to us." If war in 1962 is a great big fairy tale, what meaning have life and death?

The pleasantness, the glad hand of the group in many respects, is but the conforming surface of a deeply, though perhaps unconsciously, callous personality: Callous in that these same people can drink the weekend away impervious to the fact that in Calcutta University, 100 students die each semester from starvation and malnutrition. Callous in that they scribble down "labor" in the abstract cost columns during economics lectures unmoved by the fact that 16 million Americans are still not covered by the 1961 Minimum Wage Law. Callous in that they preach to Negroes to educate themselves when the Negro college graduate in America earns on the average two-thirds the salary of the white man with the same educational background. Callous in their incredible bragging about being "better red than dead," that not only demonstrates how deeply the mass killings of the twentieth century have sterilized our respect for the sacredness of the individual, but also becomes mindless pomposity when contrasted with the hundreds of Negroes in the South who are actually nonviolently living the words of the spiritual, "Before I'll be a slave, I'll be buried in my grave."

But callousness alone does not describe this problem. Deeper and more dangerous is the near disappearance among the students of the critical faculty—that which is expected to make fine discriminations among different political ideologies and ethical statements, that which endows the moral sense with reason, and that which refines the quality of conviction. It is this human faculty which remains untouched by much of the classroom experience and largely unused in our day-to-day-response to living. Without this faculty, we become insensitive, adapting to the dull ethics that permeate our various functional roles. As Americans, for example, we cheer loudly for Virgil Grissom and John Glenn and not so loudly for the superior performances of Gagarin and Titov. Gradually the possibility of judging as a human being disappears; being a human being is distinctly not functional and, perhaps, it might be Unpatriotic.

But this is only the visible part of this student, the part he lets us scrutinize. There is a very private as well as a public life of the powerless. Isolation soon begets a privately-constructed universe, a place of systematic study schedules, two nights a week for beer, a steady girl, early marriage—a framework infused with personality, warmth, and under control, where a fellow can at least be father of the house, however incomplete and unsatisfying it may be. This strange, deeply personal and coveted (near secret) world has been illuminated best, perhaps, by the poet Rilke, who once compared twentieth century man to a stranger who from his window looks out into the dark, abandoned street of an unfamiliar, inhospitable town. He writes:

> The new city was still to me, as though denied, and the unresponsive landscape spread its darkness as though I were not there. The nearest things did not bother to reveal themselves to me. The alley climbed to a street light. I saw how alien it was. Across the way a room was warmly lighted by a lamp. It made me feel included. They sensed this, and drew the shutters.

Amidst the growing dominance of functional over personal bonds between people, this profound detachment from the cooperative and public life, this buckling down to make a safe buck and a safer life, there still seems to be flaring the human desire for a creative neighborhood of people. But, tragically, it flares less and less, and the shutters of which Rilke speaks are drawing tighter.

How distant is this condition from the best meanings of education and social democracy?

I believe education in a democracy should be threatening and renewing—threatening in that it should critically examine the deepest understandings of life, confronting taboo, habit, ritual, and personal ethics with a withering "why," unearthing the values that society buries for security's sake, and exposing these to the sunlight of the inquiring mind; renewing in that it transmits human culture from generation to generation and place to place, transforming some parts, modifying others, concurring with still others, yet expressing reverence for the whole.

The main concern of the university should not be with the publishing of books, getting money from legislators, lobbying for federal aid, wooing the rich, producing bombs and deadly bacteria. Nor should it be with passing along the morality of the middle class, nor the morality of the white man, nor even the morality of this potpourri we call "Western society." Nor should it be with acting as a second household and church for the young man away from home, nor as a playground for twisters, neophyte drinkers, and pledge classes. Already, however, the parallels between the habits of the university and the habits of the society are many. I have listed some; include *with* these: the parallels between our academic and financial systems of credit, between competition for grades and for chamber of commerce awards, between cheating and price rigging, between the statements "attendance is a privilege, not a right" and "we reserve the right to refuse service to anyone."

The main and transcending concern of the university must be the unfolding and refinement of the moral, aesthetic, and logical capacities of men in a manner that creates genuine independence. What do I have in mind by "genuine independence"? A concern not with image or popularity, but with finding a moral meaning in life that is direct and authentic for the self. A quality of mind that is not compulsively driven by a sense of powerlessness, nor one which unthinkingly adopts values of the Top People, nor one which represses threats to its habits, but one which has full, spontaneous access to present and past experience, one which easily unites the fragmented parts of personal history, one which openly faces problems which are troubling and unresolved. An intuitive alertness to that which is capable of occurring, to that which is not yet realized, and a passion for the continuous opening of human potential. These are the qualities—the weapons—that might unravel the heavy cape of impotence, the qualities that might restore the dominance of human over functional responsibilities and bring to men once more the will and the ability to exert real influence over events as citizens.

Above all, I reject the claim that only a privileged few can be independent, the view that creativity is necessarily the function of culture-preserving elites. I believe that independence can be a fact about ordinary people. And democracy, real participating democracy, rests on the independence of the ordinary people.

Some will see a contradiction in my approval of general self-determination and my depressing characterization of the state of student culture. How, it will be asked, can I reconcile my advocacy of independence and my charge of irresponsibility? This kind of criticism, I think, rests on the silent assumption that students and people generally are *innately* apathetic, that human dullness is somehow "in the nature of things." My counter-assumption is that much of our trouble is not innate and not inevitable, but rooted in the social structures and institutions we have created. Furthermore, in many cases it is not the internal dynamic of those institutions that makes decisive decisions today, but it is very often *men*, small knots of democratically irresponsible men.

Take the college as a limited example: An authoritarian institution does not develop independent people. An authoritarian college within a society that basically values money and power, conformity and success, established habits and the status quo, does not develop independent people. When I ask these critics how they would alter things, their response usually is to further isolate the people from decision making because the transcendent value of our times, they say, is the military and economic viability of the so-called Free World. It is usually added that the government, the churches, and the press are not fulfilling their roles as builders of public morale. I do not think this response contains a remedy at all for the problems I have tried to outline. Instead of changing, it tends to aggravate the condition of the powerless in our society. It tends to obscure the values that are supposed to be at the basis of the Cold War struggle. When it was reported that a dominating response among GI's who were asked why they fought in Korea was "That's the way the ball bounces," we should not have carried on about the decline of patriotism; we should have asked ourselves: Why are these men alienated, valueless, the apathetic pawns of circumstance? What opportunities have they had to be otherwise, in politics, in their work, in their free time? When a girl says she perceives peace and war as a fairy tale, we should not bemoan her immaturity; we should ask: Why is she so rootless? What must be changed so that she will come into the society with a real, felt concern about the continued life of man?

We must have a try at bringing society under human control. We must wrest control somehow from the endless machines that grind up men's jobs, the few hundred corporations that exercise greater power over the economy and the country than in feudal societies, the vast military profession that came into existence with universal military training during our brief lifetime, the irresponsible politicians secured by the ideological overlap, the seniority system and the gerrymandered base of our political structure, and the pervasive bureaucracy that perpetuates and multiplies itself everywhere. These are the dominators of human beings, the real, definable phenomena that make human beings fall—victimized by undefinable "circumstance." Sadly, the university in America has become a part of this hierarchy of power, rather than an instrument to make men free.

It must be said, too, that the university situation in America is more a symptom than a basic cause of our problems. But a college is one place to embark on a movement of reform, a place with intellectual equipment and a reservoir of unused creativity, a place from which reason might make a last attempt to intervene in human affairs.

A really excellent university, I believe, would not be organized along corporate and authoritarian lines, but in a way that would truly activate the creative potential of students and faculty. These two communities share the real enterprise of learning, and as there can be no final unamendable Truth in a community of free inquiry, there can be no arbitrary authority structure for the relation of teacher and student. A company of scholars is a company of equals in the crucial sense that none has a premium on truth, though some may be wiser, more literate, more numerous, more knowledgeable than others. Because the faculty has more permanence and more educational training, theirs should be the primary responsibility for the direction of the university. Because education is not a one-way process, because faculty tradition must be balanced by the fresh eye of youth, and because democracy requires popular control over important decisions, students should share with professors in the developing university. Separate student government and faculty government should be abolished and replaced by a cooperative decision-making body. The organized university administration, as it now exists, should be eliminated. In the present form, administrations are increasingly staffed by individuals without backgrounds of significant scholarship, and without a primary interest in the education of students. By the very nature of their constant administrative work, these men assume greater and greater—quite oligarchical—power over the everyday and long-range progress of the university. Therefore, to think of them as "equals" with the faculty and students, is not only to say that bureaucrats should have as much say as scholars, but it is to give bureaucracy an unfair advantage which inevitably leads to dominance. Instead of this system, we should acquire a bureaucracy that is really a bureaucracy: a rational apparatus meant to service the work of the intellectual community. A bureaucracy, for instance, might take care of admissions problems, parking policies, health and medical service, staffing, business management of the dormitories, public relations. All of these functions should be subject to the democratic control of the students and faculty, although they should not be so tightly controlled as to create human problems of alienation within the bureaucracy itself. The more important administrative functions—the presidency, the academic deanships, major rules and regulations, relations with the sources of funds, curriculum content, teaching methods, class sizes—should be the direct and never-delegated concern of the students and faculty. As for the regents and trustees, the present criteria for selection, *e.g.*, wealth, political affiliation, prestige, should be subordinated to educational experience and understanding. This accomplished, regents might properly represent public interests, though with only advisory power, in university decision making.

It will be said that this activity would exhaust the scholarly community. To this I say: Better exhaustion than the present system of nearly total administrative control of the universities. It will be further said that I am being utopian and unrealistic. In response I would ask you to consider whether or not you believe that our current realisms about politics and education are solving human problems; I would then quote Norman Brown's *Life Against Death* (a psychoanalytic study of the meaning of history): "Utopian speculations . . . must come back into fashion. They are a way of affirming faith in the present moment insoluble. Today even the survival of humanity is a utopian hope." Third, I would suggest that without at least a vision of the ideal university, reformers will make no qualitative changes and may even adopt standards that their vision would oppose.

The university I envision will tolerate and even promote student exercise of democratic prerogatives. It will entertain all ideas and make them challenging. It will be culturally, racially, religiously, and internationally integrated. It will appreciate the educational benefits of testing ideas through real action.

In this good university of mine, *in loco parentis* will be replaced by the doctrine that man is meant to live, not to prepare for life. Instead of a system that is paternal and relatively closed, there will be an organic system, where ideas are sharply confronted so that man can comprehend, always developing in the tension between threat and renewal. The good university will be concerned with democracy, too: By its practices, it will counter democracy that depends on authority, elites, and specialization with one that depends on consent, individual participation, and the common intelligence that enables men to deal with confusion, anxiety, and the enormity of events.

Instead of discussing student "action" I fear I have paid more attention to the dominant trend of student "petrifaction." My hope has been to indicate my serious concern about the absence of social consciousness and action, not only within the student community but within society generally, at a time when the world needs more independently active people.

This is not to say there is no student activity on the campus. Perhaps there is more at this time than at any time during the fifties. I sense a widespread moral revival that moves in politically ambiguous directions, mostly centered among relatively creative minorities who are deeply out of phase with life in this country.

The efforts I am most moved by are those of Southern Negro students who suffer day by day, fighting for America to honor its ideals. Despite the cruelties of the machines in the South, the immoral laxity of the white community in America, the agonizing splits with families, the financial and other sacrifices required, the constance of physical danger, they go on—nearly unnoticed by the public and barely supported by the Federal Government. To be sure, they are inheritors of an historical tradition of protest, but in a real sense also they are their own leaders; they are defining the orienting policies of the struggle, they are restoring the individual personality to a creative and self-cultivating role in human affairs. Too, they are becoming one with a far more noble struggle than the degrading one between East and West; they are part of the North-South conflict between the old overdeveloped ruling elites and the masses of hungry, aspiring, utopian peoples intervening in history for the first time. I am afraid, however, that too few of us see anything exemplary about the Southern students.

Still other students—more than ever—are starting to grapple with the hard problems of war, peace, and foreign policy. Five thousand of them turned out to picket the White House and visit their Congressmen just last month, demanding American initiatives toward peace. A few hundred more participated at a high intellectual level in the First Intercollegiate Conference on Disarmament and Arms Control at Swarthmore College.

There are, finally, thousands of young conservatives who came into public significance in 1960. That I find them politically absurd does not deny the catalytic value of their social participation and the stirring they have caused among many students.

But these people are minorities; they have broken through the crust of silence. It remains for the vast majority similarly to discover that peace and war are not fairy tales, that at the midnight of Doomsday we will not turn into pumpkins (though some will be vegetating in their shelters). Every time we do not speak, we contribute to the mood of moral rigidity that grips the land. Every time we do not speak, we maintain the vacuum of public affairs. Every time we do not speak, we make harder the creation of an active public to dismantle the hierarchy of undemocratic power in America.

Do not wish to be a student in contrast to being a man. Do not study as a student, but as a man who is alive and who cares. Leave the isolated world of ideological fantasy, allow your ideas to become part of your living and your living to become part of your ideas.

All over the world the young intellectuals are breaking out of the old, stultified order. Before you call them "communist" or "extremist" or "immature," stop a moment, let yourselves be a little more insecure, so that you can listen to what they say and perhaps feel the pulse of their challenge. Their challenge politically takes many forms, with which we may agree or disagree; but the essential challenge is far deeper. It is to quit the acquiescence to political "fate," cut the confidence in business-as-usual futures, and realize that in a time of mass organization, government by expertise, success through technical specialization, manipulation by the balancing of Official Secrecy with the Soft Sell Technique, incomprehensible destructiveness of the two wars and the third which is imminent, and the Cold War which has chilled man's relation to man, the time has come for a re-assertion of the personal.

Thomas Hayden is a staff member of the Newark Community Union Project (SDS, Economic Research and Action Project), and a past president of Students for a Democratic Society. "Student Social Action" is a transcription of a talk given at the University of Michigan in spring, 1962.

Appendix: War and Foreign Policy

Every radical movement, sooner or later, comes up hard against the seemingly immobile Gibraltar that is American foreign policy. The New Left is no different. The questions of war and peace, of the developing nations, of poverty and revolution, are the most difficult and frustrating ones dealt with in this volume. A full treatment would fill a volume, and this appendix is a necessarily incomplete guide to the broad outlines of the arguments. In this area, the primacy of the Students for a Democratic Society is most apparent: from the opening shots in the original Port Huron Statement, to the recent, vigorous opposition to the Vietnam war, SDS has set the tone and the terms of the debate.

The debate, however, threatens to engulf the participants. As Jonathan Eisen indicates in his report of the January 1966 SDS Convention at the University of Illinois, the student movement has "had the courage to face everything but failure," and failure seems to be the verdict, so far, on student opposition to the war. The escalation continues, unabated by lie-ins, sit-ins, teach-ins, and pickets.

THE EDITORS

FROM THE *PORT HURON STATEMENT*

I. The Individual in the Warfare State

. . . Business and politics, when significantly militarized, affect the whole living condition of each American citizen. Worker and family depend on the Cold War for life. Half of all research and development is concentrated on military ends. The press mimics conventional cold war opinion in its editorials. In less than a full generation, most Americans accept the military-industrial structure as "the way things are." War is still pictured as one kind of diplomacy, perhaps a gloriously satisfying kind. Our saturation and atomic bombings of Germany and Japan are little more than memories of past "policy necessities" that preceded the wonderful economic boom of 1946. The fact that our once-revolutionary 20,000-ton Hiroshima Bomb is now paled by 50 megaton weapons, that our lifetime has included the creation of intercontinental ballistic missiles, that "greater" weapons are to follow, that weapons refinement is more rapid than the development of weapons of defense, that soon a dozen or more nations will have the Bomb, that one simple miscalculation could incinerate mankind: these orienting facts are but remotely felt. A shell of moral callousness separates the citizen from sensitivity to the common peril: this is the result of a lifetime saturation with horror. After all, some ask, where could we begin, even if we wanted to? After all, others declare, we can only assume things are in the best of hands. A coed at the University of Kentucky says, "We regard peace and war as fairy tales." And a child has asked in helplessness, perhaps for us all, "Daddy, why is there a cold war?"

Past senselessness permits present brutality; present brutality is a prelude to future deeds of still greater inhumanity; that is the moral history of the twentieth century, from the First World War to the present. A half century of accelerating destruction has flattened out the individual's ability to make moral distinctions; it has made people understandably give up; it has forced private worry and public silence.

To a decisive extent, the means of defense, the military technology itself, determines the political and social character of the state being defended—that is, defense mechanisms themselves in the nuclear age alter the character of the system that creates them for protection. So it has been with America, as her democratic institutions and habits have shriveled in almost direct proportion to the growth of her armaments. Decisions about military strategy, including the monstrous decision to go to war, are more and more the property of the military and industrial arms race machine, with the politicians assuming a ratifying role instead of a determining one. This is increasingly a fact not just because of the installation of the permanent military, but because of constant revolutions in military technology. The new technologies allegedly require military expertise, scientific comprehension, and the mantle of secrecy. As Congress relies more and more on the Joint Chiefs of Staff, the existing chasm between people and decision-makers becomes irreconcilably wide, and more alienating in its effects.

A necessary part of the military effort is propaganda: to "sell" the need for Congressional appropriations, to conceal various business scandals, and to convince the American people that the arms race is important enough to sacrifice civil liberties and social welfare. So confusion prevails about the national needs, while the three major services and the industrial allies jockey for power—the Air Force tending to support bombers and missilery; the Navy, Polaris and carriers; the Army, conventional ground forces and invulnerable nuclear arsenals, and all three feigning unity by support of the policy of weapons agglomeration called the "mix." Strategies are advocated on the basis of power and profit, usually more so than on the basis of national military needs. In the meantime, Congressional investigating committees—most notably the House Un-American Activities Committee and the Senate Judiciary Committee—attempt to curb the little dissent that finds its way into off-beat magazines. A huge militant anti-communist brigade throws in its support, patriotically willing to do *anything* to achieve "total victory" in the Cold War; the government advocates peaceful confrontation with international communism, then utterly pillories and outlaws the tiny

American Communist Party. University professors withdraw prudently from public issues; the very style of social science writing becomes more qualified. Needs in housing, education, minority rights, health care, land redevelopment, hourly wages, all are subordinated . . . to the primary objective of the "military and economic strength of the Free World."

What are the governing policies which supposedly justify all this human sacrifice and waste? With few exceptions they have reflected the quandaries and confusion, stagnation and anxiety, of a stalemated nation in a turbulent world. They have shown a slowness, sometimes a sheer inability to react to a sequence of new problems.

Of these problems, two of the newest are foremost: the existence of poised nuclear weapons and the revolutions against the former colonial powers. In both areas, the Soviet Union and various national Communist movements have aggravated international relations in inhuman and undesirable ways, but hardly so much as to blame only communism for the present menacing situation.

II. Deterrence Policy

. . . The accumulation of nuclear arsenals, the threat of accidental war, the possibility of limited war becoming illimitable holocaust, the impossibility of achieving final arms superiority or invulnerability, the approaching nativity of a cluster of infant atomic powers; all of these events are tending to undermine traditional concepts of power relations among nations. War can no longer be considered as an effective instrument of foreign policy, a means of strengthening alliances, adjusting the balance of power, maintaining national sovereignty, or preserving human values. War is no longer simply a forceful extension of foreign policy; it can obtain no constructive ends in the modern world. Soviet or American "megatonnage" is sufficient to destroy all existing social structures as well as value systems. Missiles have (figuratively) thumbed their nosecones at national boundaries. But America, like other countries, still operates by means of national defense and deterrence systems. These are seen to be useful so long as they are never fully used: unless we as a national entity can convince Russia that we are willing to commit the most heinous action in human history, we will be forced to commit it.

Deterrence advocates, all of them prepared at least to threaten mass extermination, advance arguments of several kinds. At one pole are the minority of open partisans of preventive war—who falsely assume the inevitability of violent conflict and assert the lunatic efficacy of striking the first blow, assuming that it will be easier to "recover" after thermonuclear war than to recover now from the grip of the Cold War. Somewhat more reluctant to advocate initiating a war, but perhaps more disturbing for their numbers within the Kennedy Administration, are the many advocates of the "counter-force" theory of aiming strategic nuclear weapons at military installations—though this might "save" more lives than a preventive war, it would require drastic, provocative, and perhaps impossible social change to separate many cities from weapon sites, it would be impossible to insure the immunity of cities after one or two counter-force nuclear "exchanges," it would generate a perpetual arms race for less vulnerability and greater weapons, power and mobility, it would make outer space a region subject to militarization, and accelerate the suspicions and arms build-ups which are incentives to precipitate nuclear action.

Others would support fighting "limited wars" which use conventional (all but atomic) weapons, backed by deterrents so mighty that both sides would fear to use them—although underestimating the implications of numerous new atomic powers on the world stage, the extreme difficulty of anchoring international order with weapons of only transient invulnerability, the potential tendency for a "losing side" to push limited protracted fighting on the soil of underdeveloped countries. Still other deterrence artists propose limited, clearly defensive and retaliatory, nuclear capacity, always potent enough to deter an opponent's aggressive designs—the best of deterrence strategems, but inadequate when it rests on the equation of an arms "stalemate" with international stability.

All the deterrence theories suffer in several common ways. They allow insufficient attention to preserving, extending, and enriching democratic values, such matters being subordinate rather than governing in the process of conducting foreign policy. Second, they inadequately realize the inherent instabilities of the continuing arms race and balance of fear. Third, they operationally tend to eclipse interest and action towards disarmament by solidifying economic, political, and even moral investments in continuation of tensions. Fourth, they offer a disinterested and even patriotic rationale for the boondoggling, belligerence, and privilege of military and economic elites. Finally, deterrence strategems invariably understate or dismiss the relatedness of various dangers; they inevitably lend tolerability to the idea of war by neglecting the dynamic interaction of problems—such as the menace of accidental war, the probable future tensions surrounding the emergence of ex-colonial nations, the imminence of several new nations joining the "Nuclear Club," the destabilizing potential of technological breakthrough by either arms race contestant, the threat of Chinese atomic might, the fact that "recovery" after World War III would involve not only human survivors but, as well, a huge and fragile social structure and culture which would be decimated perhaps irreparably by total war.

Such a harsh critique of what we are doing as a nation by no means implies that sole blame for the Cold War rests on the United States. Both sides have behaved irresponsibly—the Russians by an exaggerated lack of trust, and by much dependence on aggressive military strategists rather than on proponents of nonviolent conflict and coexistence. But we do contend, as Americans concerned with the conduct of our representative institutions, that our government has blamed the Cold War stalemate on nearly everything but its own hesitations, its own anachronistic dependence on weapons. To be sure, there is more to disarmament than wishing for it. There are inadequacies in international rulemaking institutions—which could be corrected. There are faulty inspection mechanisms—which could be perfected by disinterested scientists. There are Russian intransigency and evasiveness—which do not erase the fact that the Soviet Union, because of a strained economy, an expectant population, fears of Chinese potential, and interest in the colonial revolution, is increasingly disposed to real disarmament with real controls. But there is, too, our own reluctance to face the uncertain world beyond the Cold War, our own shocking assumption that the risks of the present are fewer than the risks of a policy re-orientation to disarmament, our own unwillingness to face the implementation of our rhetorical commitments to peace and freedom.

Today the world alternately drifts and plunges towards a terrible war—when vision and change are required, our government pursues a policy of macabre dead-end dimensions—conditioned but not justified by actions of the Soviet bloc. Ironically, the war which seems so close will not be fought between the United States and Russia, not externally between two national entities, but as an international civil war throughout the unrespected and unprotected *civitas* which spans the world.

III. The Colonial Revolution

. . . While weapons have accelerated man's opportunity for self-destruction, the counter-impulse to life and creation is superbly manifest in the revolutionary feelings of many Asian, African, and Latin American peoples. Against the individual initiative and aspiration, and social sense of organicism characteristic of these upsurges, the American apathy and stalemate stand in embarrassing contrast.

It is difficult today to give human meaning to the welter of facts that surrounds us. That is why it is especially hard to understand the facts of "underdevelopment": in India, man and beast together produced 65 percent of the nation's economic energy in a recent year, and of the remaining 35 percent of inanimately produced power almost three-fourths was obtained by burning dung. But in the United States, human and animal power together account for only one percent of the national economic energy—that is what stands humanly behind the vague term "industrialization." Even to maintain the misery of Asia today at a constant level will require a rate of growth tripling the national income and the aggregate production in Asian countries by the end of the century. For Asians to have the (unacceptable) 1950 standard of

Europeans, less than $2,000 per year for a family, national production must increase 21-fold by the end of the century, and that monstrous feat only to reach a level that Europeans find intolerable.

What has America done? During the years 1955–57 our total expenditures in economic aid were equal to one-tenth of one percent of our Gross National Product. Prior to that time it was less; since then it has been a fraction higher. Immediate social and economic development is needed—we have helped little, seeming to prefer to create a growing gap between "have" and "have not" rather than to usher in social revolutions which would threaten our investors and our military alliances. The new nations want to avoid power entanglements that will open their countries to foreign domination—and we have often demanded loyalty oaths. They do not see the relevance of uncontrolled free enterprise in societies without accumulated capital and a significant middle class—and we have looked calumniously on those who would not try "our way." They seek empathy—and we have sided with the old colonialists, who now are trying to take credit for "giving" all the freedom that has been wrested from them, or we "empathize" when pressure absolutely demands it.

With rare variation, American foreign policy in the Fifties was guided by a concern for foreign investment and a negative anti-Communist political stance linked to a series of military alliances, both undergirded by military threat. We participated unilaterally—usually through the Central Intelligence Agency—in revolutions against governments in Laos, Guatemala, Cuba, Egypt, Iran. We permitted economic investment to decisively affect our foreign policy: sugar in Cuba, oil in the Middle East, diamonds in South Africa (with whom we trade more than with any African nation). More exactly: America's "foreign market" in the late Fifties, including exports of goods and services plus overseas sales by American firms, averaged about $60 billion annually. This represented twice the investment of 1950, and it is predicted that the same rate of increase will continue. The reason is obvious; *Fortune* said in 1958, "foreign earnings will more than double in ten years, more than twice the probable gain in domestic profits."

These investments are concentrated primarily in the Middle East and Latin America, neither region being an impressive candidate for long-run stability, political caution, and lower-class tolerance that American investors typically demand.

Our pugnacious anti-communism and protection of interests has led us to an alliance inappropriately called the "Free World." It includes four major parliamentary democracies: ourselves, Canada, Great Britain, and India. It also has included through the years Batista, Franco, Verwoerd, Salazar, De Gaulle, Boun Oum, Ngo Diem, Chiang Kai Shek, Trujillo, the Somozas, Saud, Ydigoras—all of these non-democrats separating us deeply from the colonial revolutions.

Since the Kennedy administration began, the American government seems to have initiated policy changes in the colonial and underdeveloped areas. It accepted "neutralism" as a tolerable principle; it sided more than once with the Angolans in the United Nations; it invited Souvanna Phouma to return to Laos after having overthrown his neutralist government there; it implemented the Alliance for Progress that President Eisenhower proposed when Latin America appeared on the verge of socialist revolutions; it made derogatory statements about the Trujillos; it cautiously suggested that a democratic socialist government in British Guiana might be necessary to support; in inaugural oratory, it suggested that a moral imperative was involved in sharing the world's resources with those who have been previously dominated. These were hardly sufficient to heal the scars of past activity and present associations, but nevertheless they were motions away from the Fifties. But quite unexpectedly, the President ordered the Cuban invasion, and while the American press railed about how we had been "shamed" and defied by that "monster Castro," the colonial peoples of the world wondered whether our foreign policy had really changed from its old imperialist ways (we had never supported Castro, even on the eve of his taking power, and had announced early that "the conduct of the Castro government toward foreign private enterprise in Cuba" would be a main State Department concern). Any heralded changes in our foreign policy are now further suspect in the wake of the Punta Del Este foreign ministers' conference where the five countries representing most of Latin America refused to cooperate in our plans to further "isolate" the Castro government.

Ever since the colonial revolution began, American policy makers have reacted to new problems with old "gunboat" remedies, often thinly disguised. The feeble but desirable efforts of the Kennedy administration to be more flexible are coming perhaps too late, and are of too little significance to really change the historical thrust of our policies. The hunger problem is increasing rapidly, mostly as a result of the world-wide population explosion that cancels out the meager triumphs gained so far over starvation. The threat of population to economic growth is simply documented: in 1960–70 population in Africa south of the Sahara will increase 14 percent; in South Asia and the Far East by 22 percent; in North Africa 26 percent; in the Middle East by 27 percent; in Latin America 29 percent. Population explosion, no matter how devastating, is neutral. But how long will it take to create a relation of trust between America and the newly-developing societies? How long to change our policies? And what length of time do we have?

The world is in transformation. But America is not. It can race to industrialize the world, tolerating occasional authoritarianisms, socialisms, neutralisms along the way—or it can slow the pace of the inevitable and default to the eager and self-interested Soviets and, much more importantly, to mankind itself. Only mystics would guess we have opted thoroughly for the first. Consider what our people think of this, the most urgent issue on the human agenda. Fed by a bellicose press, manipulated by economic and political opponents of change, drifting in their own history, they grumble about "the foreign aid waste," or about "that beatnik down in Cuba," or how "things will get us by" . . . thinking confidently, albeit in the usual bewilderment, that Americans can go right on as always, five percent of mankind producing forty percent of its goods.

IV. The Industrialization of the World

. . . Many Americans are prone to think of the industrialization of the newly-developed countries as a modern form of American *noblesse*, undertaken sacrificially for the benefit of others. On the contrary, the task of world industrialization, of eliminating the disparity between the have and have-not nations, is as important as any issue facing America. The colonial revolution signals the end of an era for the old Western powers and a time of new beginnings for most of the people of the earth. In the course of these upheavals, many problems will emerge: American policies must be revised or accelerated in several ways.

1. The United States' principal goal should be creating a world where hunger, poverty, disease, ignorance, violence, and exploitation are replaced as central features by abundance, reason, love, and international cooperation.

To many this will seem the product of juvenile hallucination: but we insist that it is a more realistic goal than is a world of nuclear stalemate. Some will say this is a hope beyond all bounds: but it is far better to us to have positive vision than a "hard-headed" resignation. Some will sympathize, but claim it is impossible: if so, then we, not Fate, are the responsible ones, for we have the means at our disposal. *We should not give up the attempt for fear of failure.*

2. We should undertake here and now a fifty-year effort to prepare for all nations the conditions of industrialization.

Even with far more capital and skill than we now export to emerging areas, serious prophets expect that two generations will pass before accelerating industrialism is a world-wide act. The needs are numerous: every nation must build an adequate infrastructure (transportation, communication, land resources, waterways) for future industrial growth; there must be industries suited to the rapid development of differing raw materials and other resources; education must begin on a continuing basis for everyone in the society, especially including engineering and technical training; technical assistance from outside sources must be adequate to meet present and long-term needs; atomic power plants must spring up to make electrical energy available. With

America's idle productive capacity, it is possible to begin this process immediately without changing our military allocations. This might catalyze a "peace race" since it would demand a response of such magnitude from the Soviet Union that arms spending and "coexistence" spending would become strenuous, perhaps impossible, for the Soviets to carry on simultaneously.

3. We should not depend significantly on private enterprise to do the job.

Many important projects will not be profitable enough to entice the investment of private capital. The total amount required is far beyond the resources of corporate and philanthropic concerns. The new nations are suspicious, legitimately, of foreign enterprises dominating their national life. World industrialization is too huge an undertaking to be formulated or carried out by private interests. Foreign economic assistance is a national problem, requiring long-range planning, integration with other domestic and foreign policies, and considerable public debate and analysis. Therefore the Federal government should have primary responsibility in this area.

4. We should not lock the development process into the Cold War: we should view it as a way of ending that conflict.

When President Kennedy declared that we must aid those who need aid because it is right, he was unimpeachably correct—now principle must become practice. We should reverse the trend of aiding corrupt anti-Communist regimes. To support dictators like Diem while trying to destroy ones like Castro will only enforce international cynicism about American "principle," and is bound to lead to even more authoritarian revolutions, especially in Latin America where we did not even consider foreign aid until Castro had challenged the status quo. We should end the distinction between Communist hunger and anti-Communist hunger. To feed only anti-Communists is to directly fatten men like Boun Oum, to incur the wrath of real democrats and to distort our own sense of human values. We must cease seeing development in terms of communism and capitalism. To fight communism by capitalism in the newly-developing areas is to fundamentally misunderstand the international hatred of imperialism and colonialism and to confuse the needs of nineteenth-century industrial America with those of contemporary nations.

Quite fortunately, we are edging away from the Dullesian "either-or" foreign policy ultimatum towards an uneasy acceptance of neutralism and nonalignment. If we really desire the end of the Cold War, we should now welcome nonalignment—that is, the creation of whole blocs of nations concerned with growth and with independently trying to break out the Cold War apparatus.

Finally, while seeking disarmament as the genuine deterrent, we should shift from financial support of military regimes to support of national development. Real security cannot be gained by propping up military defenses, but only through the hastening of political stability, economic growth, greater social welfare, improved education. Military aid is temporary in nature, a "shoring up" measure that only postpones crisis. In addition, it tends to divert the allocations of the nation being defended to supplementary military spending (Pakistan's budget is 70 percent oriented to defense measures). Sometimes it actually creates crisis situations, as in Latin America where we have contributed to the growth of national armies which are opposed generally to sweeping democratization. Finally, if we are really generous, it is harder for corrupt governments to exploit economic aid unfairly—especially if it is so plentiful that rulers cannot blame the absence of real reforms on anything but their own power lusts.

5. America should show its commitment to democratic institutions not by withdrawing support from undemocratic regimes, but by making domestic democracy exemplary.

World-wide amusement, cynicism, and hatred toward the United States as a democracy is not simply a Communist propaganda trick, but an objectively justifiable phenomenon. If respect for democracy is to be international, then the significance of democracy must emanate from American shores, not from the "soft sell" of the United States Information Agency.

> 6. America should agree that public utilities, railroads, mines, and plantations, and other basic economic institutions should be in the control of national, not foreign, agencies.

The destiny of any country should be determined by its nationals, not by outsiders with economic interests within. We should encourage our investors to turn over their foreign holdings (or at least 50 percent of the stock) to the national governments of the countries involved.

> 7. Foreign aid should be given through international agencies, primarily the United Nations.

The need is to eliminate political overtones, to the extent possible, from economic development. The use of international agencies, with interests transcending those of American or Russian self-interest, is the feasible means of working on sound development. Second, internationalization will allow more long-range planning, integrate development plans adjacent countries and regions may have, and eliminate the duplication built into national systems of foreign aid. Third, it would justify more strictness of supervision than is now the case with American foreign aid efforts, but with far less chance of suspicion on the part of the developing countries. Fourth, the humiliating "hand-out" effect would be replaced by the joint participation of all nations in the general development of the earth's resources and industrial capacities. Fifth, it would eliminate national tensions, e.g., between Japan and some Southeast Asian areas, which now impair aid programs by "disguising" nationalities in the common pooling of funds. Sixth, it would make easier the task of stabilizing the world market prices of basic commodities, alleviating the enormous threat that decline in prices of commodity exports might cancel out the gains from foreign aid in the new nations. Seventh, it would improve the possibilities of non-exploitative development, especially in creating "soft-credit" rotating-fund agencies which would not require immediate progress or financial return. Finally, it would enhance the importance of the United Nations itself, as the disarming process would enhance the UN as a rule-enforcement agency.

8. Democratic theory must confront the problems inherent in social revolutions.

For Americans concerned with the development of democratic societies, the anti-colonial movements and revolutions in the emerging nations pose serious problems. We need to face the problems with humility: after 180 years of constitutional government we are still striving for democracy in our own society. We must acknowledge that democracy and freedom do not magically occur, but have roots in historical experience; they cannot always be demanded for any society at any time, but must be nurtured and facilitated. We must avoid the arbitrary projection of Anglo-Saxon democratic forms onto different cultures. Instead of democratic capitalisms we should anticipate more or less authoritarian variants of socialism and collectivism in many emergent societies.

But we do not abandon our critical faculties. Insofar as these regimes represent a genuine realization of national independence, and are engaged in constructing social systems which allow for personal meaning and purpose where exploitation once was, economic systems which work for the people where once they oppressed them, and political systems which allow for the organization and expression of minority opinion and dissent, we recognize their revolutionary and positive character. Americans can contribute to the growth of democracy in such societies not by moralizing, nor by indiscriminate prejudgment, but by retaining a critical identification with these nations, and by helping them to avoid external threats to their independence. Together with students and radicals in these nations we need to develop a reasonable theory of democracy which is concretely applicable to the cultures and conditions of hungry people.

HEADS YOU WIN, TAILS WE LOSE

A Report on the SDS Convention by Jonathan Eisen

Urbana, Illinois, January 2, 1966

For the past week I have been attending a national membership conference of the Students for a Democratic Society, assiduously taking notes, watching the notables, interviewing, listening. In light of the fact that the SDS is the largest and probably most important left-wing student organization in the country (about 3,500 members), such a conference and its portents and implications are not without significance. As the totem for thousands of kids around the country concerned and tremulous over the Vietnam balloon, SDS has taken on a position of leadership—moral, political and strategic—which it has probably never known before. And as the focus of attention for the national press, Evans and Novak, the FBI and sundry others, its fulminations are now more influential than before, when the organization was the youth group of the venerable but decrepit League for Industrial Democracy.

The SDS has had a hard time coming to terms with its new importance on the national scene, and like many organizations in the past, is groping around trying to reduce the hiatus between necessity and its rather inadequate structural capabilities. One of the tasks of the conference was to grapple with the hard fact that unless the SDS can overcome its organizational limitations, its influence and magnetism are likely to fade rapidly. And Vietnam is the hangup.

As Mike O'Hanlon from the Berkeley Vietnam Day Committee phrased it, the problem resides in the nature of the issue itself. In the civil rights movement, while participants may have been beaten, jailed, maimed, even murdered, there was at least the pervasive conviction that history was consonant with its aims, that "We Shall Overcome."

But in the case of the war in Vietnam, the movement falters, and escalates its tactics in the absence of anything else which might be politically provocative and effective. As O'Hanlon puts it, "The movement has had the courage to face anything except failure." Profoundly pessimistic over possibilities of the New Left's swinging any political weight to halt the hostilities, O'Hanlon and his people are still pushing, still urging further action and analysis—for what else is there to do?

Others, like Don Weatherall, a young Negro student from Chicago, have been inducted and have refused to serve. He has contended that to serve in the army at this time would subject him to charges of being a war criminal. He bases his defense on the conclusion reached at the Nuremburg trials. For him the way to stop this war and future wars like it is for individuals to refuse to subordinate their conscience to the demands of the state. No trial date has been set for Weatherall, but the feeling is that his case may be significant. In any event it is symptomatic of the way in which the New Left is responding to the justifications being proffered by the Johnson consensus.

Despair, however, governs many of the conference-goers. One senior from Philadelphia (who prefers to remain anonymous) is making clandestine arrangements to escape to Canada as soon as he can, or to hide in storm sewers if he is drafted.

There is something odd (not crazy) about the SDS people facing the war, and it seems pervasive. The storm sewer kid is exemplary. The debate over contingency plans for when a full-blown crisis emerges (war with China, the bombing of Hanoi), as to the advisability of a student strike, or another international day of protest, or a Peace Draft, or another march on Washington involving civil disobedience, is illustrative. Nobody knows what to do, really. And they're losing their grip thinking about it.

No one, including SDS members, can long live in such psychically rending circumstances. And so a major effort is being made to "get off the Vietnam hangup" and adopt a more multifaceted approach which will serve to link up Vietnam with what they see as the essential rot and corruption of American society. The handling of this is enlightening, if somewhat confusing. The theory goes that Vietnam is merely a symbol, an instance of the driving forces of American power and ideology. There will be more Vietnams, perhaps again in Cuba, perhaps somewhere else in South America. The Dominican Republic incident is illustrative: America is now committed to protecting its colonial empire from nationalist uprisings. Liberalism laid bare is imperialism; the ideology of America is materialism, anti-communism, and order.

The conference was convened partly to formulate an ideology (if ideologies are in fact amenable to *formulation*, which is doubtful) to oppose American liberalism. In any case this was not done, but the thrust of the purpose is important: on the one hand SDS wants to extricate itself from leadership of the peace movement, to "get off" the Vietnam issue and focus more on "radicalizing" American youth. Partly recognizing the futility of action projects which circumvent political success, and partly for other than strategic reasons, Vietnam is seen as debilitating. And some rather wispy utopianism shows through the organization fabric: SDS is not out merely to radicalize the American youth, to educate students—it's out for power, it's out to change the dominant ideology on the American continent. If it can't extricate America from Southeast Asia, it can formulate an alternative ideology which excludes imperialism and offer this to America (listening). And when once adopted, there will be no more Vietnams. Rather than war protests which are immediately futile, and obviously destined to the historical scrapheap, the organization is trying to aim at the "complete social transformation of America" through an "alternative ideology." In light of the elephantine but vague proportions of this undertaking, O'Hanlon's remarks about the movement's courage to face anything but failure are terribly correct. The leadership knows that no movement hangs together very long by failing.

If SDS starts emphasizing education, ideology, and radicalizing American youth—diversifying its approach—it's likely that given complete failure in the Vietnam issue, the organization will not face complete breakdown. In fact, the more protean, the less the organization is conducive to failure or success in conventional terms: moreover SDS will succeed in a sense if it merely attracts more students to its fold, even if it does not substantially alter the structure of American liberalism, which it is not likely to do. Furthermore, it will continue to channel discontent into organizational outlets, and thereby enhance its standing on the left. So long as it does not function as a convulsive group responding viscerally to each crisis perpetrated by the American elite it will flourish, or at least survive. But so long as American youth is preoccupied with Vietnam and the threat of central war which it implies, SDS is probably destined to wither if it does not come up with something soon in the way of success—like peace. Parenthetically, some SDS people are now predicting a gradual drift into fascism if America is forced to evacuate Vietnam or offer a substantive compromise. A rehearsal of the "stab in the back" motif is seen in the works. But if America "wins" by crushing the NLF and North Vietnam, this too will be disastrous, since it will no doubt lead to further adventuristic attempts other places by the American policy makers. Heads you win, tails we lose. The current diplomatic peace offensive is seen, moreover, as an attempt to contain the peace movement by providing the excuse to escalate further, and the feeling is that Johnson is out for big game. No wonder the leadership is trying to switch tracks. The left is on the ropes.

A few words about the people and the factions, and then I'm through. As with any political organization—especially, it seems, those on the left—SDS is replete with discrete and often dissonant strains. The most interesting is the "emotional anarchism" strain which has given rise to fascinating behavior. A year or so ago was spawned the "cult of love" which reliable informants describe to me as a faction which heartily believed that no radical humanism could stand aloft unless the exponents ardently loved each other. Thus klaches and circles and hand-holding where each would proclaim undying selfless love for the other and all. Unfortunately, however, there were those who did not love, like those fellow SDS'ers in the New York office. Those who did not love were impure. So the national office was moved from the Babylon of New York to the Elysian fields of (yes) Chicago. Funny in a way but somehow revealing of a romanticism which reaches into the very heart of the movement itself. Hal Draper laments the anti-organizational posture of the FSM people, the antipathy for all types of bureaucracy—including that of their own organization. And there is much of this too in SDS. Last year there was something afoot to abolish several national positions and even the National Office itself. Regional, local autonomy was the word. Freedom meant the lack of control from all sources—including the "control" from Chicago. Here at the conference there was still a remnant or two of this wafting through the meetings.

In fact this emotive anarchism led to serious repercussions within SDS and partly to the severance of all formal bonds with the League for Industrial Democracy. That the LID has since gone to some pains to renovate itself and make some token accommodations to the ardor of the young people has not served to mitigate the split which many feel is now irrevocable. Tom Kahn, author of "The Unfinished Revolution"—one of the most influential pamphlets of the early Sixties for the student civil rights movement—arrived and was met with unremitting hostility from the far left of the organization, partly for his advocacy of coalitions with liberal organizations, but also for his leadership role in the LID. Harrington, Kahn, Irving Howe and others of the "democratic left" are coming increasingly under the barrage of the SDS folks, often for sound organizational reasons—like their preoccupation with anti-communism—but also for refusing to relinquish their trust in the democratic system (democratic in SDS quotes).

In response to these trends, if trends they are, many people in the old guard of SDS—Al Haber, Bob Ross, Todd Gitlin, Paul Booth, Lee Webb, Steve Max and others—apparently (nothing is certain) have begun reasserting their leadership, not for power but to nudge the organization back into more functional, more effective and more politically relevant roles. Other old guarders (all under 30) keep the organization viable on the local level: Rennie Davis in Chicago (working on organizing the poor in an organization called JOIN—Jobs or Income Now), Tom Hayden in Newark (at this writing he is in Hanoi with Herbert Aptheker and Staughton Lynd), and Paul Potter in Cleveland constitute much of the impetus and theoretical leadership for the continuing SDS projects. That at least some of these projects have met with recognition, if not success, is evinced in the efforts of Shriver's office to build a rapport with the Newark office and to co-opt some of the projects for the administration. For Shriver is shrewd enough to recognize that SDS has something that the Job Corps and similar poverty agencies with their millions of dollars cannot approach: an eagerness to build a consciousness among the poor of their power and dignity and their abilities to map out their own life, if properly organized, against the dominant political and economic hierarchies. And it is the old guard that has made more than a start at utilizing the ideology of democracy (participatory democracy) within the community, although not without friction within the SDS: in fact the tenacity of the top strata of the organization is a source of continuing resentment, and there is a new move to organize a "Movement for a Democratic Society" to draw off the older SDS'ers and recruit non-students. Where this push is destined is, like nearly everything else in the movement, unclear.

Some kind of conclusion is probably in order, but the problem is finding an appropriate handle. Something about the ideology, perhaps. But this is foggy, and more a Weltanschauung, an amalgamation of vulgar Marxism, humanism, Freudianism, populism and romanticism: what can you say? Maybe something about what they're doing: but the conference was a morass, a labyrinth, a marathon of procedural amendments, non-sequiturs, soul-searching and maneuvering, partying and arguing, plenaries which went nowhere, proposals unheeded, undebated; terminology which only the most in of the ingroup could comprehend, much less care about; and a few who were too far gone to participate in anything but getting girls. Pages and pages of proposals, prospectuses, amendments, workshop resolutions, recommendations, counter-recommendations, hasseling and dancing to the Beatles. Now it's the Lindy, the camp dance to do.

SDS is people who are withdrawing from the larger society, but who are still looking for a radical vocation around which to cluster or construct their community. It is people conscious of the lures of the big world but hating that big world and knowing that alternatives to it are most often swallowed up or crushed flat. The movement is also an island as well as an agent of change, a community in itself, and members look at one another from a closeness which betrays their desire to build moats from as well as bridges to the larger society. Hence the dress, the hair, the argot: the fraternity, the railing against the machine, the anomaly, the ferreting for basics, roots; the use of the word "comrade" has died out; the spirit remains, and makes the New Left look more like a large family than a political force.

Jon Eisen is a student at the University of Edinburgh, Scotland. A former editor of The Activist, *Mr. Eisen has written for* motive, *the* Illinois Political, *and other journals. This article originally appeared in* The Activist, *March 1966.*

LET US SHAPE THE FUTURE

by Carl Oglesby

Seven months ago at the April March on Washington, Paul Potter, then President of Students for a Democratic Society, stood in approximately this spot and said that we must name the system that creates and sustains the war in Vietnam—name it, describe it, analyze it, understand it, and change it.

Today I will try to name it—to suggest an analysis which, to be quite frank, may disturb some of you—and to suggest what changing it may require of us.

We are here again to protest a growing war. Since it is a very bad war, we acquire the habit of thinking it must be caused by very bad men. But we only conceal reality, I think, to denounce on such grounds the menacing coalition of industrial and military power, or the brutality of the blitzkrieg we are waging against Vietnam, or the ominous signs around us that heresy may soon no longer be permitted. We must simply observe, and quite plainly say, that this coalition, this blitzkrieg, and this demand for acquiescence are creatures, all of them, of a Government that since 1932 has considered itself to be fundamentally *liberal.*

The original commitment in Vietnam was made by President Truman, a mainstream liberal. It was seconded by President Eisenhower, a moderate liberal. It was intensified by the late President Kennedy, a flaming liberal. Think of the men who now engineer that war—those who study the maps, give the commands, push the buttons, and tally the dead: Bundy, McNamara, Rusk, Lodge, Goldberg, the President himself. They are not moral monsters. They are all honorable men. They are all liberals.

But so, I'm sure, are many of us who are here today in protest. To understand the war, then, it seems necessary to take a closer look at this American liberalism. Maybe we are in for some surprises. Maybe we have here two quite different liberalisms: one authentically humanist; the other not so human at all

Not long ago I considered myself a liberal and if someone had asked me what I meant by that, I'd perhaps have quoted Thomas Jefferson or Thomas Paine, who first made plain our nation's unprovisional commitment to human rights. But what do you think would happen if these two heroes could sit down now for a chat with President Johnson and McGeorge Bundy?

They would surely talk of the Vietnam war. Our dead revolutionaries would soon wonder why their country was fighting against what appeared to be a revolution. The living liberals would hotly deny that it is one: there are troops coming in from outside, the rebels get arms from other countries, most of the people are not on their side, and they practice terror against their own. Therefore: *not* a revolution.

What would our dead revolutionaries answer? They might say: "What fools and bandits, sirs, you make then of us. Outside help? Do you remember Lafayette? Or the three thousand British freighters the French navy sunk for our side? Or the arms and men we got from France and Spain? And what's this about terror? Did you never hear what we did to our own Loyalists? Or about the thousands of rich American Tories who fled for their lives to Canada? And as for popular support, do you not know that we had less than one-third of our people with us? That, in fact, the colony of

New York recruited more troops for the British than for the revolution? Should we give it all back?"

Revolutions do not take place in velvet boxes. They never have. It is only the poets who make them lovely. What the National Liberation Front is fighting in Vietnam is a complex and vicious war. This war is also a revolution, as honest a revolution as you can find anywhere in history. And this is a fact which all our intricate official denials will never change.

But it doesn't make any difference to our leaders anyway. Their aim in Vietnam is really much simpler than this implies. It is to safeguard what they take to be American interests around the world against revolution or revolutionary change, which they always call communism—as if that were that. In the case of Vietnam, this interest is, first, the principle that revolution shall not be tolerated anywhere, and second, that South Vietnam shall never sell its rice to China—or even to North Vietnam.

There is simply no such thing now, for us, as a just revolution —never mind that for two-thirds of the world's people the Twentieth Century might as well be the Stone Age; never mind the melting poverty and hopelessness that are the basic facts of life for most modern men; and never mind that for these millions there is now an increasingly perceptible relationship between their sorrow and our contentment.

Can we understand why the Negroes of Watts rebelled? Then why do we need a devil theory to explain the rebellion of the South Vietnamese? Can we understand the oppression in Mississippi, or the anguish that our Northern ghettoes makes epidemic? Then why can't we see that our proper human struggle is not with communism or revolutionaries, but with the social desperation that drives good men to violence, both here and abroad?

To be sure, we have been most generous with our aid, and in Western Europe, a mature industrial society, that aid worked. But there are always political and financial strings. And we have never shown ourselves capable of allowing others to make those traumatic institutional changes that are often the prerequisites of progress in colonial societies. For all our official feeling for the millions who are enslaved to what we so self-righteously call the yoke of communist tyranny, we make no real effort at all to crack through the much more vicious right-wing tyrannies that our businessmen traffic with and our nation profits from every day. And for all our cries about the international Red conspiracy to take over the world, we take only pride in the fact of our six thousand military bases on foreign soil.

We gave Rhodesia a grave look just now—but we keep on buying her chromium, which is cheap because black slave labor mines it.

We deplore the racism of Verwoerd's facist South Africa—but our banks make big loans to that country and our private technology makes it a nuclear power.

We are saddened and puzzled by random back-page stories of revolt in this or that Latin American state—but are convinced by a few pretty photos in the Sunday supplement that things are getting better, that the world is coming our way, that change from disorder can be orderly, that our benevolence will pacify the distressed, that our might will intimidate the angry.

Optimists, may I suggest that these are quite unlikely fantasies? They are fantasies because we have lost that mysterious social desire for human equity that from time to time has given us genuine moral drive. We have become a nation of young, bright-eyed, hard-hearted, slim-waisted, bullet-headed make-out artists. A nation—may I say it?—of beardless liberals.

You say I am being hard? Only think.

This country, with its thirty-some years of liberalism, can send 200,000 young men to Vietnam to kill and die in the most dubious of wars, but it cannot get 100 voter registrars to go into Mississippi.

What do you make of it?

The financial burden of the war obliges us to cut millions from an already pathetic War on Poverty budget. But in almost the same breath, Congress appropriates one hundred forty million dollars for the Lockheed and Boeing companies to compete with each other on the supersonic transport project—that Disneyland creation that will cost us all about two billion dollars before it's done.

What do you make of it?

Many of us have been earnestly resisting for some years now the idea of putting atomic weapons into West German hands, an action that would perpetuate the division of Europe and thus the Cold War. Now just this week we find out that, with the meagerest of security systems, West Germany has had nuclear weapons in her hands for the past six years.

What do you make of it?

Some will make of it that I overdraw the matter. Many will ask: What about the other side? To be sure, there is the bitter ugliness of Czechoslovakia, Poland, those infamous Russian tanks in the streets of Budapest. But my anger only rises to hear some say that sorrow cancels sorrow, or that *this* one's shame deposits in *that* one's account the right to shamefulness.

And others will make of it that I sound mighty anti-American. To these, I say: Don't blame *me* for *that!* Blame those who mouthed my liberal values and broke my American heart.

Just who might they be, by the way? Let's take a brief factual inventory of the latter-day Cold War.

In 1953 our Central Intelligence Agency managed to overthrow Mossadegh in Iran, the complaint being his neutralism in the Cold War and his plans to nationalize the country's oil resources to improve his people's lives. Most evil aims, most evil man. In his place we put in General Zahedi, a World War II Nazi collaborator. New arrangements on Iran's oil gave twenty-five-year leases on forty per cent of it to three U.S. firms, one of which was Gulf Oil. The C.I.A.'s leader for this coup was Kermit Roosevelt. In 1960 Kermit Roosevelt became a vice president of Gulf Oil.

In 1954, the democratically-elected Arbenz of Guatemala wanted to nationalize a portion of United Fruit Company's plantations in his country, land he needed badly for a modest program of agrarian reform. His government was overthrown in a C.I.A.-supported right-wing coup. The following year, General Walter

Bedell Smith, director of the C.I.A. when the Guatemala venture was being planned, joined the board of directors of the United Fruit Company.

Comes 1960 and Castro cries we are about to invade Cuba. The Administration sneers, "poppycock," and we Americans believe it. Comes 1961 and the invasion. Comes with it the awful realization that the United States Government had lied.

Comes 1962 and the missile crisis, and our Administration stands prepared to fight global atomic war on the curious principle that another state does not have the right to its own foreign policy.

Comes 1963 and British Guiana, where Cheddi Jagan wants independence from England and a labor law modelled on the Wagner Act. And Jay Lovestone, the AFL-CIO foreign policy chief, acting, as always, quite independently of labor's rank and file, arranges with our Government to finance an eleven-week dock strike that brings Jagan down, ensuring that the state will remain *British* Guiana, and that any workingman who wants a wage better than fifty cents a day is a dupe of communism.

Comes 1964. Two weeks after Undersecretary Thomas Mann announces that we have abandoned the *Alianza's* principle of no aid to tyrants, Brazil's Goulart is overthrown by the vicious right-winger, Ademar Barros, supported by a show of American gunboats at Rio de Janeiro. Within twenty-four hours, the new head of state, Mazzilli, receives a congratulatory wire from our President.

Comes 1965. The Dominican Republic. Rebellion in the streets. We scurry to the spot with twenty thousand neutral Marines and our neutral peacemakers—like Ellsworth Bunker, Jr., Ambassador to the Organization of American States. Most of us know that our neutral Marines fought openly on the side of the junta, a fact that the Administration still denies. But how many also know that what was at stake was our new Caribbean Sugar Bowl? That this same neutral peacemaking Bunker is a board member and stock owner of the National Sugar Refining Company, a firm his father founded in the good old days, and one which has a major interest in maintaining the status quo in the Dominican Republic? Or that the President's close personal friend and advisor, our new Supreme Court Justice Abe Fortas, has sat for the past nineteen years on the board of the Sucrest Company, which imports blackstrap molasses from the Dominican Republic? Or that the rhetorician of corporate liberalism and the late President Kennedy's close friend, Adolf Berle, was chairman of that same board? Or that our roving ambassador Averill Harriman's brother Roland is on the board of National Sugar? Or that our former ambassador to the Dominican Republic, Joseph Farland, is a board member of the South Puerto Rico Sugar Co., which owns two hundred and seventy-five thousand acres of rich land in the Dominican Republic and is the largest employer on the island—at about one dollar a day?

Neutralists! God save the hungry people of the world from such neutralists!

We do not say these men are evil. We say, rather, that good men can be divided from their compassion by the institutional system that inherits us all. Generation in and out, we are put to use. People become instruments. Generals do not hear the screams of the bombed; sugar executives do not see the misery of the cane cutters: for to do so is to be that much *less* the general, that much *less* the executive.

The foregoing facts of recent history describe one main aspect of the estate of Western liberalism. Where is our American humanism here? What went wrong?

Let's stare our situation coldly in the face. All of us are born to the colossus of history, our American corporate system—in many ways an awesome organism. There is one fact that describes it: With about five percent of the world's people, we consume about half the world's goods. We take a richness that is in good part not our own, and we put it in our pockets, our garages, our split-levels, our bellies, and our futures.

On the *face* of it, it is a crime that so few should have so much at the expense of so many. Where is the moral imagination so abused as to call this just? Perhaps many of us feel a bit uneasy in our sleep. We are not, after all, a cruel people. And perhaps we don't really need this super-dominance that deforms others. But what can we do? The investments are made. The financial ties are established. The plants abroad are built. Our system *exists.* One is swept up into it. How intolerable—to be born moral, but addicted to a stolen and maybe surplus luxury. Our goodness threatens to become counterfeit before our eyes—unless we change. But change threatens us with uncertainty—at least.

Our problem, then, is to justify this system and give its theft another name—to make kind and moral what is neither, to perform some alchemy with language that will make this injustice seem a most magnanimous gift.

A hard problem. But the Western democracies, in the heyday of their colonial expansionism, produced a hero worthy of the task.

Its name was free enterprise, and its partner was an *illiberal liberalism* that said to the poor and the dispossessed: What we acquire of your resources we repay in civilization: the white man's burden. But this was too poetic. So a much more hardheaded theory was produced. This theory said that colonial status is in fact a *boon* to the colonized. We give them technology and bring them into modern times.

But this deceived no one but ourselves. We were delighted with this new theory. The poor saw in it merely an admission that their claims were irrefutable. They stood up to us, without gratitude. We were shocked—but also confused, for the poor seemed again to be right. How long is it going to be the case, we wondered, that the poor will be right and the rich will be wrong?

Liberalism faced a crisis. In the face of the collapse of the European empires, how could it continue to hold together our twin need for richness and righteousness? How can we continue to sack the ports of Asia and still dream of Jesus?

The challenge was met with a most ingenious solution: the ideology of anti-Communism. This was the bind: We cannot call revolution bad, because we started that way ourselves, and because it is all too easy to see why the dispossessed should rebel. So we will call revolution Communism. And we will reserve for ourselves the right to say what Communism means. We take note of revolution's enormities, wrenching them where necessary from their historical context and often exaggerating them, and say: Behold, Communism is a bloodbath. We take note of those reactionaries who stole the revolution, and say: Behold, Communism is a betrayal of the people. We take note of the revolution's need to consolidate itself, and say: Behold, Communism is a tyranny.

It has been all these things, and it will be these things again, and we will never be at a loss for those tales of atrocity that comfort us so in our self-righteousness. Nuns will be raped and bureaucrats will be disembowelled. Indeed, revolution is a *fury*. For it is a letting loose of outrages pent up sometimes over centuries. But the more brutal and longer-lasting the supression of this energy, all the more ferocious will be its explosive release.

Far from helping Americans deal with this truth, the anti-Communist ideology merely tries to disguise it so that things may stay the way they are. Thus, it depicts our presence in other lands not as a coercion, but a protection. It allows us even to say that the napalm in Vietnam is only another aspect of our humanitarian love—like those exorcisms in the Middle Ages that so often killed the patient. So we say to the Vietnamese peasant, the Cuban intellectual, the Peruvian worker: "You are better dead than Red. If it hurts or if you don't understand why—sorry about that."

This is the action of *corporate liberalism*. It performs for the corporate state a function quite like what the Church once performed for the feudal state. It seeks to justify its burdens and protect it from change. As the Church exaggerated this office in the Inquisition, so with liberalism in the McCarthy time—which, if it was a reactionary phenomenon, was still made possible by our anti-Communist corporate liberalism.

Let me then speak directly to humanist liberals. If my facts are wrong, I will soon be corrected. But if they are right, then you may face a crisis of conscience. Corporatism or humanism: which? For it has come to that. Will you let your dreams be used? Will you be a grudging apologist for the corporate state? Or will you help try to change it—not in the name of this or that blueprint or ism, but in the name of simple human decency and democracy and the vision that wise and brave men saw in the time of our own Revolution?

And if your commitment to human values is unconditional,

then disabuse yourselves of the notion that statements will bring change, if only the right statements can be written, or that interviews with the mighty will bring change if only the mighty can be reached, or that marches will bring change if only we can make them massive enough, or that policy proposals will bring change if only we can make them responsible enough.

We are dealing now with a colossus that does not want to be changed. It will not change itself. It will not cooperate with those who want to change it. Those allies of ours in the Government—are they really our allies? If they *are*, then they don't need advice, they need *constituencies;* they don't need study groups, they need a *movement*. And if they are *not*, then all the more reason for building that movement with a most relentless conviction.

There are people in this country today who are trying to build that movement, who aim at nothing less than a humanist reformation. And the humanist liberals must understand that it is this movement with which their own best hopes are most in tune. We radicals know the same history that you liberals know, and we can understand your occasional cynicism, exasperation, and even distrust. But we ask you to put these aside and help us risk a leap. Help us find enough time for the enormous work that needs doing here. Help us build. Help us shape the future in the name of plain human hope.

Carl Ogelsby is an immediate past president of the Students for a Democratic Society. He is presently at work on a book on "corporate capitalism and American foreign policy." This article was written as a speech to the March on Washington to End the War in Vietnam on November 27, 1965.

THE CRISIS OF COLD WAR IDEOLOGY

by Paul Booth

I. *Facing the American Leviathan*

We face America the leviathan. Our nation attempts throughout the world to guard by force an order of power relations in which established American interests are respected and achieved. Everywhere American reality conflicts with our values: to our assertion of the dignity of individuals, of the values of love, honesty, reason, and equality, America responds with war, manipulation, and the selfish concentration of wealth.

The America which we face denies democracy—it is a nation in which the crucial economic decisions which affect us all are made by corporate managers and bankers, in which millions of people are dependent on the indulgence of public welfare systems over which they have no control, *in which the decisions of war and peace are made by a clique of advisers and experts*. Can this be called democracy? We understand democracy to be that system of rule in which the people make the decisions.

With every escalation of the war in Vietnam has come an increased awareness at home that the Cold War strategy is having no impact on the root problem of Revolution. The unrest in the Black ghettoes gives ample indication that the war on poverty and its accompanying housing and education programs are having no impact on poverty in America.

We speak as a new American left—a new generation of radical democrats trying to point a way out of the crisis. Our vision for the reconstruction of America comes out of our experience as products of the dominant culture and as activists fighting its most obvious injustices, and out of our democratic values as people seeking a decent and humane order, recognizing the inherent equality of men, and freeing their capacities for love, reason, and creativity.

We speak as a new American left—affirming the heritage of Americans who have championed the cause of the people against corporate power, populists of the nineteenth century, Socialists of the early 1900's and workers who built the industrial unions. While we reject the dogmas and sectarianism of the Old Left, we adopt as our own the best features of the idea of Socialism that moved them. At the same time, we develop an understanding of and a program to change the managed society of the '60s. But ours is a time of crisis for that leviathan. The old explanations provide no direction, the old programs of liberalism are washouts. Violence in Vietnam and poverty at home give daily evidence of the crisis. The lives of our whole generation give further evidence of the disintegration of the old standards. Young Americans are no longer impressed by the old morality or the old patriotism: neither Lyndon's war nor Lady Bird's beautification campaign turns us on. Nor are we content to take our places among the managers and the managed. Both the Cold War ideology and the liberal domestic program are failures, and the country knows it.

We speak as a new American left—committed to the achievement of political power in our time. We seek a redistribution of power in our society in favor of disenfranchised people who live in ghettoes, white and black, north and south, who work in factories, who are passive consumers of the culture, who are segregated systematically from their fellow-men. We seek political power so that men may at last prevail over the arrangements of society in which a few control the destinies of all.

These commitments set an intellectual agenda. The first task of the crisis is to identify its key questions and work to find the answers around which a strategy of change can be built.

II. *United States and the Third World*

Con los pobres de la tierra, quiero yo mi siempre echar.—Marti

Vietnam is the flaming symbol to the world of the American arrogance that has already made itself felt in the day-to-day representation of our country by diplomats and businessmen and tourists. In Vietnam it is a more serious matter than the kind of misunderstanding of or scorn for another country's symbols and customs that has previously caused bitterness and mistrust. It is now arrogance toward human life.

However the war's strategists calculate the ramifications of this bombing mission or that rural pacification scheme, it is clear that Vietnamese lives are not assigned a heavy weight. From time to time we hear that the fighting man in the sentry has respect for the VC opponents as "plucky and determined," but the overall operating assumption is that the VC are bandits and desperadoes; any kind of torture is justified to repay such acts of desperate terrorism as the bombings of Saigon restaurants and the executions of village headmen. Civilians—and there are now over a million refugees in Saigon who have fled the bombings of their villages—are pawns in the game, to be relocated from their village according to one General's notion of "strategic hamlets," to be kept under meticulous police observation and control in the truly totalitarian schemes known as "rural pacification." Buddhist and other anti-Communist nationalists are a disruptive force who must be repressed because their activity works objectively to the advantage of the Communists: neutralists are banned from the "free elections" even though non-alignment was the hope of the Geneva Conventions we claim to honor. The North Vietnamese, bombed to fulfill the requirements of LBJ's devil theory, are utterly hapless—even if they withdrew all support from the Southern Liberation Front, we would still have to bomb them. As for our allies, their soldiers are "apathetic" according to our GI's, who now do most of the fighting.

Why Vietnam? The Cold War is one answer. The balance of power among Great Powers must be respected; in particular, China must be contained. Russia is proving a willing participant in Great Power politics, and China must also refrain from destabilizing that balance. "Wars of Liberation" are the most widespread threat to international stability and China advocates those wars. Chinese Communism is a virile alternative to the pattern of oligarchic and military dominance in the Third World, to the growing desperation of the masses of people in those countries. So the war is pre-eminently a demonstration of our power to contain Communism a few hundred miles from the borders of Red China.

When Dean Rusk complains that he has put out peace feelers but the Chinese are never at the other end of the phone, he means that they don't want to participate in a conversation with us as Great Power to Great Power. When we announce that we want to contain China, not isolate her, we mean for China to pick up the receiver and tell Dean Rusk that she will assume the style of a Great Power, and not champion the cause of a small nationalism against another Great Power.

Why Vietnam? The American response to revolution is the other answer. In practice, our nation is a powerful opponent of revolutionary change, and a startlingly successful opponent. Although our leaders make rhetorical gestures acknowledging the radical disparities between rich and poor throughout the Third World and the desperate need for economic development, these are frequently vague phrases. When they contain promises, as did the Alliance for Progress, promising backing for land reform, tax reform, and opposition to military rule, they are betrayed down the line. In practice our Peace Corps is an insignificant gesture next to the Marine Corps and the Exploitation Corps.

Throughout the Third World, the force of nationalism is increasingly powerful. The desire for independent development has not been quenched by the end of colonialism; in many countries this has only created an increased expectation that now the New Nations could determine their own economic courses, international course, cultural course. Where Western investors have warped the economies by channeling all energy into the extraction of primary products, the New Nations have attempted to develop a neutralist force. Where our businesses have propagated the culture of Frigidaires and Coca-Cola, the New Nations have sought to recreate national identity, and bring to life their own heritages. Increasingly, American power in the Sixties has worked to limit the choices for nationalists. We are the agent of polarization, our terms are "freedom or Communism." Nationalists and revolutionists must inevitably become those "Communists" under the impact of our military might, for we now intervene consistently against the *revolutionaries*. And when we support Ky against the Buddhists,

Balaguer against Bosch, Castelo-Branco against Goulart, Boumedienne against Ben Bella—and support them powerfully, not merely in rhetoric—we demonstrate how completely we are committed to Counter-Revolution. It should be no surprise that movements like the Vietnamese Liberation Front—which advocate land redistribution—have popular support, while the U.S. is increasingly hated. Our local collaborators, true to the spirit of foreign aid, "help themselves." But Vietnam represents the current arena of the fight to defeat any and all revolutions, and so fight it we must, and to the bitter end. And with whatever means at our disposal: the Air Force, the Army, the Special Forces, General Lansdale and his Rural Pacifiers, the AID teams, everyone is told to "Do your thing." It is almost as if we wish to build *and* burn our way into the hearts of the Vietnamese so that they would not desire land, and would not desire a Vietnamese nation. Experience shows that the anti-Communist leaders of our dreams have not developed who could both rally popular support and modernize.

But poverty is the overwhelming problem of these countries. This is the poverty of desperate hunger; Gerassi tells us, "Three-fourths of Latin Americans are constantly hungry. The average daily calorie intake is 1,200, when normal subsistency is considered 2,400 (and our average in the United States is 3,100). Many Latin Americans actually die from starvation. In Haiti peasants are forced to trap skinny pigeons for food. In Peru and Chile, many eat every other day, and often average as low as 500 calories daily."

This is also the poverty of radical inequality, where the masses are hungry and diseased and a very few are as rich as the opulent Americans they imitate. This is the real instability, of millions not knowing where the next meal will come from. By any criteria of judgment, by any humane values, these disparities require a radical solution.

The Cold War is deeply embedded in our culture. America misunderstands the turbulence in the underdeveloped world by interpreting it as the product of the struggle between east and west blocs. The emotions on which insurgencies in the Third World draw are genuine and intense—they come from the demands for national integrity and for relief from poverty. This revolutionary upsurge is a challenge to the assumption on which our leaders work—that concerted political movements are invariably the products of manipulation and subversion. We *are so accustomed to top-down control in our own society that we forget that man is capable* of doing the opposite—*of working to change the conditions of his oppression.*

THE AMERICAN PRESENCE

In the world, the American presence is truly awe-inspiring. A sixty-year commitment to the extension of American influence has made our country the Great Power that towers over the others. The power of American fighting men is visible in forty-eight countries, the power of our investors is felt in several dozen more. Friendly regimes show their loyalties at the turn of each year when they take out full-page ads in the New York *Times* Review of the Year's Business:

Thailand Welcomes Foreign Investment

". . . The state guarantees against expropriation or nationalization of private industry . . . A new promoted industry will be exempt from income tax for a period of five years . . . Thailand possesses vast amounts of natural resources and also large, peaceful, cheap and adaptable labor forces awaiting to be developed with the assistance of foreign capital. . . ."

This is a statement of pride from Thailand as recorded in the New York *Times.* Page after page, its annual international financial report is a testimony of the virtues of stability, the accepted object of government in most countries of the underdeveloped world. The question is, however, stability for whom?

That vaunted stability is the slogan of the American ambition to manage the whole world. In practice, stability acquires more meaning than the benevolent wish of Dean Rusk's rhetoric that all countries could have the same domestic tranquility that America has. It means:

• Stable currencies, so that foreign investors can be sure that when they enter into a transaction the rate of return on that loan or investment will not be obliterated by inflation. This is known as the Austerity Policy (hold the line on wages and projects of social spending), such as practiced by President Arturo Alexsandri of Chile between 1958 and 1963. He did bring down annual inflation from 38 per cent to 10 per cent, but even with the U.S. forking out 70 per cent of the cost, his economic development plan brought annual growth of 1.4 per cent, compared to a population growth of 2.5 per cent. Unemployment rose to 18 per cent.

• Stable policies, so that the alliance system of the Cold War created by Acheson and Dulles will not be disturbed. Four dozen countries are tied into our network of alliances, and when one moves from being pro-U.S. to neutralism, as Iraq did in 1958, we send the Marines to the neighboring countries, or we encourage the local military to dump the regime, as in Brazil in 1961 and 1964—where the crime was not neutralism but an independent foreign policy extending trade relations to Russia, China, and East Germany.

• Stable policing of internal forces of unrest, so that "Communists" and other movements that might bring about regimes less respectful of the virtues of the other stabilities get nipped in the bud. To train police, John Kennedy created the famous Special Forces as an independent unit, and through U.S. military aid missions has them training civic action teams in rural counter-insurgency and police forces in urban tactics. They are at work in dozens of countries, and in Peru and Colombia (and others we aren't told about) they are going up into hills as advisors, just like Vietnam.

In order to make possible the coup that replaced Patrice Lumumba in the Congo, we provided the cash so that Joseph Mobuto could pay his troops. One year after FDR declared the Good Neighbor policy, our ambassador gave his blessing to Anastasio Somoza's proposal to assassinate the Nicaraguan hero Sandino; the Somozas then ruled by terror for twenty-five years.

• Stable relations for American-owned industries. After Leonel

Brizola nationalized the International Telephone and Telegraph subsidiary in Brazil's Rio Grande do Sul state, Senator Bourke Hickenlooper led a successful move to cut any country out of foreign aid that confiscated U.S. business without adequate (by our terms) compensation. One country that has been cut off is Ceylon —in July 1962 Mrs. Bandaranaike, the Prime Minister, nationalized Esso, Shell, and Caltex filling stations and oil depots, and said, "The best form of foreign aid the U.S. can give to small countries is to abstain from interfering in their affairs." Generally we have been more successful in warding off such efforts; in Guatemala in 1954 we sent the CIA to overthrow a regime that was nibbling away at our plantations, and in Iran in 1950 the CIA overthrew Mossadegh to prevent nationalization of the oil industry. In the Dominican Republic we let Bosch fall because he proposed to keep collectivized the sugar plantations formerly owned by the deposed Trujillo family. Our interference is almost never of the openness of the Dominican affair—generally our diplomacy, military aid, threats of sanctions by international banking institutions which we dominate, and political meddling of the covert and clandestine varieties will do the trick. Of course, none of these weapons is used against the regime of South Africa, where the annual rate of return on our $500 million worth of investments is over 20 per cent. In fact, the U.S. banking community together with the International Monetary Fund actually bailed out that country during its 1961 financial crisis.

• Stable day-to-day politics. This turns out to be a set of dubious freedoms, like the freedom from strikes, the freedom from overly harsh press criticism, the freedom from parliamentary opposition, etc. The Corporacion Minera de Boliva (COMIBOL) placed the following ad in the New York *Times:*

"The first stage in the recent history of the Tin mines began on October 31, 1952, when the mines were nationalized.

"With the advent of the Military Junta in 1964, COMIBOL entered into the second phase of its existence. Under the Presidency of a distinguished and dynamic Bolivian Army Colonel and top management of a well-known American Engineer, this enormous mining enterprise . . . today offers an entirely new perspective. Their main objective is to transform COMIBOL into a profitable industrial enterprise . . .

"Labor union arrogance exercised by Communists has been abolished.

"The principle of authority has been firmly established . . .

"The new economic and financial outlook offered today by COMIBOL, and the advantageous terms of Bolivia's Investment Law sanctioned by the Military Junta, have prompted foreign and local capital to boost Bolivia's mining activities. . . ." In country after country in the underdeveloped world we support right-wing dictatorships of the most brutal kind; we outfit their armies, encourage U.S. businesses to invest there, underwrite their budgets, and otherwise treat them like honest and forthright partners in progress. Of the scores of military juntas and dictators in the world, only Pakistan and Egypt can even make the excuse of using their power for economic development.

These problems are deepening, just as the hope of resolving them becomes progressively dimmer. The questions of our times are not: Is America the foe of change? or, Is there a need for revolution? We know the answers to these. But we must grapple with the growing gap between rich and poor countries and the lack of progress toward economic development, the increasing irrelevance of these countries to American prosperity, and the growing number of setbacks incurred by the political elements in the Third World which have been in the leadership of revolution.

The Prospects for Economic Change

The maintenance of the *status quo* social relations in the underdeveloped world has been achieved basically through the export of primary commodities to the industrial regions of the world. The revenues necessary for maintaining conservative regimes in power have come from taxes on revenues from these export products and from the sale of concessions for their exploitation. The dependence cannot be over-exaggerated; in Venezuela, oil revenues, which account for 92 per cent of foreign exchange, accounted for approximately *two-thirds* of the 1962 national budget. The ability to import, especially to import luxury consumer goods, repay foreign loans, and otherwise "carry on" economically is hinged irrevocably to these products in these so-called hacienda-export economies. Typically this is a dependence on one or two items; in Latin America, the average proportion of export revenues derived from the country's single leading export is well over 50 per cent. And so fluctuations in the commodity prices are of critical importance to the stability of these regimes. Coffee and sugar prices have often fluctuated by as much as 50 per cent in one year. Moreover, there has been in the post-war era a general overall tendency to depress the prices of these commodities, a phenomenon which Raul Prebisch, in his report as Secretary-General to the UN Conference on Trade and Development (UNCD), identified as a major cause of the increasing gap between the rich and poor nations. The United States is the leading opponent of international stabilization and regulation of commodity prices; this is partly due to a desire to protect domestic industries, and partly to our unwillingness to cut into the profits made by the American firms who do the importing, or even to pass the added costs on to American consumers. The industrialized countries generally support this policy, including, as Cuba and Romania point out, the Soviet Union, which uses the prevailing world market prices in relations to its allies.

But it is the desperate need to defend the prices of traditional exports that led to the formation of what became known as the bloc of 75 at the UN trade conference in 1964. For the most part these are regimes without the slightest interest in attacking the deeper problems of land distribution, or of discouraging U.S. investment in their countries. But they recognize the increasingly marginal economic role of the Third World: While exports throughout the world rose by 7.1 per cent from 1950–62, exports from the Third World rose by 3.4 per cent. And, their share of world trade fell from 32 per cent to 21 per cent. And this reflects not only the deterioration in terms of trade affecting the value of exports, but the fact that the underdeveloped countries are supplying a decreasing share of primary products as developed countries become less dependent through technological advances. And although developments such as the coffee agreement in Africa and the Latin American and Central American Free Trade Areas are admirable, they are a minor relief to the major pattern of trade relations which go on between individual underdeveloped countries; between 1952 and 1960, according to UNCTD, while the value of international trade was increasing by 7.1 per cent, the value of trade among the countries of the Third World increased 1.8 per cent.

If the trade picture holds little prospect of easing the desperate poverty of the Third World, the vistas for industrial development can hardly be said to be hopeful. What industrial development does take place will do so against the backdrop of rapidly increasing population and labor force. By the year 2000, the population of the poor countries will more than double, reaching 4 billion. New industries, especially if they are modernly equipped and if they replace more primitive labor-intensive economic activity, will not have a marked effect on employment for years to come. Thus, as has happened in the last decade, new population will have to be employed in agriculture in order to avoid starvation or it will accumulate in the slums of the cities.

It is impossible to avoid the conclusion that the major stumbling-block to progress in the Third World is the way inequality is so thoroughly the principle of economic structure. In the agricultural sector this is glaring.

The productivity of both land and labor are low in the Third World due to these structural considerations. The Food and Agriculture Organization, however, estimates that over half the world's population suffers from hunger or crippling malnutrition. In Latin America, only three countries can claim that more than 50 per cent of their agricultural population are owners of their own land or even tenants or co-op members or workers on their own account. The extent of out-and-out peonage is further illustrated by the fact Gerasi records that in 1961 1.2 per cent of the farms accounted for 71.6 per cent of farm land, not counting Cuba and Bolivia. (Even counting them in, the top 1.5 per cent of the farms account for 65 per cent of the land.) The output on the large estates is very low. Other consequences in agrarian society of this maldistribution result from the monopoly on political power of the oligarchy, who spend as little as possible on schools thereby perpetuating illiteracy which retards significantly any agricultural development—and other social investment in health and communications. Where land reforms have been enacted, it has become imperative to supplement them with improved roads and with the distribution of agricultural equipment to the peasants, thereby revealing how underdeveloped the agricultural economy has been.

Another dramatic demonstration of the structural causes of continued poverty in the Third World—in this case the foreign ownership of land—is provided by the fruit trade. Latin America grows 70 per cent of the world's bananas, and sells half of these abroad. But only a minor proportion of the profits—under 30 per cent—ends up in the budgets of the governments concerned, most of it is retained by United Fruit, and to a lesser extent, Standard Fruit. In addition, United Fruit owns the railroads and trolleys and shipping fleet and several ports.

The oligarchies which dominate the countries of Latin America, Africa, and Asia, are hardly Calvinists, reinvesting the money they earned in further development. On the contrary, Ibn Saud with his fleet of Cadillacs is the model for the poor half of the world. A very slim proportion of property income gets reinvested; the level of consumption is very high, as is the proportion of savings saved in Swiss banks. Because the governments are firmly in the hands of the rich, the highest tax a Latin American country levies on its richest income bracket is 37 per cent (and evasion is rife).

American policy decidedly is *not* determined on the basis of a sympathetic response to these dilemmas. Witness the fate of Chester Bowles, who did recognize the "revolution of rising expectations"; he was given the post of Under Secretary of State for Political Affairs under Kennedy but was quickly sidetracked when it became clear his views were eccentric. Or the fate of the Alliance for Progress, not a development program at all (its small development allocations represented no increase in funds over the Eisenhower years), but an increased effort to promote financial stability though softer—lower-interest—loans in friendly countries. The capital improvements we have financed include new roads to United Fruit plantations, docks for our tankers in Venezuela's ports, etc.

The motivation behind our foreign policy is explained to a considerable extent by the needs of our economic empire. Foreign investments constitute 5 per cent of all U.S. investment; but bring in 11 per cent of our profits. Investments in underdeveloped countries account for 2 per cent of all American capital at work, but 8 per cent of profits. The Survey of Current Business of the Department of Commerce also tells us that the rate of return on investment in the Third World is 15 per cent a year. Over half of our overseas investment is in the control of 45 giant corporations. In 1960, America withdrew $1.1 billion in profits and interest from South America, and sent in $1.0 billion in new private investment and all *public lending*, a net capital drain. In 1964, dealing with direct (not portfolio) investment in the whole Third World of $13.032 billion, we invested with new private capital and reinvested profits $687 million in these countries, and repatriated $2,179 million from these countries in earnings. This is not, however, a complete explanation, since the militance of our foreign policy extends throughout the world, into countries where our businessmen have little or no influence or interests.

The Defeat of Nationalism

The worldwide design of America is the defeat of independent forces, and this design is being carried out in the Sixties with remarkable success. It was around the time that our generation came to an awareness of foreign policy—with the Bay of Pigs invasion —that the men of power were recognizing that the real threat to U.S. interests came from the underdeveloped world, not Russia. Together with this recognition came experimentation with counter-insurgency, readjustment of the defense machinery to meet limited wars, and a new political rhetoric. The Johnson Administration has relied heavily on armed forces in Vietnam, but its use of the CIA and other instruments has been extensive and effective.

There has been no tidal wave of revolution. Every style of revolutionary leadership, from the most radical Chinese-style insurgencies, to mass communist parties, to one-party nationalist regimes, to constitutionalist reformers, have been dealt defeats at the hand of their own domestic reactionaries and American power.

Defeats for the left have taken a number of forms. They include:

Foreign Armies. In Vietnam, it is clear to everyone, the regime would not last a minute beyond the withdrawal of U.S. forces. The size of the American troop commitment has been steadily escalated to meet the need, and constitute a virtual occupying force, committed to stay there until the NLF is obliterated. The guerilla war in the countryside has been contained, to all appearances. By our presence, South Vietnamese government forces have been freed to defeat neutralist uprisings among the students and Buddhists—a setback as well to the NLF's strategy. While in Vietnam, U.S. planes have been available to strafe emplacements of left-wing Pathet Lao forces in Laos, which have in the past, by virtue of coalition with neutralists, tried to keep control of the country out of the hands of the CIA-fed Gen. Nosavan.

That our fighting men are useful against the non-Communist left as well was demonstrated in the Dominican Republic, when a group of nationalist military men at the head of a constitutionalist popular revolt in the capital chased the local *gorilas* (apes, Latin term for junta generals) onto an island. U.S. troops along with token contingents from military regimes in Latin America kept law and order while the police forces and hoodlum squads of the old junta terroized the left, jailing and assassinating so many on a scale so reminiscent of Trujillo (who killed over 500,000 people in his thirty-two years) that the countryside voted for the right-wing Presidential candidate in the hope of a return of stability.

Another military operation that succeeded was the sending of British troops to East Africa in 1965 after the independence of Zanzibar revealed a revolutionary regime. These troops guaranteed against troop revolts in Kenya and Uganda.

Mercenaries. In the case of a genuine civil war, the addition of trained foreign troops can be critically important. In the Congo, where the U.S. served as paymaster, white mercenaries put down the Simba uprising (which had a Lumumbist political flavoring) in a fierce reminder that Europeans have always outdone Africans in torture and brutality.

Massacre. The worst massacre since Hitler has been perpetrated in Indonesia, against the Communists (PKI) and sympathizers. Over 500,000 lives have been taken since the October 1st, 1965, abortive Colonels uprising, which the Generals pinned on the innocent PKI. The new regime, in addition to moving toward peace with Malaysia, has declared a policy of hospitality to foreign capital. This is renewed testimony to the weaknesses of a left in an underdeveloped country where the means of violence have been built up either through external influence (like U.S. military aid) or military adventures of the regime. Other massacres have been perpetrated in the Sixties, including a similar, though smaller, Ba'athist purge of Communists in Iraq. The technique is becoming uncomfortably conventional in the modern world, used by all sides. The State Department, of course, doesn't sponsor such action. But the absence of any, even mild, disapproval for this mass murder deprives the U.S. of the right to stand on the world stage and condemn, on the basis of general humanitarian principles, the violence of parties we happen to oppose. What end could our leaders possibly imagine to justify such means?

Police force. Guerrilla efforts are in bad shape throughout the Third World. Any expectation (fostered by the victory of Castro against the tottering Batista rule) that the Latin American *ancien regime* was foredoomed should be laid to rest. In Venezuela, where 70 per cent of the population is in cities, urban guerrillas have been turned back and forced into the hills, while left-wing Congressmen and students have been shot down in the streets. The FALN guerrillas talk of a ten-year fight. In Colombia, where U.S. Special Forces train the police, "pacification" has eliminated political bandits, and the revolutionary priest Torres has been assassinated. The same story seems to hold for Peru and Brazil. In these countries where military regimes maintain strict order, the best that can be hoped for is a kind of Political Cycle in which the left-wing Opposition alternates between open and parliamentary struggle when it can, and the building of a peasant base when urban activity is outlawed.

Bloody guerrilla wars are taking place in Portuguese Africa at the present time, but the chance of victory for the Africans has been diminished by the establishment of an independent racist regime in Rhodesia, and the new legitimacy of apartheid in Southwest Africa. In other countries where guerrilla movements have the strength of long struggle (that is a partial explanation of the tenacity of the NLF in Vietnam), such as Guatemala and Philippines, the regimes are under some strain.

Local military coups. One of the chiefs of the U.S. military mission in Uruguay told John Gerassi: "Don't worry. The new Uruguayan army has been well indoctrinated, especially the officers. Whatever they do, if they seize power, they'll be with us. When I first came here, I was very depressed about the army. The boys looked like a bunch of boys, and they didn't give a damn about what the government was doing. Now they care enough to keep it in line. . . . That's my doing, in part at least."

U.S. foreign policy has been well served by the officers of three continents. Coups have displaced more than a dozen independent nationalist regimes, some elected and some personal regimes representing the movement that ended colonialism in those countries. If the early sixties were a period of exuberant assertion of "positive neutralism"—the activists of nonaligned nations meddling against the Cold War—the late sixties seem to be the defeat of the first generation of nationalist leadership.

In Ghana, Nkrumah has fallen, and his regime's corruption is being exposed every day. Independent foreign policies have been wiped out in Latin America, with the fall of Quadros and then Goulart from coups in Brazil, and the coups in Bolivia, Ecuador, Argentina. Ben Bella has fallen from a coup at the hands of Gen. Boumedienne. Other military juntas have succeeded neutralist regimes in Dahomey, Congo (Brazzaville), and Rwanda. The coups in the Middle East have been too numerous to follow, while Socialist regimes have been displaced, and Nasser has been isolated in Egypt.

Although the most notable nationalist authoritarian regimes have proved more vulnerable than would have been expected, other styles have not fared any better. Attempts to gain power through electoral means have been thwarted in a number of countries: in Guyana, the British gerrymandered the legislature and stirred up interracial hostility to deprive Cheddi Jagan of a chance to rule. In Chile, where illiterates cannot vote, the Socialist-Communist electoral alliance failed to elect Allende to the Presidency in a two-way 1964 contest with the Christian Democrat Frei, backed by right-wing money.

The upshot of all these defeats is that the militant wing of the Organization of African Unity is now composed of Guinea, Tanzania, and Mali, almost alone. Of the six regimes that voted abstentions on the American proposal to eject Cuba from the OAS, four have fallen to military coups, leaving only Chile and Mexico with an independent foreign policy. Of the first generation of nationalist leaders, only Nasser, Toure, and Castro remain. One minimal condition for the attractiveness of a model is success, and alternatives to China and the American Way become fewer and fewer as time goes by.

One group of nations has been paraded by American liberals as a genuine alternative: it includes India, Venezuela, Puerto Rico, and sometimes Formosa and Japan. Formosa, of course, is a dictatorship. Japan is a developed country, where the old elite took the leadership in economic development. In India, Venezuela, and Puerto Rico, however, local capital has been subordinated to foreign capital. In Venezuela since 1957 a Social Democratic banner flies from a regime that obeys the dictates of the coalition between foreign oil interests and the local oligarchy. In Puerto Rico and India there is, by contrast, a great deal of industrial development, but this is controlled by foreign investors. In India local capitalists originally objected and had to be kept in line by the Government. In all three countries development is lopsided in the direction of high and fast profits, and social spending remains low.

The late sixties may well be a new period of defeat for the radicals throughout the world. In the early fifties, when America was in a period of frigidity, things were "closing down" as well in Russia; these developments fed on each other. Then Hungary, Nasser; Montgomery, Alabama; the Soviet thaw, and a number of other developments forced the world open to change. The possibilities for change in America are related to the fortunes of popular forces in the Third World. This relationship is not the romantic hope held by some American "leftists," of an anti-imperialist world, led by China, surrounding and isolating America, the citadel of world reaction. Rather, it is a complementary relationship; many of the enemies are the same, and many of the issues are parallel. A major unanswered question is the real dependence of American corporate enterprise on foreign investment opportunities; a deeper understanding of that complex subject might give some direction to our strategy.

The failure to develop economic independence and the failure to maintain political independence also indicate that the next generation of radicals will have to make a more fundamental assessment of economic power-relationships. It has been primarily American efforts that have narrowed the range of choices open to developing countries. To restrain American rapaciousness must continue to be the first aim of our efforts; but secondly, we want to press for a foreign policy of encouragement to popular rule and economic development.

Paul Booth is a former national secretary of the Students for a Democratic Society. This article was written as a position discussion paper for the SDS National Council Meeting in August 1966, and is reprinted from New Left Notes *(July 29, 1966), an SDS publication.*